BRIAN BORU

IRELAND'S WARRIOR KING

DAMIEN GOODFELLOW

THE O'BRIEN PRESS
DUBLIN

DEDICATION
DEDICATED TO A TRUE WARRIOR, CULLEN KENNEDY.

ACKNOWLEDGEMENTS
THANK YOU SO MUCH TO LILLY AND JOE GOODFELLOW FOR THEIR PATIENCE AND CONSTANT ENCOURAGEMENT. TO PADRAIG BURKE FOR HIS ADVICE, SUPPORT AND FRIENDSHIP. TO HELEN CARR, EMMA BYRNE, MICHAEL O'BRIEN AND EVERYONE AT THE O'BRIEN PRESS; I COULD NEVER HAVE DONE IT WITHOUT THEIR ADVICE AND PROFESSIONALISM.

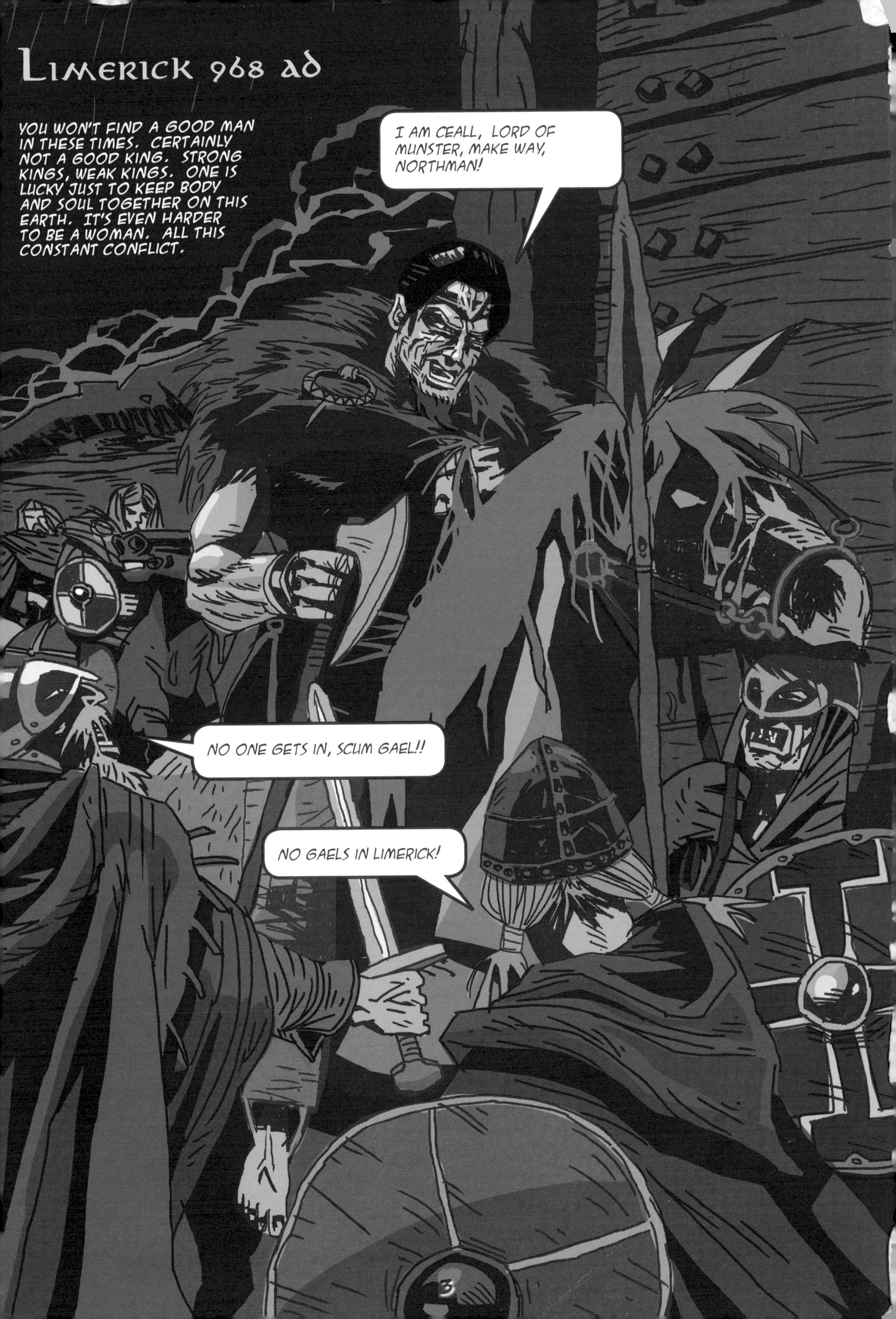
LIMERICK 968 AD
YOU WON'T FIND A GOOD MAN IN THESE TIMES. CERTAINLY NOT A GOOD KING. STRONG KINGS, WEAK KINGS. ONE IS LUCKY JUST TO KEEP BODY AND SOUL TOGETHER ON THIS EARTH. IT'S EVEN HARDER TO BE A WOMAN. ALL THIS CONSTANT CONFLICT.
I AM CEALL, LORD OF MUNSTER, MAKE WAY, NORTHMAN!
NO ONE GETS IN, SCUM GAEL!!
NO GAELS IN LIMERICK!
3

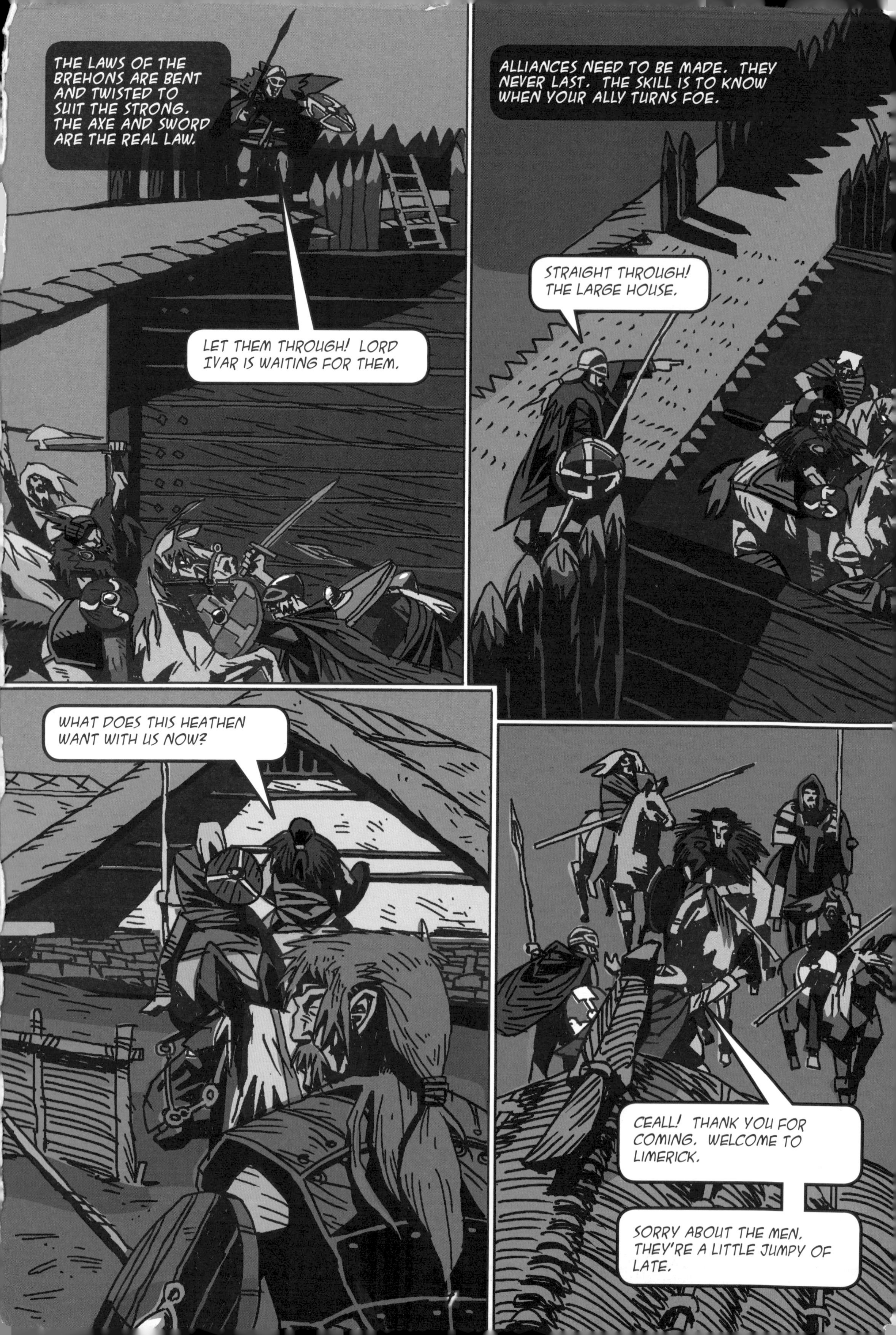
THE LAWS OF THE BREHONS ARE BENT AND TWISTED TO SUIT THE STRONG. THE AXE AND SWORD ARE THE REAL LAW.
LET THEM THROUGH! LORD IVAR IS WAITING FOR THEM.
ALLIANCES NEED TO BE MADE. THEY NEVER LAST. THE SKILL IS TO KNOW WHEN YOUR ALLY TURNS FOE.
STRAIGHT THROUGH! THE LARGE HOUSE.
WHAT DOES THIS HEATHEN WANT WITH US NOW?
CEALL! THANK YOU FOR COMING. WELCOME TO LIMERICK.
SORRY ABOUT THE MEN. THEY'RE A LITTLE JUMPY OF LATE.

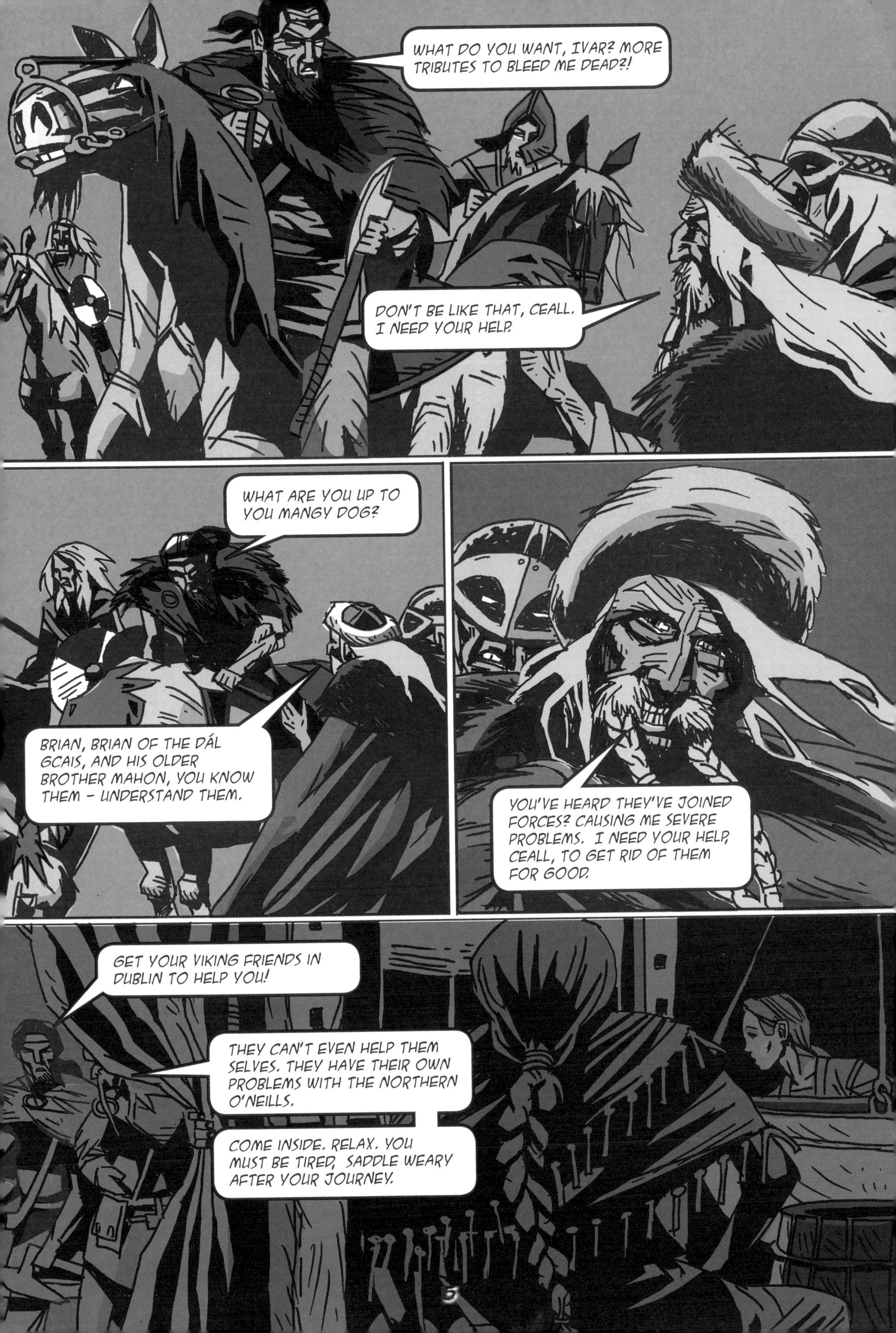
WHAT DO YOU WANT, IVAR? MORE TRIBUTES TO BLEED ME DEAD?!
DON'T BE LIKE THAT, CEALL. I NEED YOUR HELP.
WHAT ARE YOU UP TO YOU MANGY DOG?
BRIAN, BRIAN OF THE DÁL GCAIS, AND HIS OLDER BROTHER MAHON, YOU KNOW THEM – UNDERSTAND THEM.
YOU'VE HEARD THEY'VE JOINED FORCES? CAUSING ME SEVERE PROBLEMS. I NEED YOUR HELP, CEALL, TO GET RID OF THEM FOR GOOD.
GET YOUR VIKING FRIENDS IN DUBLIN TO HELP YOU!
THEY CAN'T EVEN HELP THEM SELVES. THEY HAVE THEIR OWN PROBLEMS WITH THE NORTHERN O'NEILLS.
COME INSIDE. RELAX. YOU MUST BE TIRED, SADDLE WEARY AFTER YOUR JOURNEY.

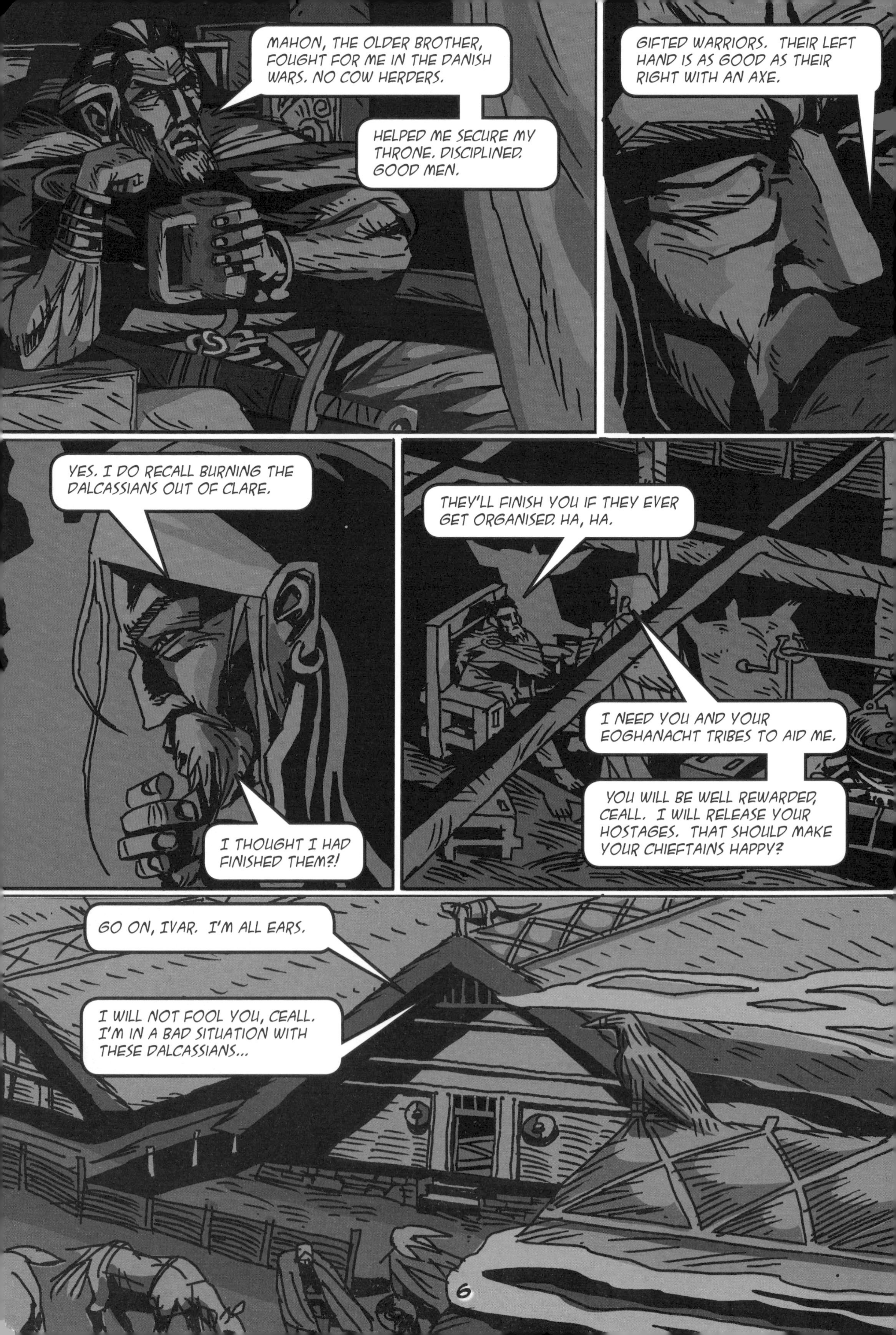
MAHON, THE OLDER BROTHER, FOUGHT FOR ME IN THE DANISH WARS. NO COW HERDERS.
HELPED ME SECURE MY THRONE. DISCIPLINED. GOOD MEN.
GIFTED WARRIORS. THEIR LEFT HAND IS AS GOOD AS THEIR RIGHT WITH AN AXE.
YES. I DO RECALL BURNING THE DALCASSIANS OUT OF CLARE.
I THOUGHT I HAD FINISHED THEM?!
THEY'LL FINISH YOU IF THEY EVER GET ORGANISED. HA, HA.
I NEED YOU AND YOUR EOGHANACHT TRIBES TO AID ME.
YOU WILL BE WELL REWARDED, CEALL. I WILL RELEASE YOUR HOSTAGES. THAT SHOULD MAKE YOUR CHIEFTAINS HAPPY?
GO ON, IVAR. I'M ALL EARS.
I WILL NOT FOOL YOU, CEALL. I'M IN A BAD SITUATION WITH THESE DALCASSIANS...

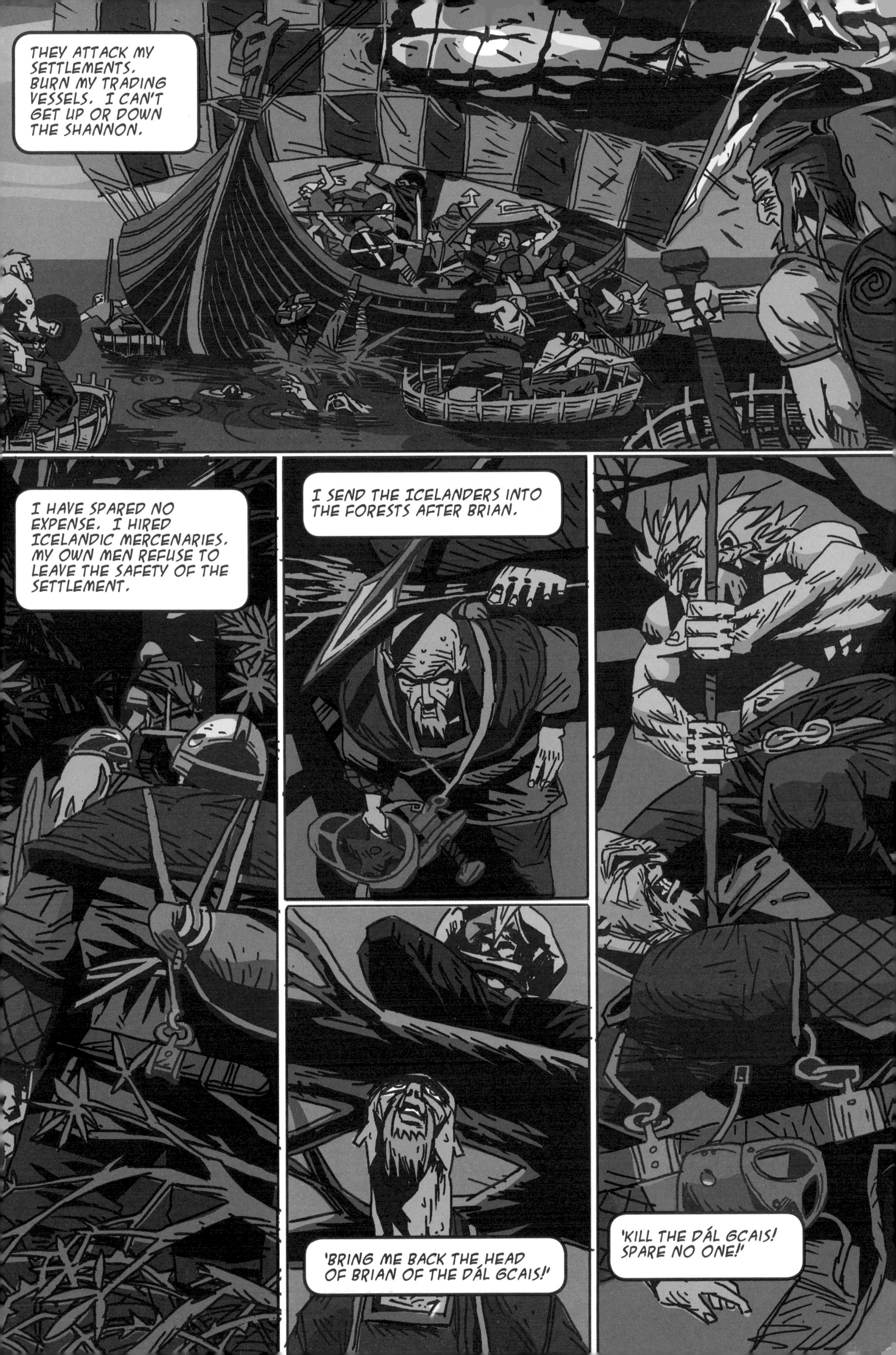
THEY ATTACK MY SETTLEMENTS. BURN MY TRADING VESSELS. I CAN'T GET UP OR DOWN THE SHANNON.
I HAVE SPARED NO EXPENSE. I HIRED ICELANDIC MERCENARIES. MY OWN MEN REFUSE TO LEAVE THE SAFETY OF THE SETTLEMENT.
I SEND THE ICELANDERS INTO THE FORESTS AFTER BRIAN.
'BRING ME BACK THE HEAD OF BRIAN OF THE DÁL GCAIS!'
'KILL THE DÁL GCAIS! SPARE NO ONE!'

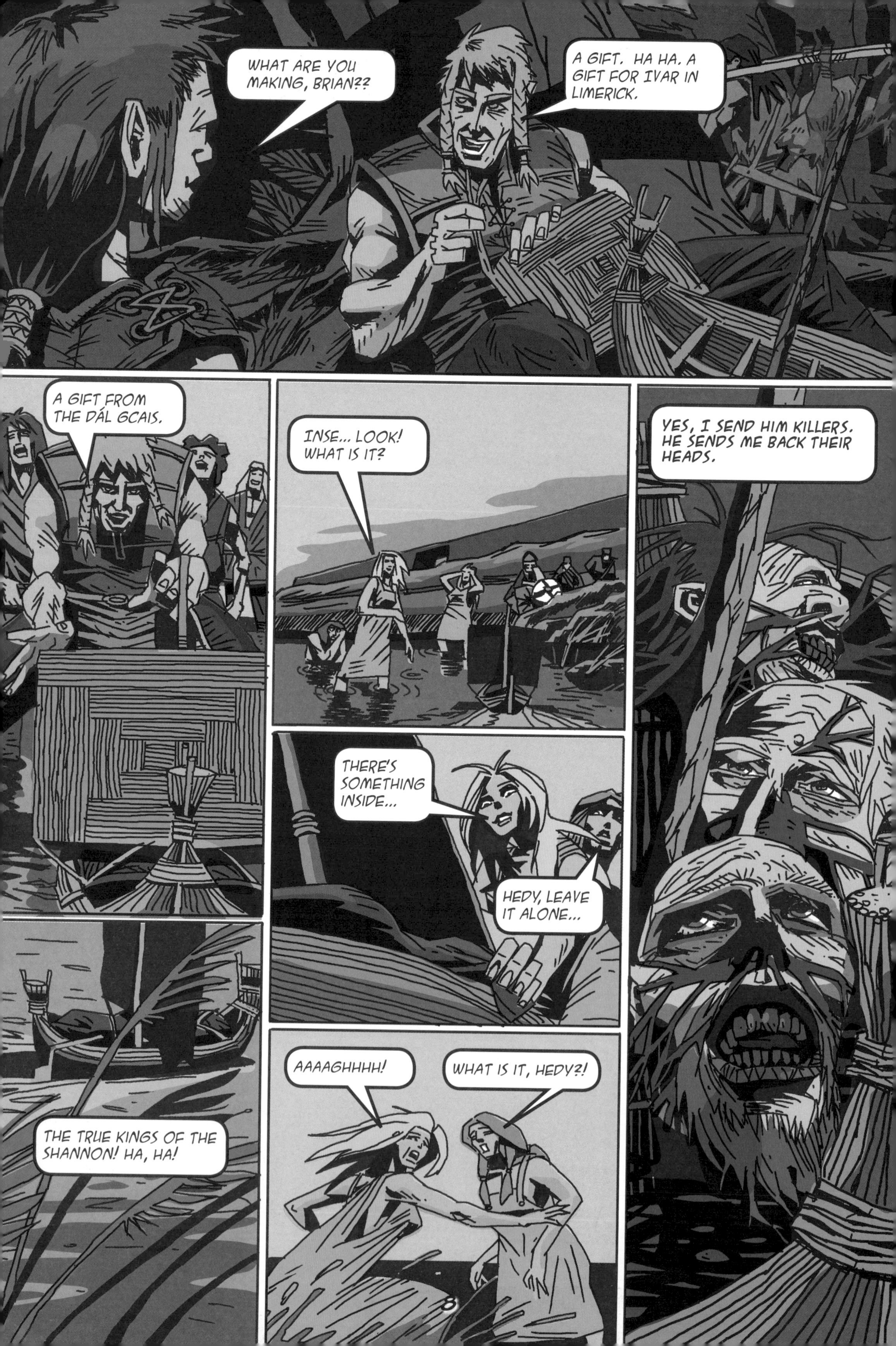
WHAT ARE YOU MAKING, BRIAN??
A GIFT. HA HA. A GIFT FOR IVAR IN LIMERICK.
A GIFT FROM THE DÁL GCAIS.
THE TRUE KINGS OF THE SHANNON! HA, HA!
INSE... LOOK! WHAT IS IT?
THERE'S SOMETHING INSIDE...
HEDY, LEAVE IT ALONE...
AAAAGHHHH!
WHAT IS IT, HEDY?!
YES, I SEND HIM KILLERS. HE SENDS ME BACK THEIR HEADS.

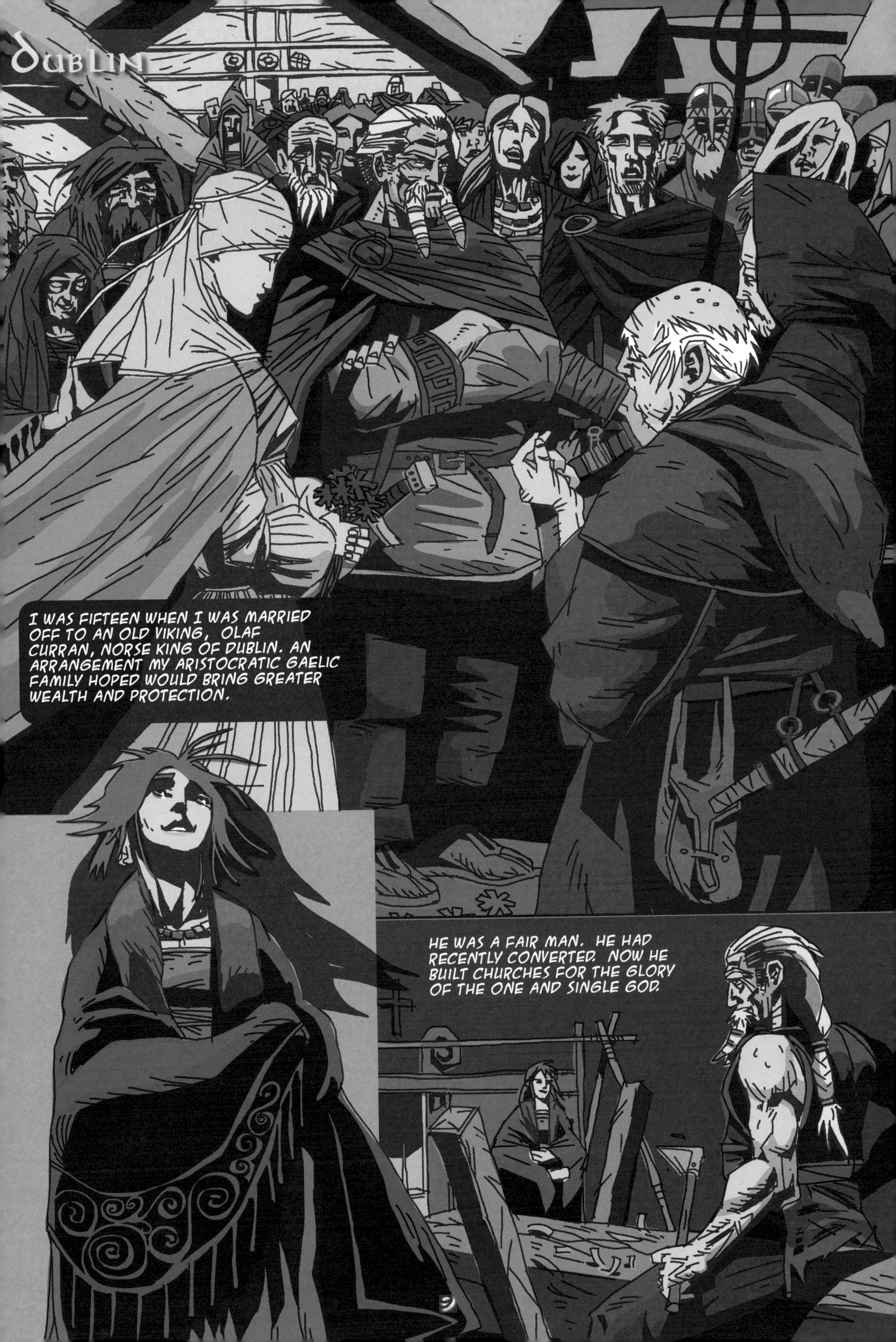
DUBLIN
I WAS FIFTEEN WHEN I WAS MARRIED OFF TO AN OLD VIKING, OLAF CURRAN, NORSE KING OF DUBLIN. AN ARRANGEMENT MY ARISTOCRATIC GAELIC FAMILY HOPED WOULD BRING GREATER WEALTH AND PROTECTION.
HE WAS A FAIR MAN. HE HAD RECENTLY CONVERTED. NOW HE BUILT CHURCHES FOR THE GLORY OF THE ONE AND SINGLE GOD.

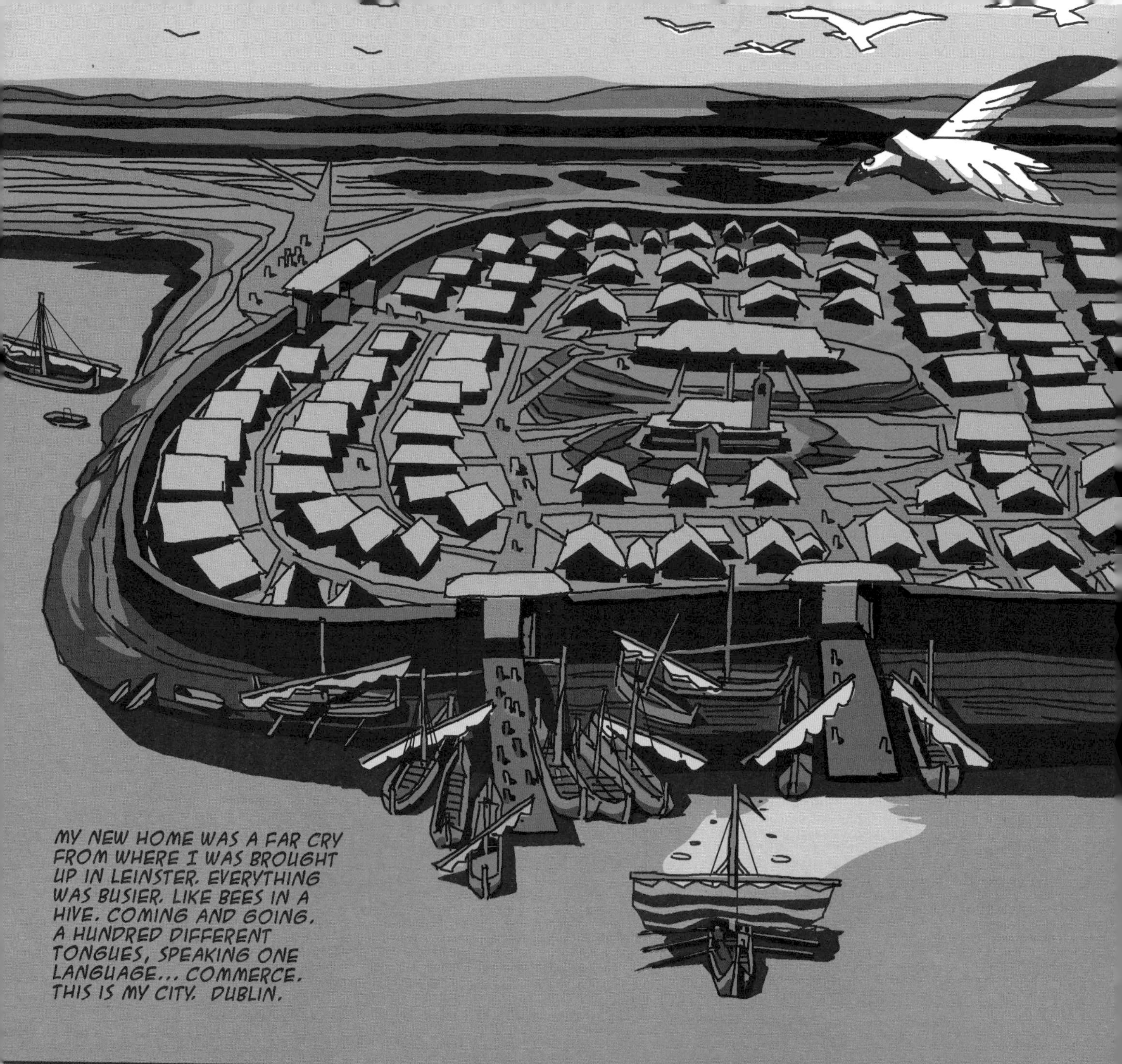
MY NEW HOME WAS A FAR CRY FROM WHERE I WAS BROUGHT UP IN LEINSTER. EVERYTHING WAS BUSIER. LIKE BEES IN A HIVE. COMING AND GOING. A HUNDRED DIFFERENT TONGUES, SPEAKING ONE LANGUAGE... COMMERCE. THIS IS MY CITY. DUBLIN.

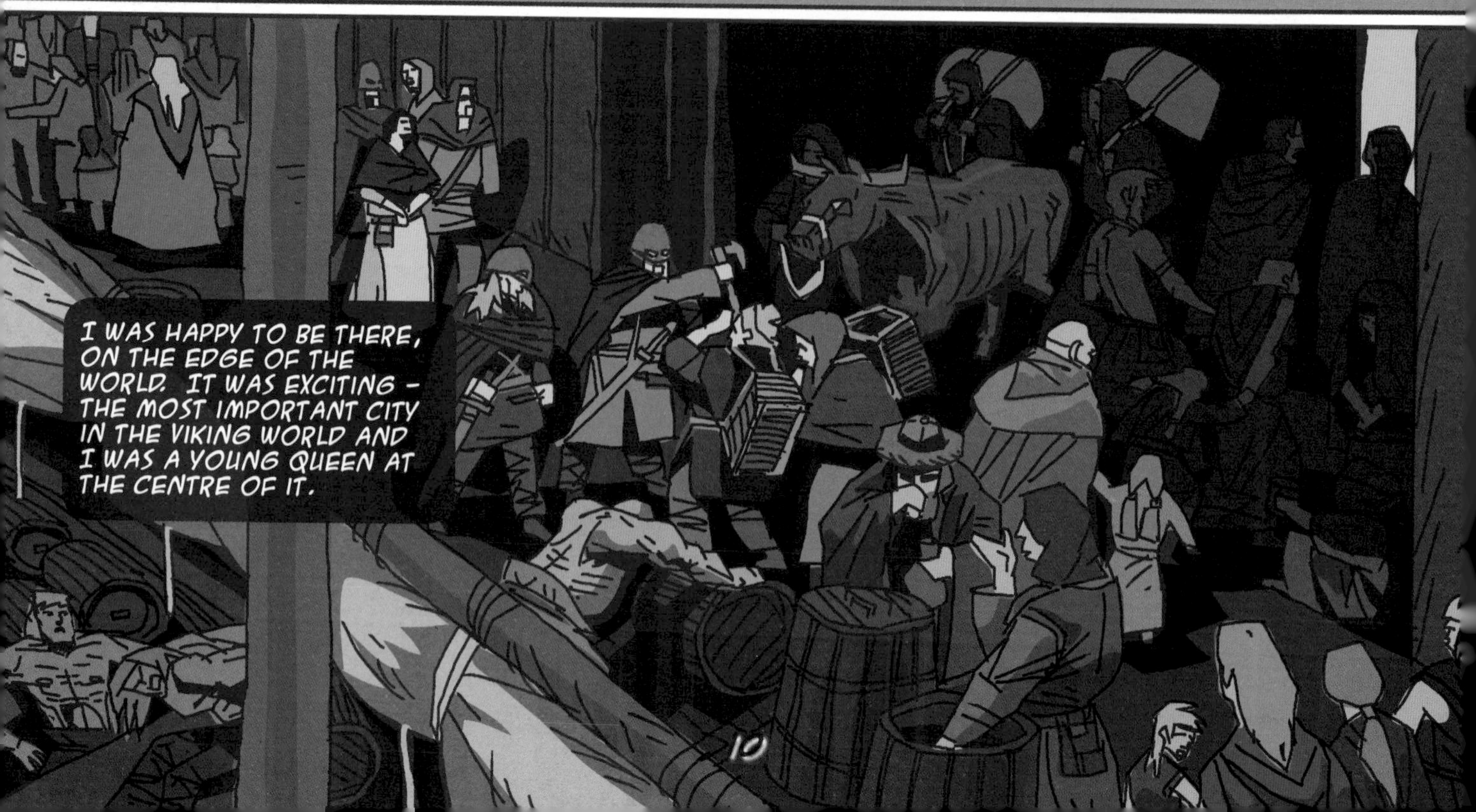
I WAS HAPPY TO BE THERE, ON THE EDGE OF THE WORLD. IT WAS EXCITING - THE MOST IMPORTANT CITY IN THE VIKING WORLD AND I WAS A YOUNG QUEEN AT THE CENTRE OF IT.

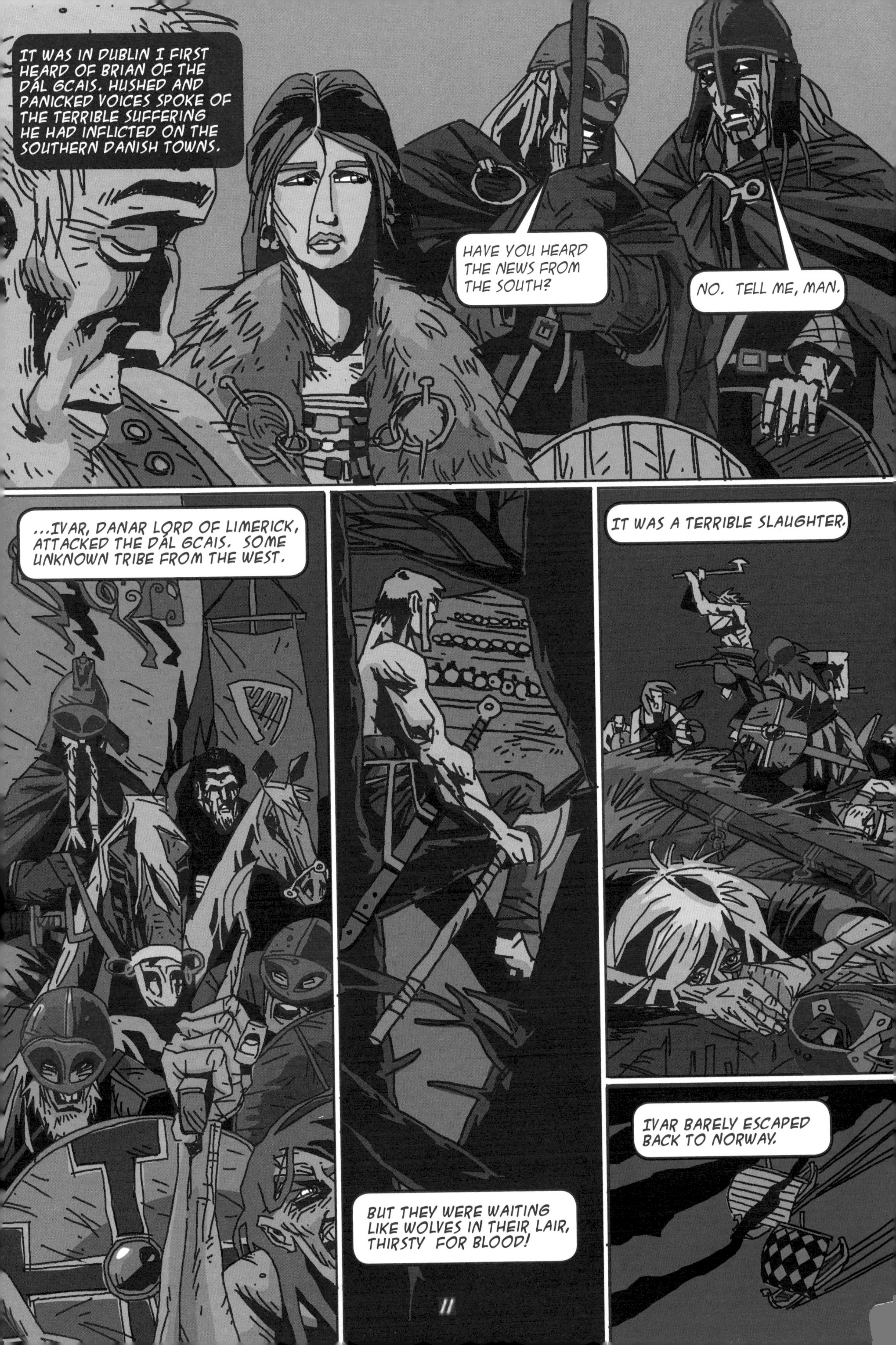
IT WAS IN DUBLIN I FIRST HEARD OF BRIAN OF THE DÁL GCAIS. HUSHED AND PANICKED VOICES SPOKE OF THE TERRIBLE SUFFERING HE HAD INFLICTED ON THE SOUTHERN DANISH TOWNS.
HAVE YOU HEARD THE NEWS FROM THE SOUTH?
NO. TELL ME, MAN.
...IVAR, DANAR LORD OF LIMERICK, ATTACKED THE DÁL GCAIS. SOME UNKNOWN TRIBE FROM THE WEST.
BUT THEY WERE WAITING LIKE WOLVES IN THEIR LAIR, THIRSTY FOR BLOOD!
IT WAS A TERRIBLE SLAUGHTER.
IVAR BARELY ESCAPED BACK TO NORWAY.

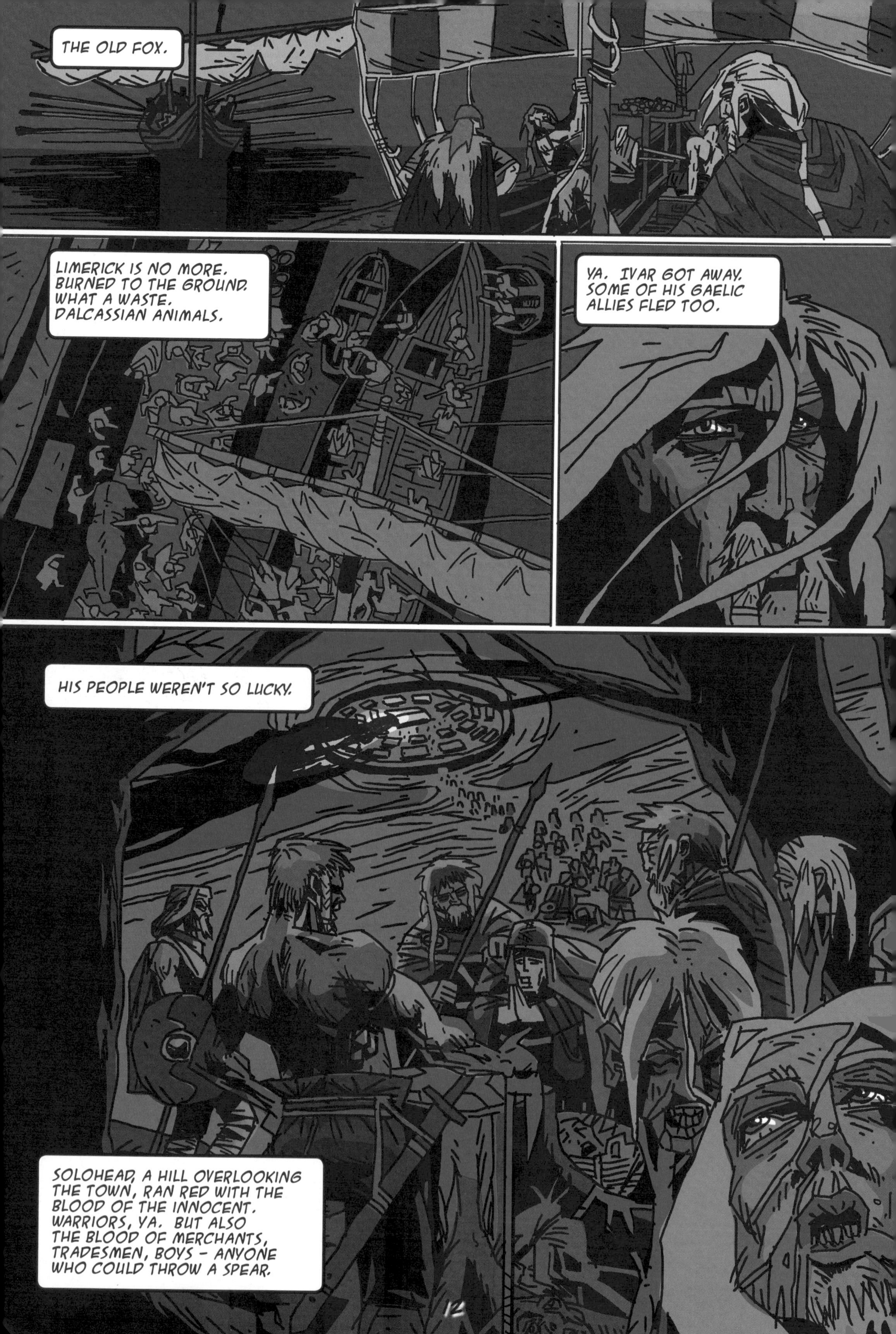
THE OLD FOX.
LIMERICK IS NO MORE. BURNED TO THE GROUND. WHAT A WASTE. DALCASSIAN ANIMALS.
YA. IVAR GOT AWAY. SOME OF HIS GAELIC ALLIES FLED TOO.
HIS PEOPLE WEREN'T SO LUCKY.
SOLOHEAD, A HILL OVERLOOKING THE TOWN, RAN RED WITH THE BLOOD OF THE INNOCENT. WARRIORS, YA. BUT ALSO THE BLOOD OF MERCHANTS, TRADESMEN, BOYS – ANYONE WHO COULD THROW A SPEAR.

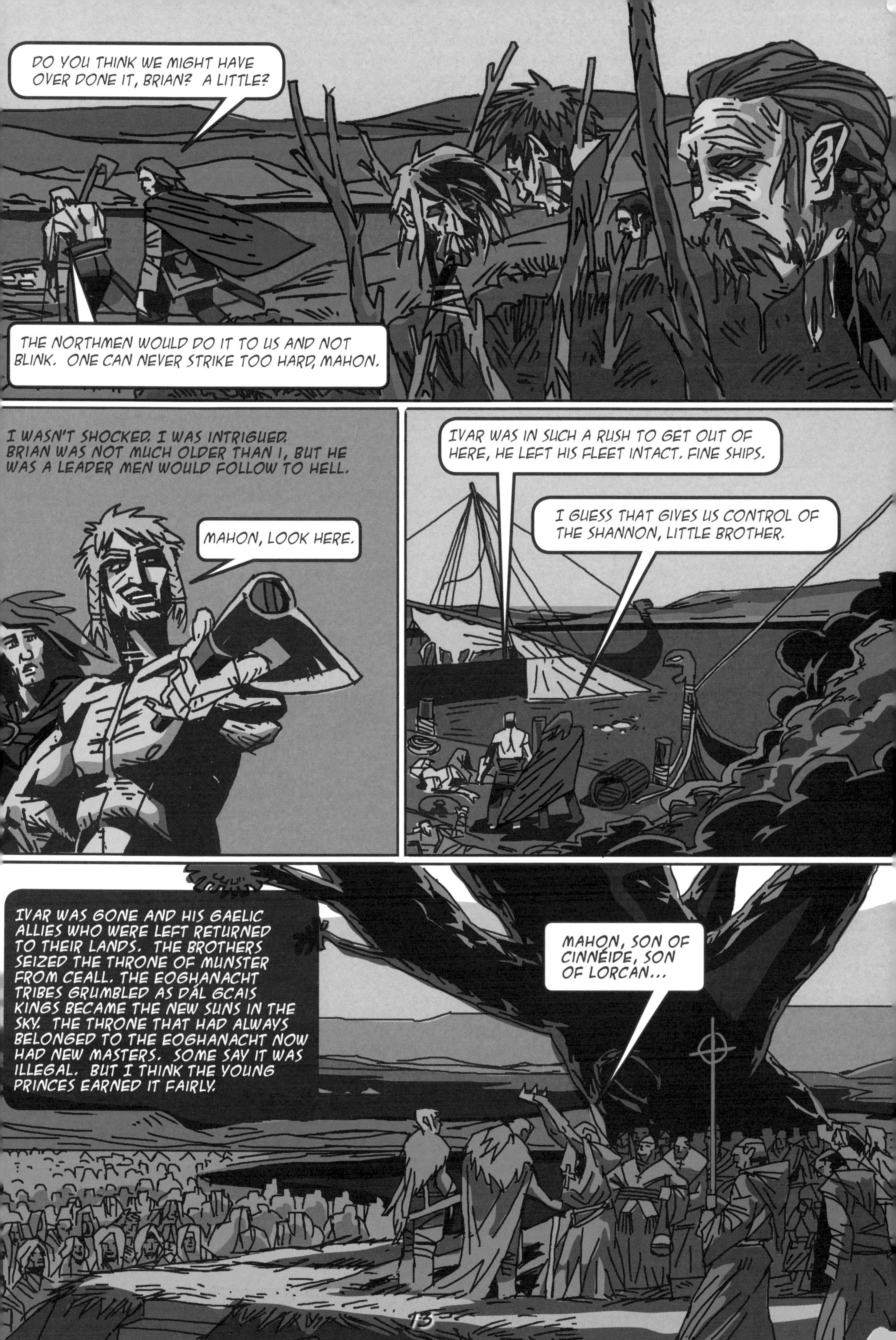

DO YOU THINK WE MIGHT HAVE OVER DONE IT, BRIAN? A LITTLE?
THE NORTHMEN WOULD DO IT TO US AND NOT BLINK. ONE CAN NEVER STRIKE TOO HARD, MAHON.
I WASN'T SHOCKED. I WAS INTRIGUED. BRIAN WAS NOT MUCH OLDER THAN I, BUT HE WAS A LEADER MEN WOULD FOLLOW TO HELL.
MAHON, LOOK HERE.
IVAR WAS IN SUCH A RUSH TO GET OUT OF HERE, HE LEFT HIS FLEET INTACT. FINE SHIPS.
I GUESS THAT GIVES US CONTROL OF THE SHANNON, LITTLE BROTHER.
IVAR WAS GONE AND HIS GAELIC ALLIES WHO WERE LEFT RETURNED TO THEIR LANDS. THE BROTHERS SEIZED THE THRONE OF MUNSTER FROM CEALL. THE EOGHANACHT TRIBES GRUMBLED AS DÁL GCAIS KINGS BECAME THE NEW SUNS IN THE SKY. THE THRONE THAT HAD ALWAYS BELONGED TO THE EOGHANACHT NOW HAD NEW MASTERS. SOME SAY IT WAS ILLEGAL. BUT I THINK THE YOUNG PRINCES EARNED IT FAIRLY.
MAHON, SON OF CINNÉIDE, SON OF LORCAN...

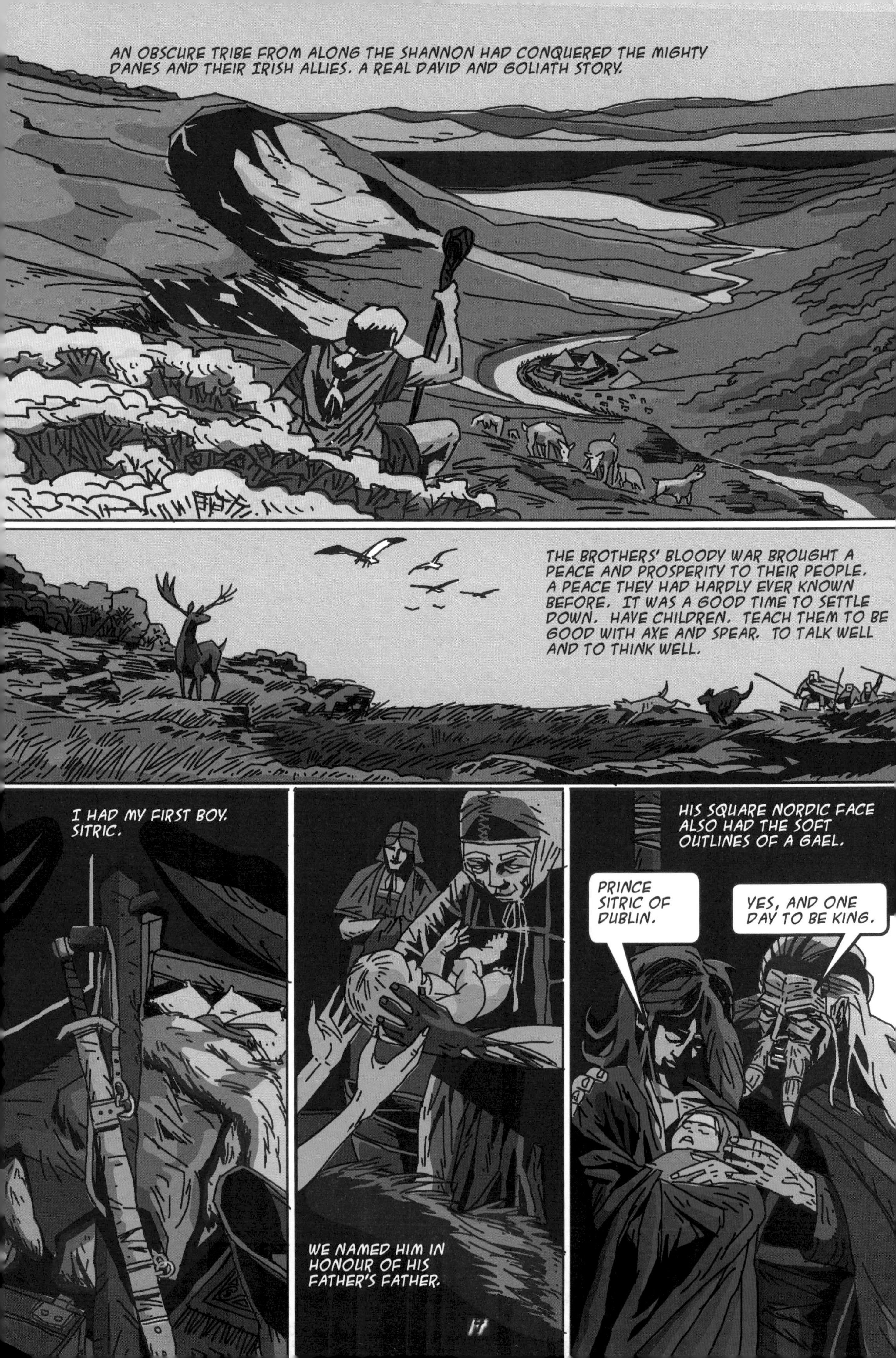
AN OBSCURE TRIBE FROM ALONG THE SHANNON HAD CONQUERED THE MIGHTY DANES AND THEIR IRISH ALLIES. A REAL DAVID AND GOLIATH STORY.
THE BROTHERS' BLOODY WAR BROUGHT A PEACE AND PROSPERITY TO THEIR PEOPLE. A PEACE THEY HAD HARDLY EVER KNOWN BEFORE. IT WAS A GOOD TIME TO SETTLE DOWN. HAVE CHILDREN. TEACH THEM TO BE GOOD WITH AXE AND SPEAR. TO TALK WELL AND TO THINK WELL.
I HAD MY FIRST BOY. SITRIC.
WE NAMED HIM IN HONOUR OF HIS FATHER'S FATHER.
HIS SQUARE NORDIC FACE ALSO HAD THE SOFT OUTLINES OF A GAEL.
PRINCE SITRIC OF DUBLIN.
YES, AND ONE DAY TO BE KING.

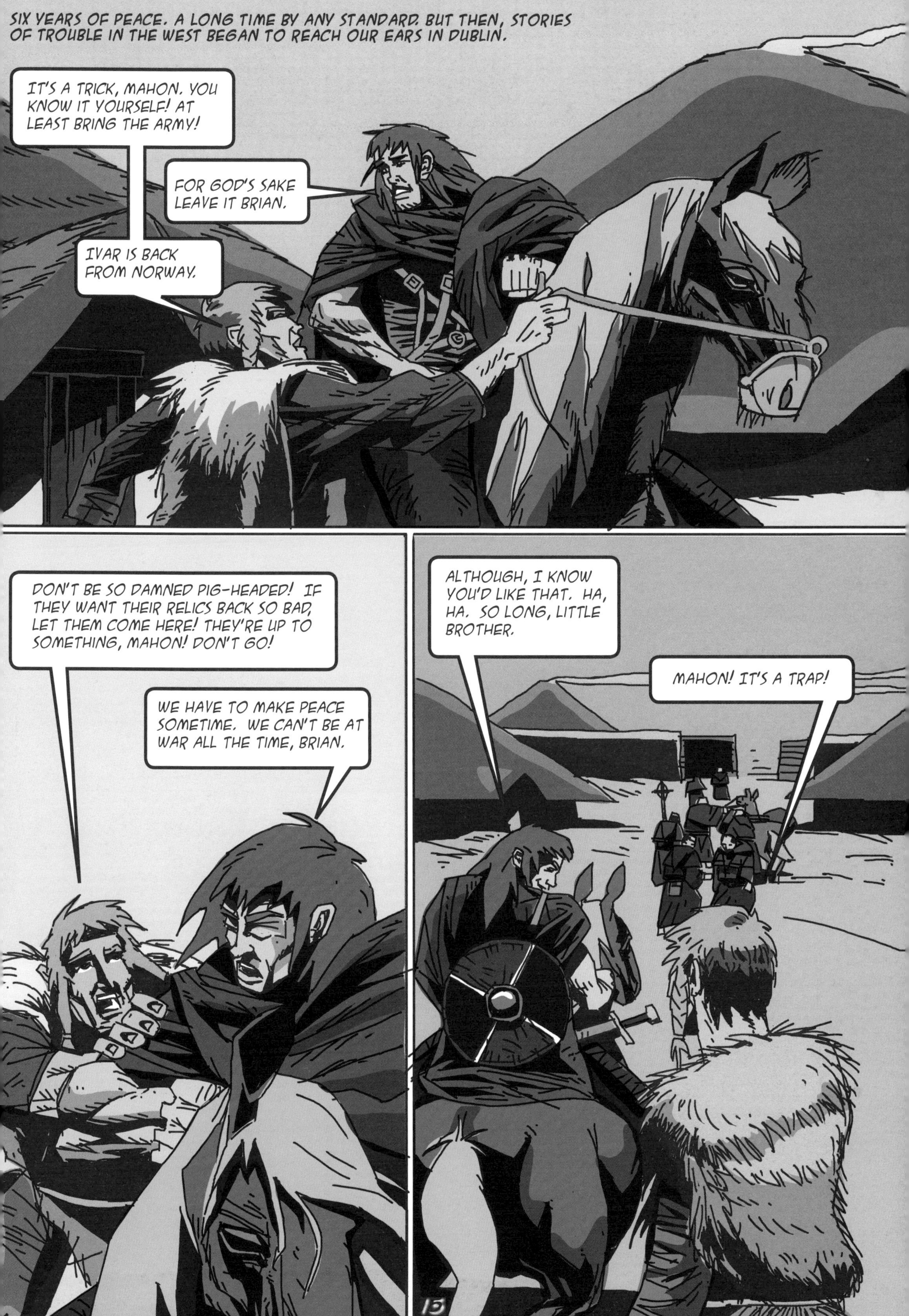
SIX YEARS OF PEACE. A LONG TIME BY ANY STANDARD. BUT THEN, STORIES OF TROUBLE IN THE WEST BEGAN TO REACH OUR EARS IN DUBLIN.
IT'S A TRICK, MAHON. YOU KNOW IT YOURSELF! AT LEAST BRING THE ARMY!
FOR GOD'S SAKE LEAVE IT BRIAN.
IVAR IS BACK FROM NORWAY.
DON'T BE SO DAMNED PIG-HEADED! IF THEY WANT THEIR RELICS BACK SO BAD, LET THEM COME HERE! THEY'RE UP TO SOMETHING, MAHON! DON'T GO!
WE HAVE TO MAKE PEACE SOMETIME. WE CAN'T BE AT WAR ALL THE TIME, BRIAN.
ALTHOUGH, I KNOW YOU'D LIKE THAT. HA, HA. SO LONG, LITTLE BROTHER.
MAHON! IT'S A TRAP!

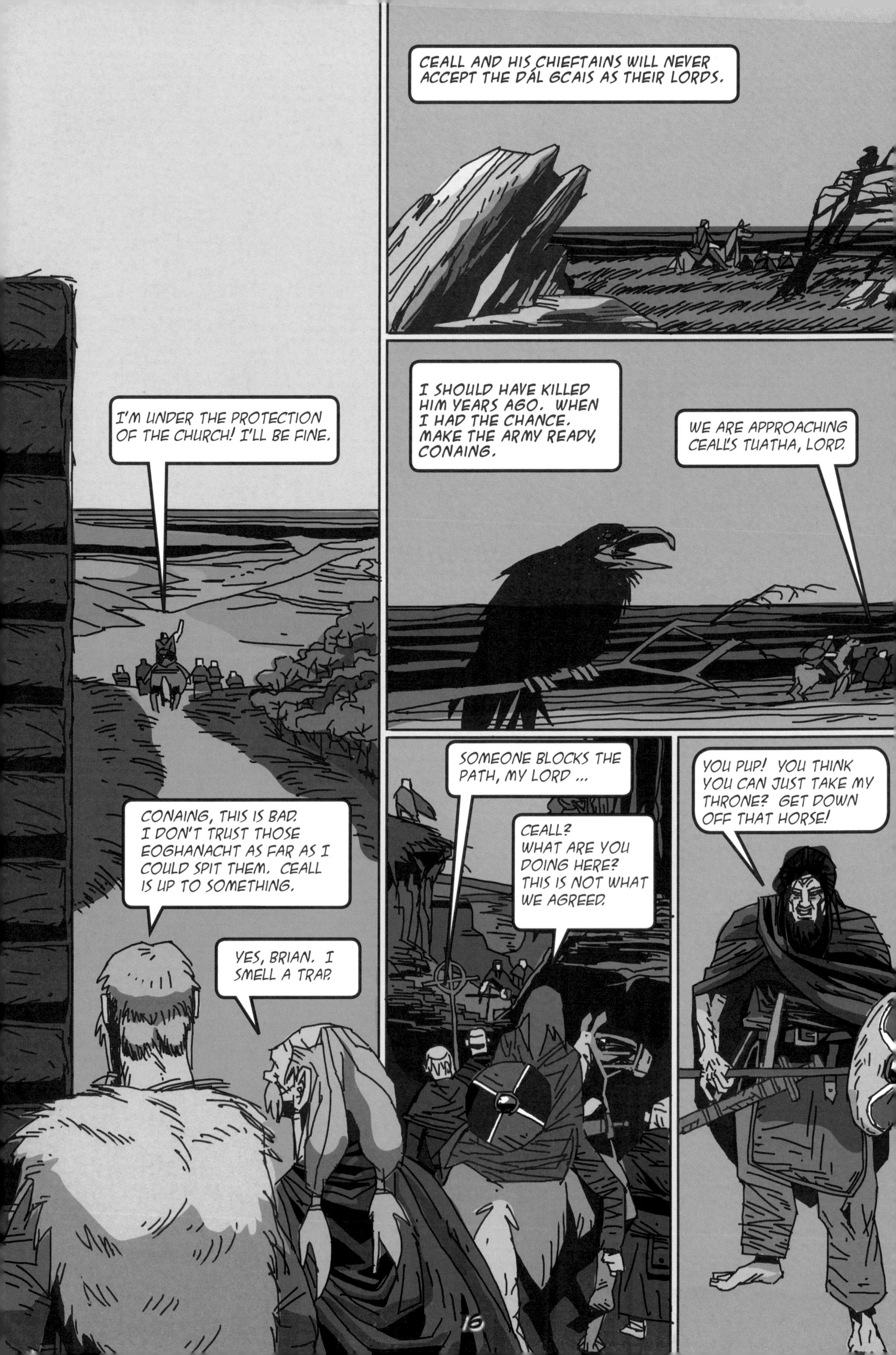
I'M UNDER THE PROTECTION OF THE CHURCH! I'LL BE FINE.
CONAING, THIS IS BAD. I DON'T TRUST THOSE EOGHANACHT AS FAR AS I COULD SPIT THEM. CEALL IS UP TO SOMETHING.
YES, BRIAN. I SMELL A TRAP.
CEALL AND HIS CHIEFTAINS WILL NEVER ACCEPT THE DÁL GCAIS AS THEIR LORDS.
I SHOULD HAVE KILLED HIM YEARS AGO. WHEN I HAD THE CHANCE. MAKE THE ARMY READY, CONAING.
WE ARE APPROACHING CEALL'S TUATHA, LORD.
SOMEONE BLOCKS THE PATH, MY LORD ...
CEALL? WHAT ARE YOU DOING HERE? THIS IS NOT WHAT WE AGREED.
YOU PUP! YOU THINK YOU CAN JUST TAKE MY THRONE? GET DOWN OFF THAT HORSE!

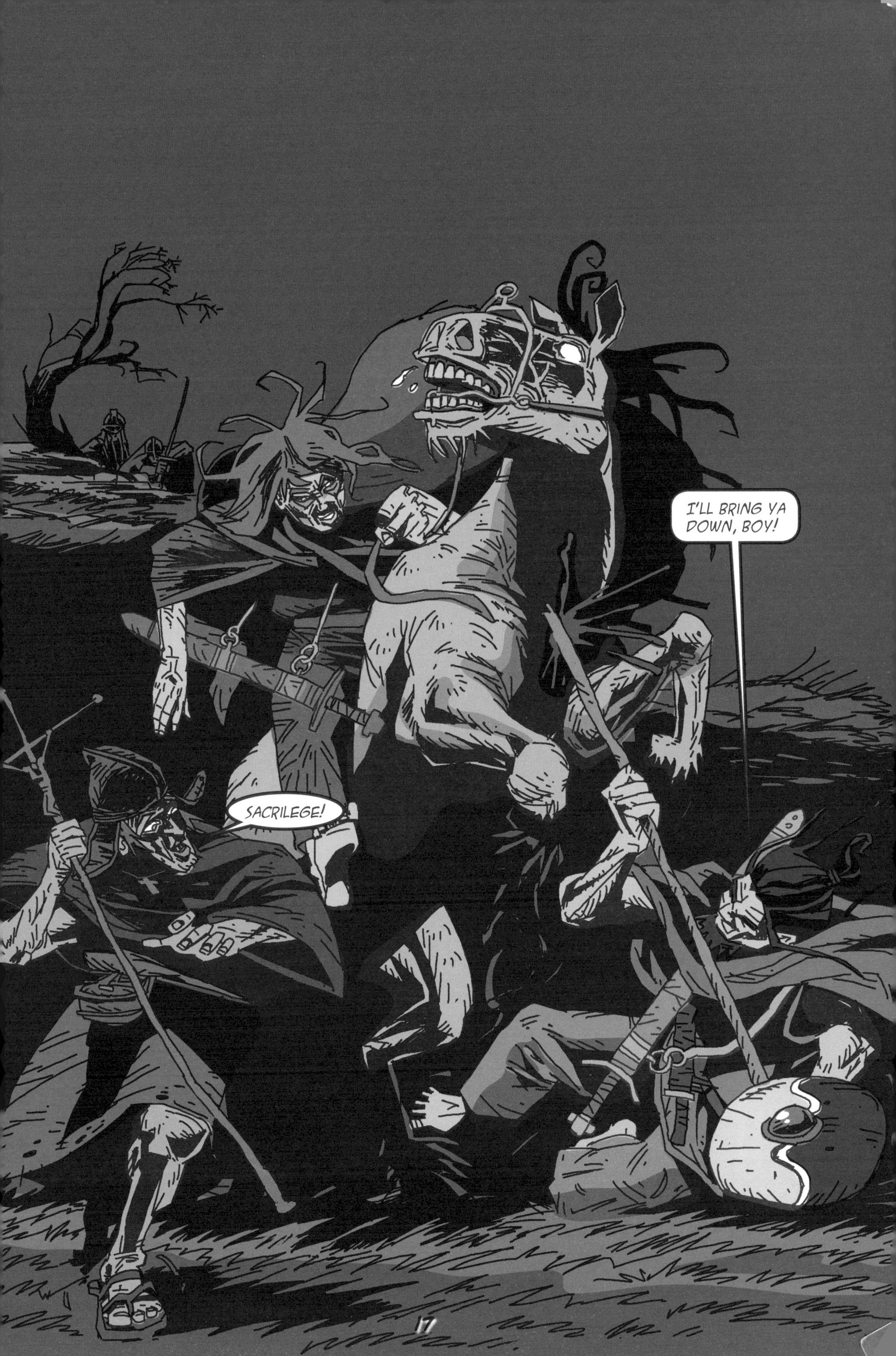
I'LL BRING YA DOWN, BOY!
SACRILEGE!

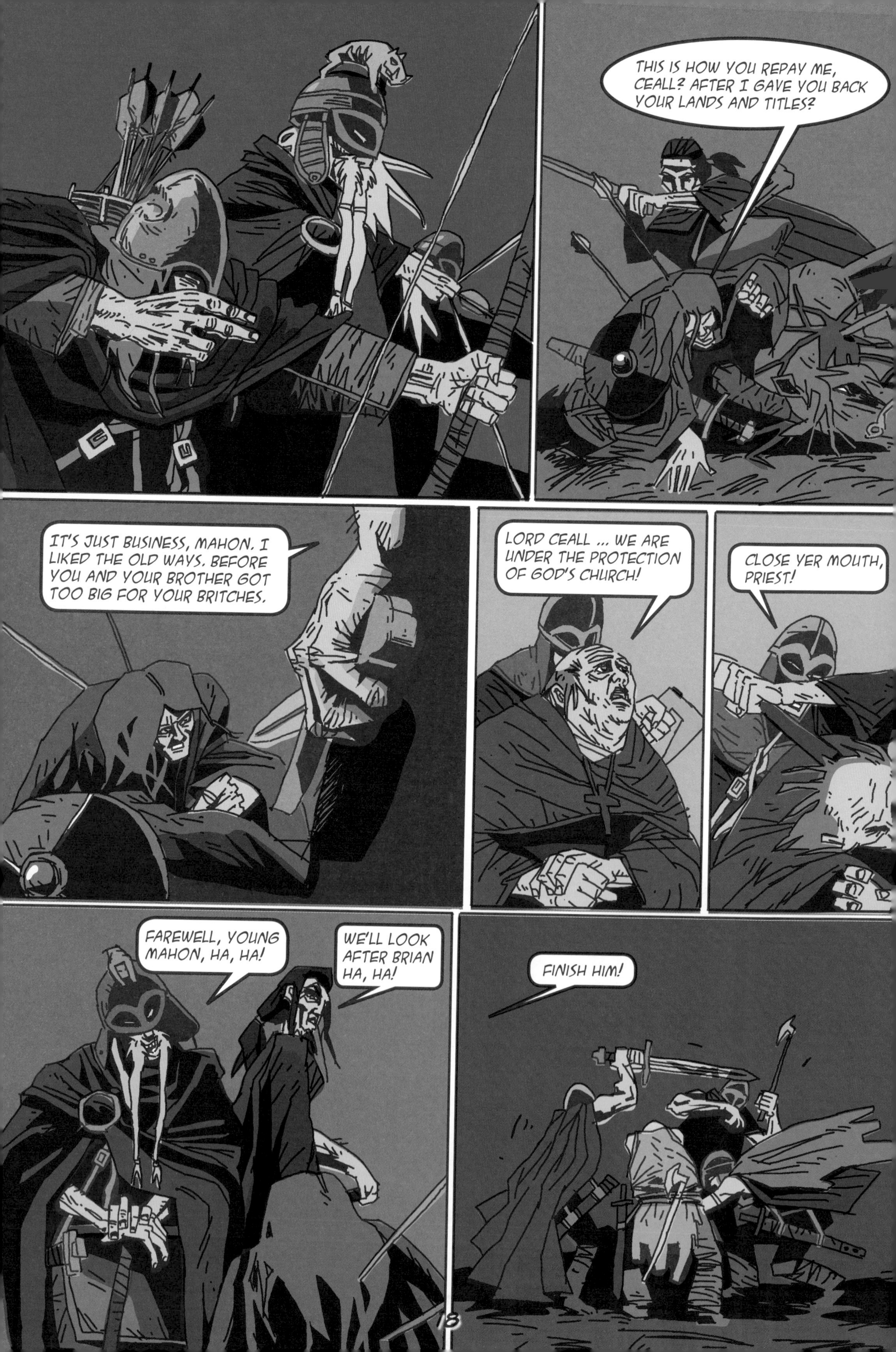
THIS IS HOW YOU REPAY ME, CEALL? AFTER I GAVE YOU BACK YOUR LANDS AND TITLES?
IT'S JUST BUSINESS, MAHON. I LIKED THE OLD WAYS. BEFORE YOU AND YOUR BROTHER GOT TOO BIG FOR YOUR BRITCHES.
LORD CEALL ... WE ARE UNDER THE PROTECTION OF GOD'S CHURCH!
CLOSE YER MOUTH, PRIEST!
FAREWELL, YOUNG MAHON, HA, HA!
WE'LL LOOK AFTER BRIAN HA, HA!
FINISH HIM!

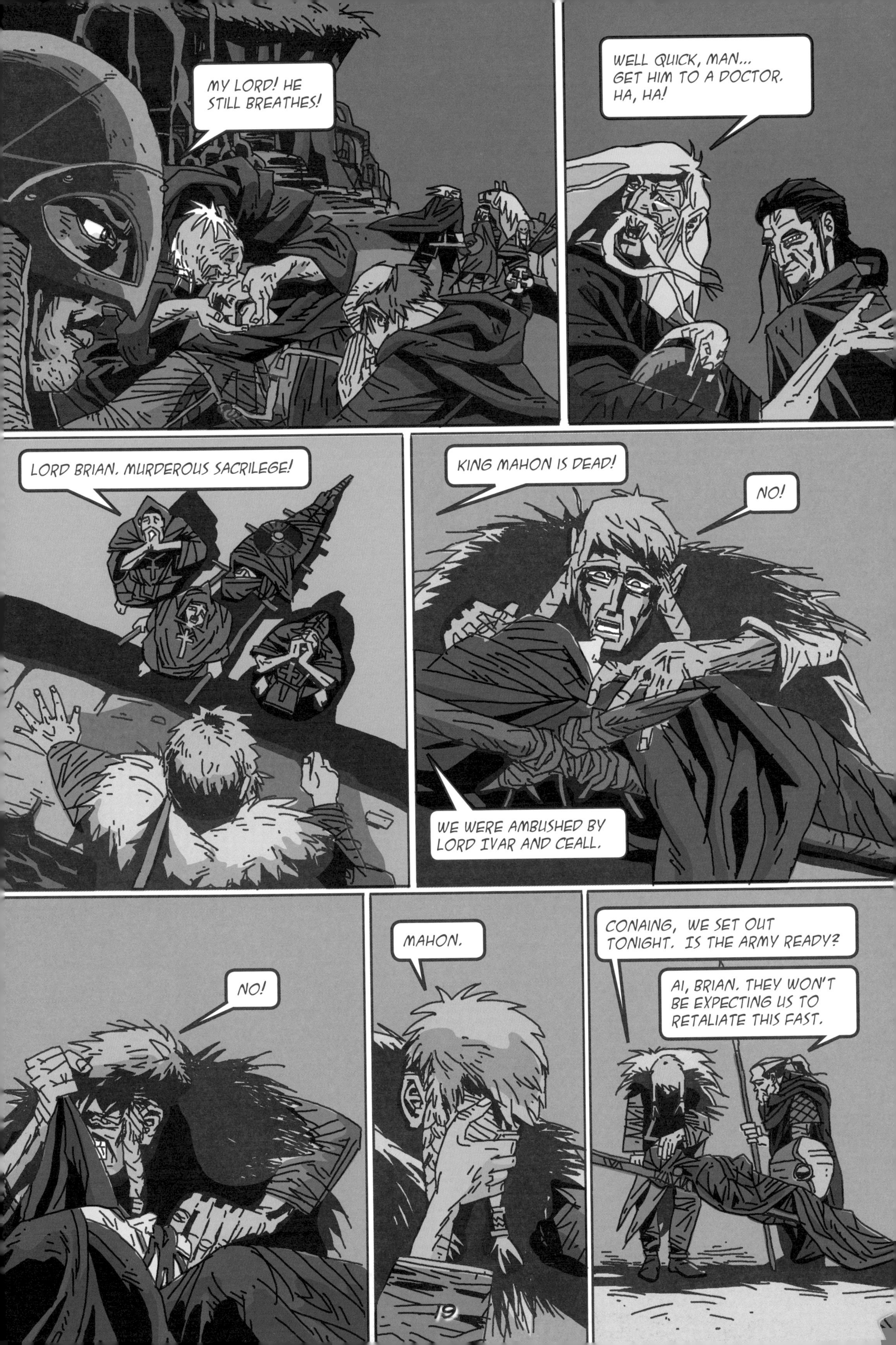
MY LORD! HE STILL BREATHES!
WELL QUICK, MAN... GET HIM TO A DOCTOR. HA, HA!
LORD BRIAN. MURDEROUS SACRILEGE!
KING MAHON IS DEAD!
NO!
WE WERE AMBUSHED BY LORD IVAR AND CEALL.
NO!
MAHON.
CONAING, WE SET OUT TONIGHT. IS THE ARMY READY?
AI, BRIAN. THEY WON'T BE EXPECTING US TO RETALIATE THIS FAST.

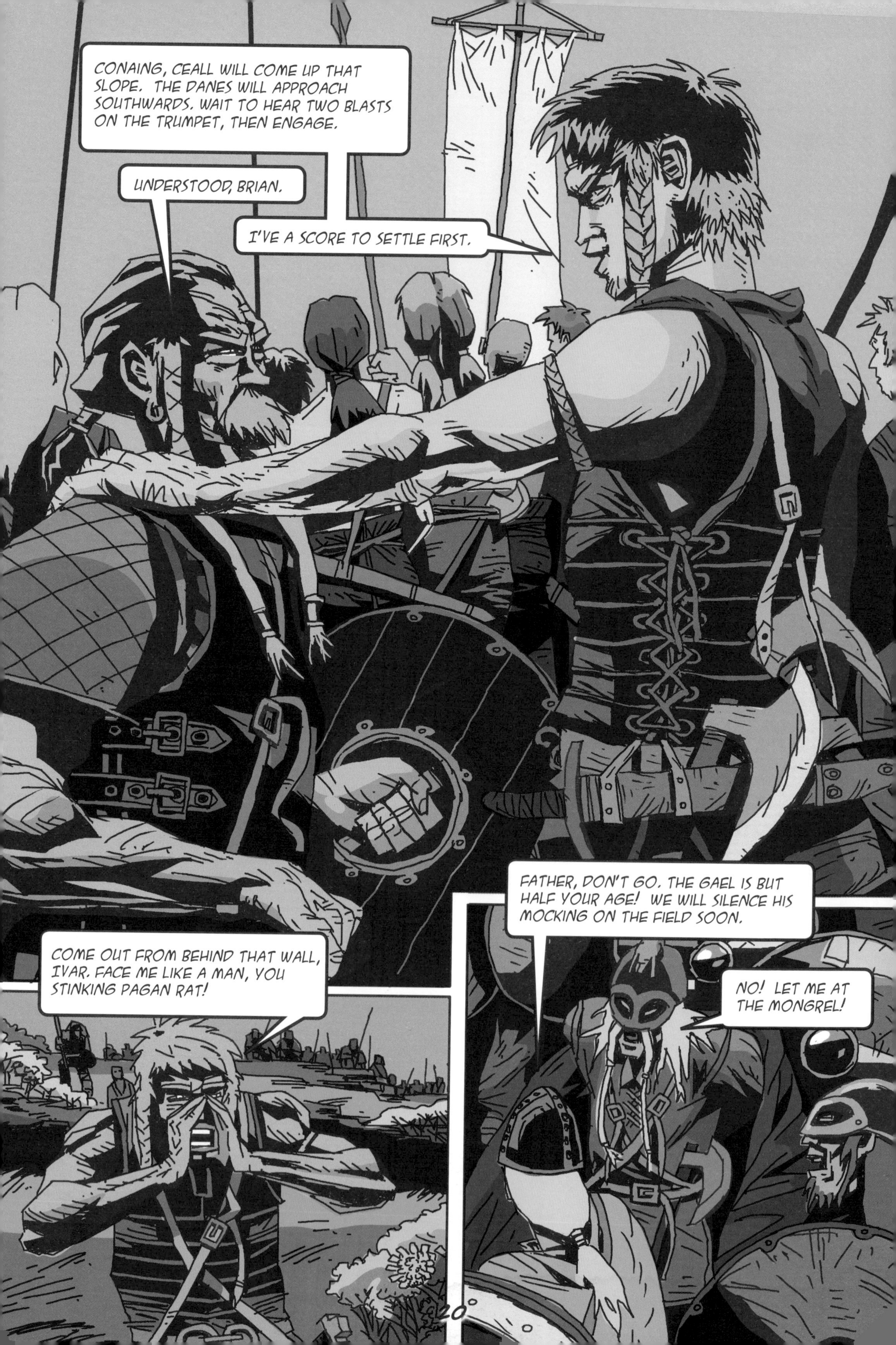

CONAING, CEALL WILL COME UP THAT SLOPE. THE DANES WILL APPROACH SOUTHWARDS. WAIT TO HEAR TWO BLASTS ON THE TRUMPET, THEN ENGAGE.
UNDERSTOOD, BRIAN.
I'VE A SCORE TO SETTLE FIRST.
COME OUT FROM BEHIND THAT WALL, IVAR. FACE ME LIKE A MAN, YOU STINKING PAGAN RAT!
FATHER, DON'T GO. THE GAEL IS BUT HALF YOUR AGE! WE WILL SILENCE HIS MOCKING ON THE FIELD SOON.
NO! LET ME AT THE MONGREL!

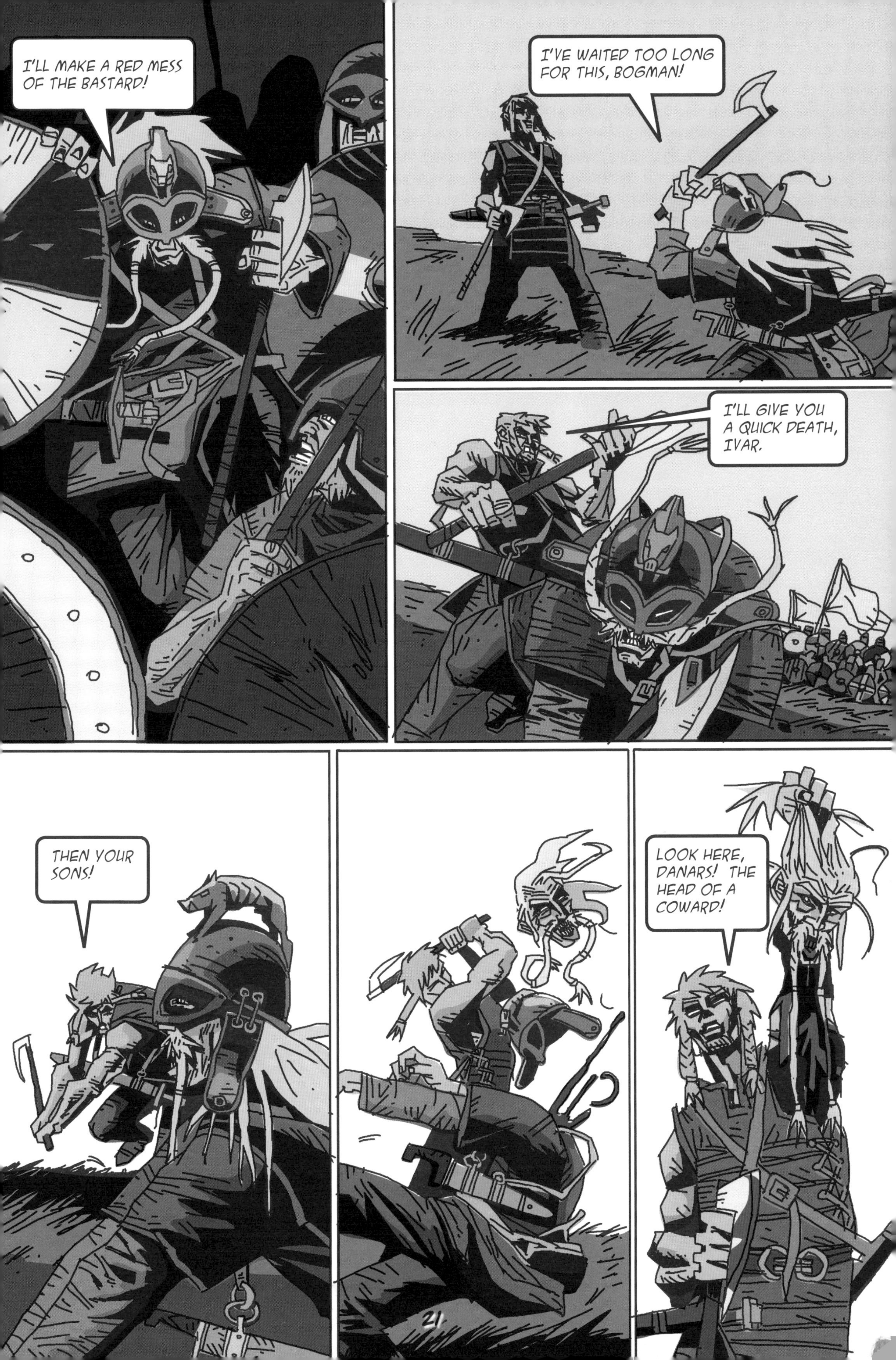
I'LL MAKE A RED MESS OF THE BASTARD!
I'VE WAITED TOO LONG FOR THIS, BOGMAN!
I'LL GIVE YOU A QUICK DEATH, IVAR.
THEN YOUR SONS!
LOOK HERE, DANARS! THE HEAD OF A COWARD!

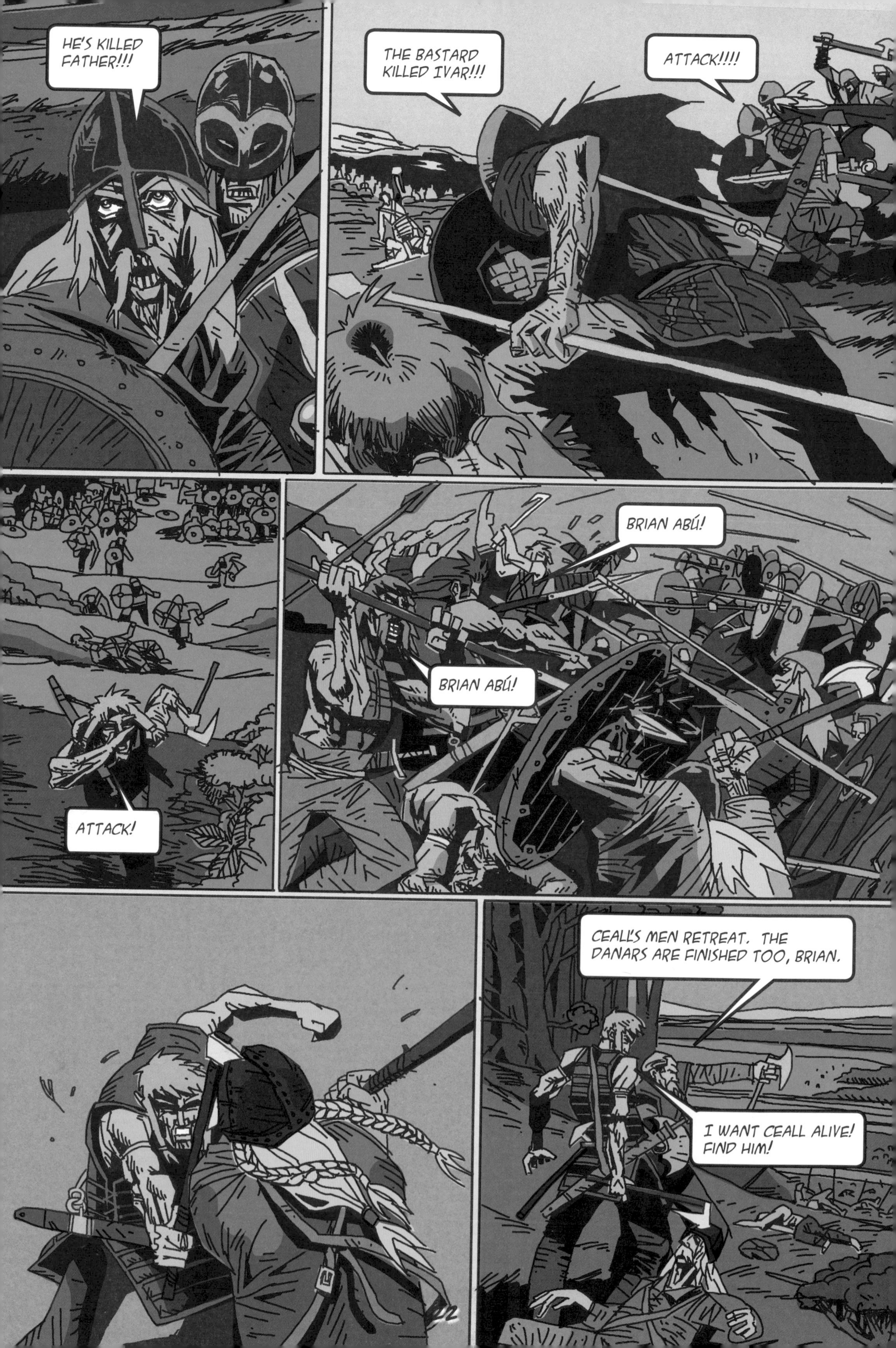
HE'S KILLED FATHER!!!
THE BASTARD KILLED IVAR!!!
ATTACK!!!!
ATTACK!
BRIAN ABÚ!
BRIAN ABÚ!
CEALL'S MEN RETREAT. THE DANARS ARE FINISHED TOO, BRIAN.
I WANT CEALL ALIVE! FIND HIM!

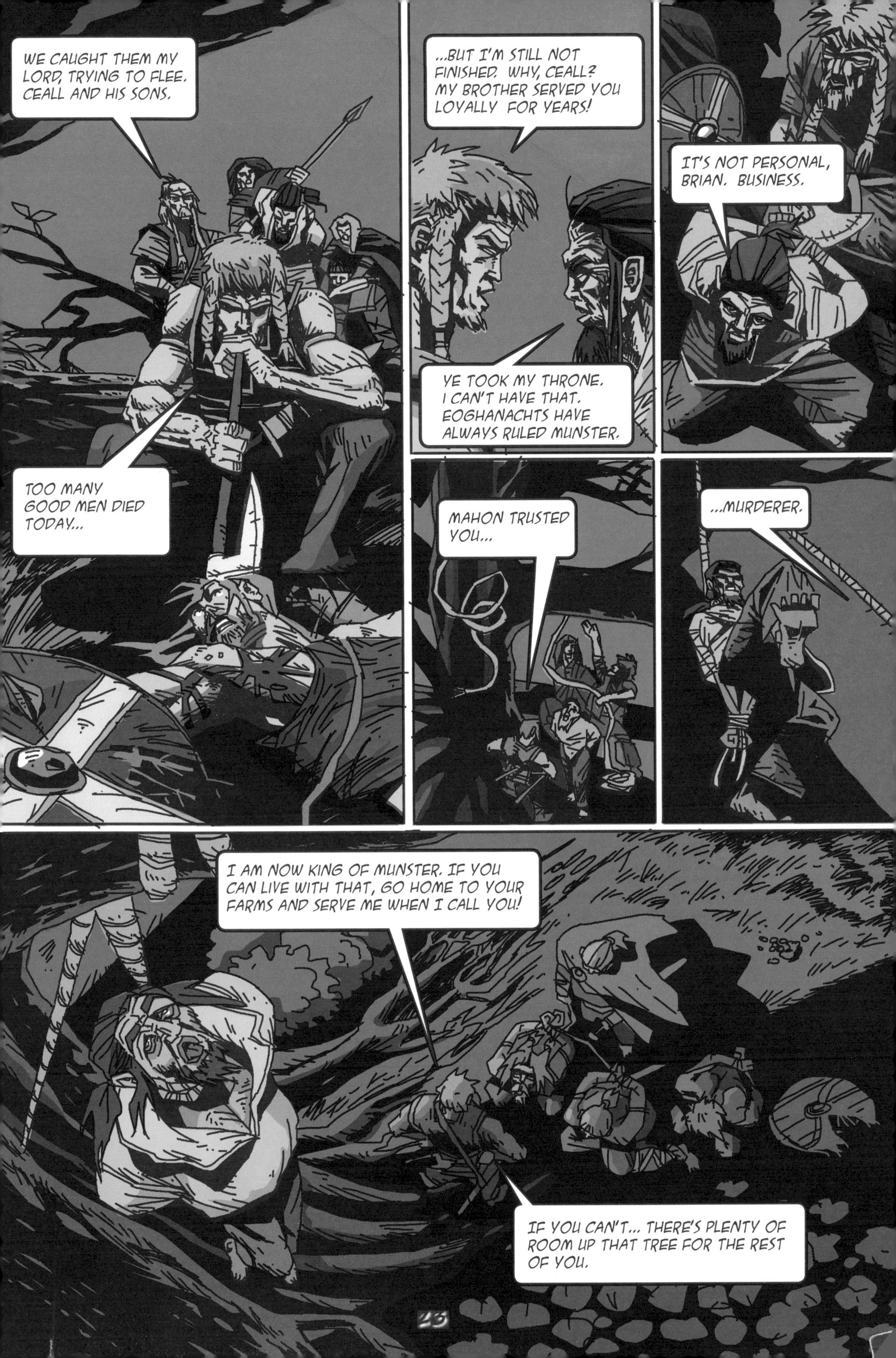
WE CAUGHT THEM MY LORD, TRYING TO FLEE. CEALL AND HIS SONS.
TOO MANY GOOD MEN DIED TODAY...
...BUT I'M STILL NOT FINISHED. WHY, CEALL? MY BROTHER SERVED YOU LOYALLY FOR YEARS!
YE TOOK MY THRONE. I CAN'T HAVE THAT. EOGHANACHTS HAVE ALWAYS RULED MUNSTER.
IT'S NOT PERSONAL, BRIAN. BUSINESS.
MAHON TRUSTED YOU...
...MURDERER.
I AM NOW KING OF MUNSTER. IF YOU CAN LIVE WITH THAT, GO HOME TO YOUR FARMS AND SERVE ME WHEN I CALL YOU!
IF YOU CAN'T... THERE'S PLENTY OF ROOM UP THAT TREE FOR THE REST OF YOU.

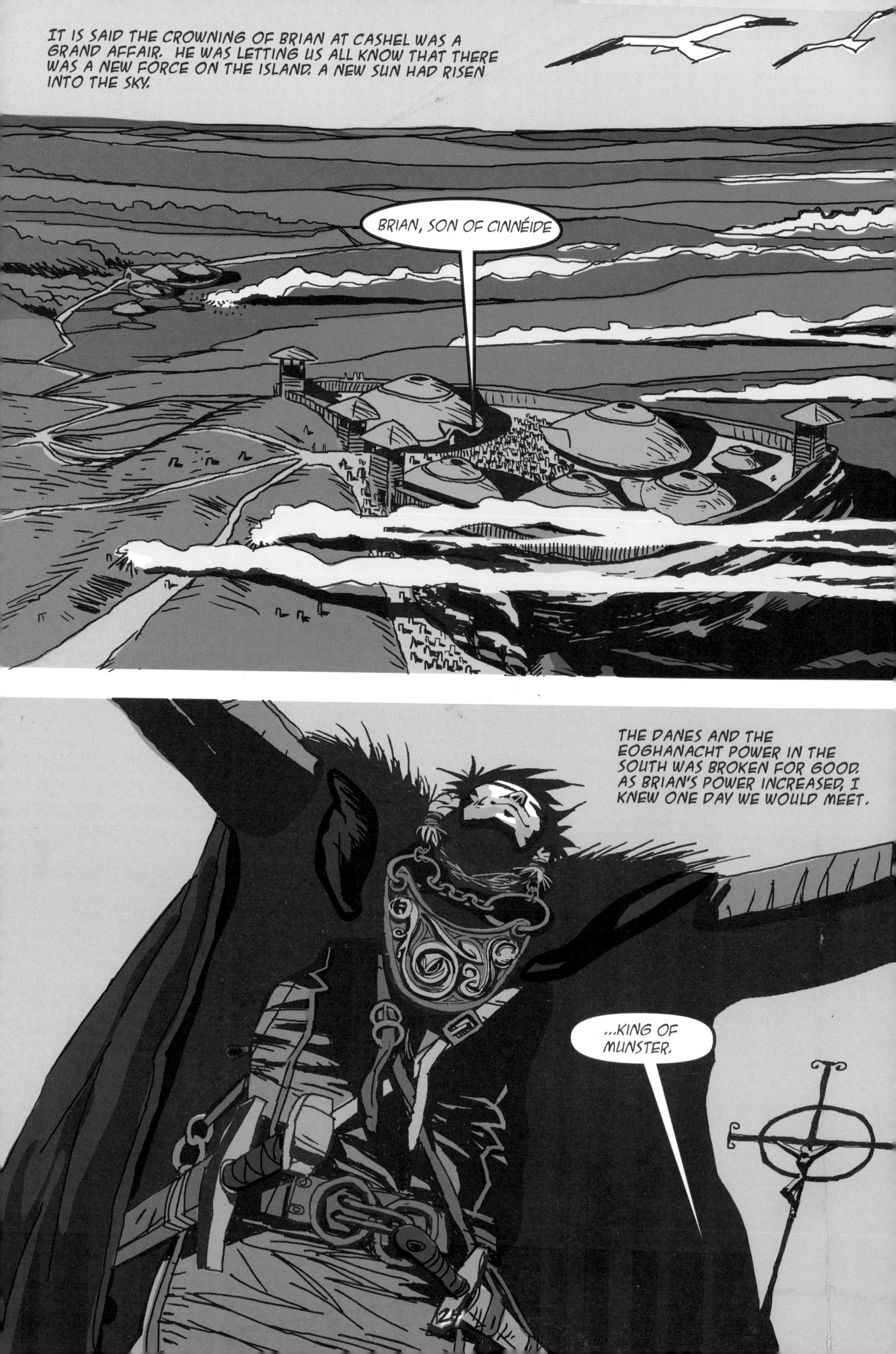
IT IS SAID THE CROWNING OF BRIAN AT CASHEL WAS A GRAND AFFAIR. HE WAS LETTING US ALL KNOW THAT THERE WAS A NEW FORCE ON THE ISLAND. A NEW SUN HAD RISEN INTO THE SKY.
BRIAN, SON OF CINNÉIDE
THE DANES AND THE EOGHANACHT POWER IN THE SOUTH WAS BROKEN FOR GOOD. AS BRIAN'S POWER INCREASED, I KNEW ONE DAY WE WOULD MEET.
...KING OF MUNSTER.

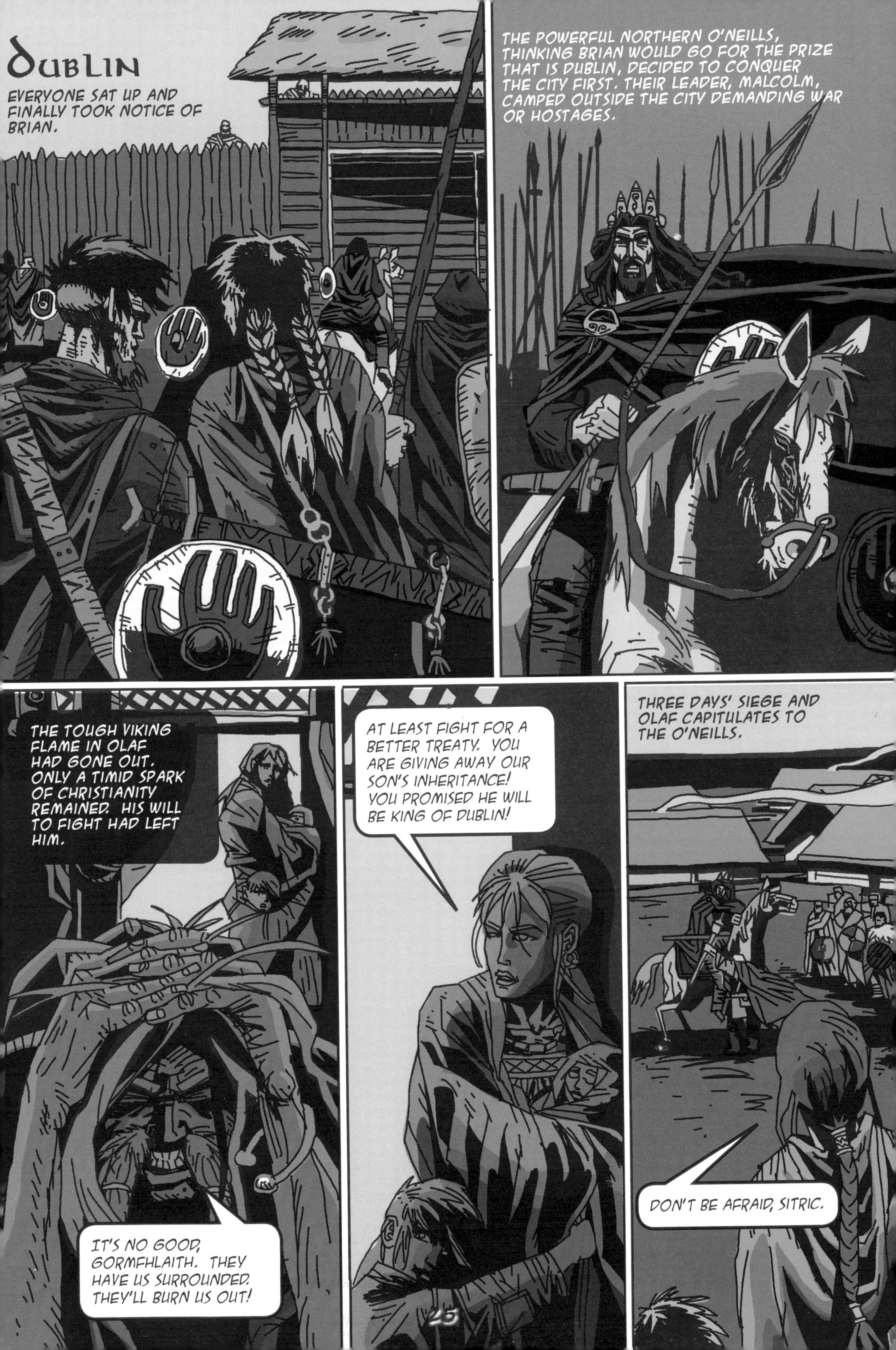
DUBLIN
EVERYONE SAT UP AND FINALLY TOOK NOTICE OF BRIAN.
THE POWERFUL NORTHERN O'NEILLS, THINKING BRIAN WOULD GO FOR THE PRIZE THAT IS DUBLIN, DECIDED TO CONQUER THE CITY FIRST. THEIR LEADER, MALCOLM, CAMPED OUTSIDE THE CITY DEMANDING WAR OR HOSTAGES.
THE TOUGH VIKING FLAME IN OLAF HAD GONE OUT. ONLY A TIMID SPARK OF CHRISTIANITY REMAINED. HIS WILL TO FIGHT HAD LEFT HIM.
IT'S NO GOOD, GORMFHLAITH. THEY HAVE US SURROUNDED. THEY'LL BURN US OUT!
AT LEAST FIGHT FOR A BETTER TREATY. YOU ARE GIVING AWAY OUR SON'S INHERITANCE! YOU PROMISED HE WILL BE KING OF DUBLIN!
THREE DAYS' SIEGE AND OLAF CAPITULATES TO THE O'NEILLS.
DON'T BE AFRAID, SITRIC.

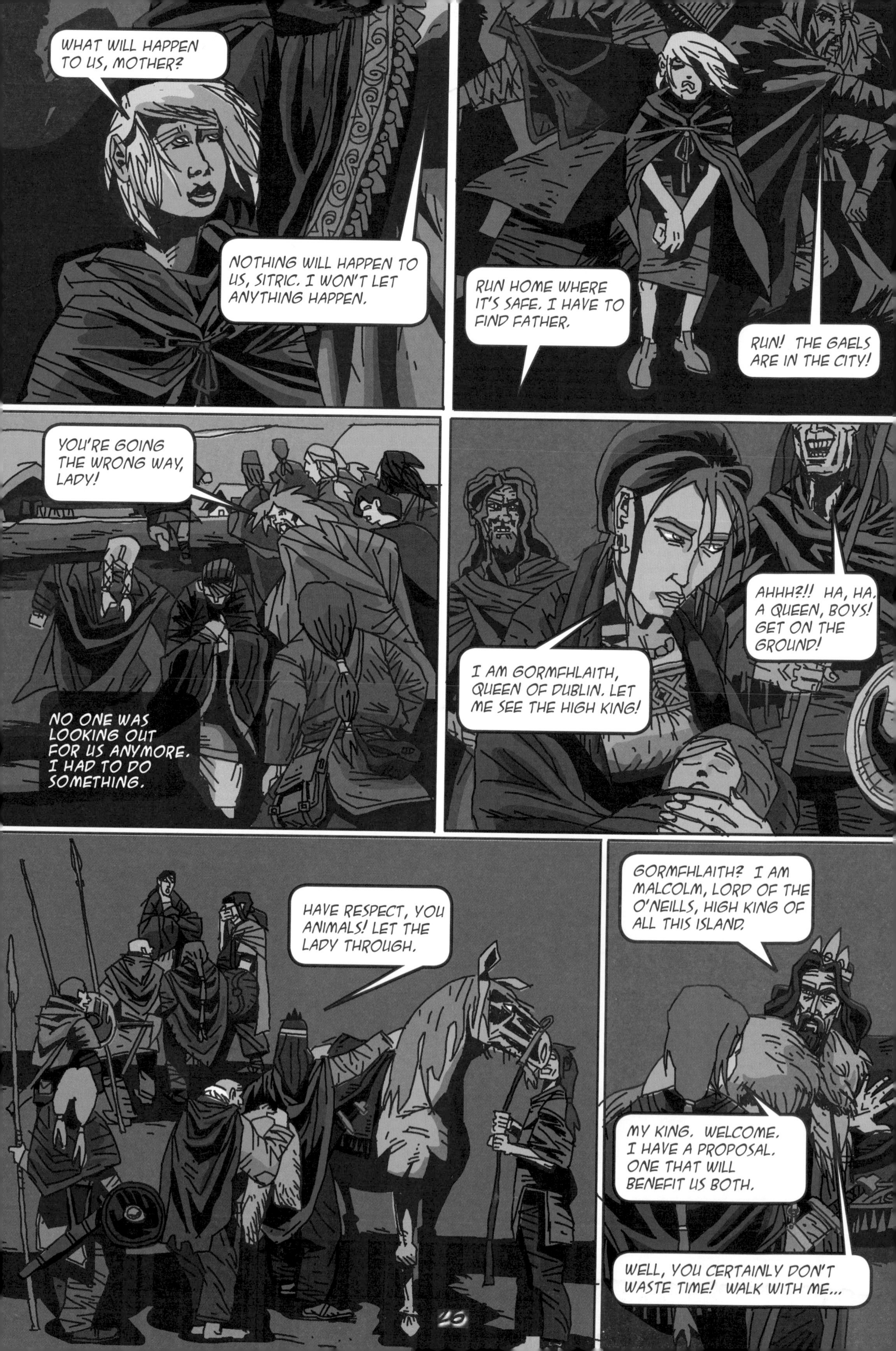
WHAT WILL HAPPEN TO US, MOTHER?
NOTHING WILL HAPPEN TO US, SITRIC. I WON'T LET ANYTHING HAPPEN.
RUN HOME WHERE IT'S SAFE. I HAVE TO FIND FATHER.
RUN! THE GAELS ARE IN THE CITY!
YOU'RE GOING THE WRONG WAY, LADY!
NO ONE WAS LOOKING OUT FOR US ANYMORE. I HAD TO DO SOMETHING.
I AM GORMFHLAITH, QUEEN OF DUBLIN. LET ME SEE THE HIGH KING!
AHHH?!! HA, HA. A QUEEN, BOYS! GET ON THE GROUND!
HAVE RESPECT, YOU ANIMALS! LET THE LADY THROUGH.
GORMFHLAITH? I AM MALCOLM, LORD OF THE O'NEILLS, HIGH KING OF ALL THIS ISLAND.
MY KING. WELCOME. I HAVE A PROPOSAL. ONE THAT WILL BENEFIT US BOTH.
WELL, YOU CERTAINLY DON'T WASTE TIME! WALK WITH ME...

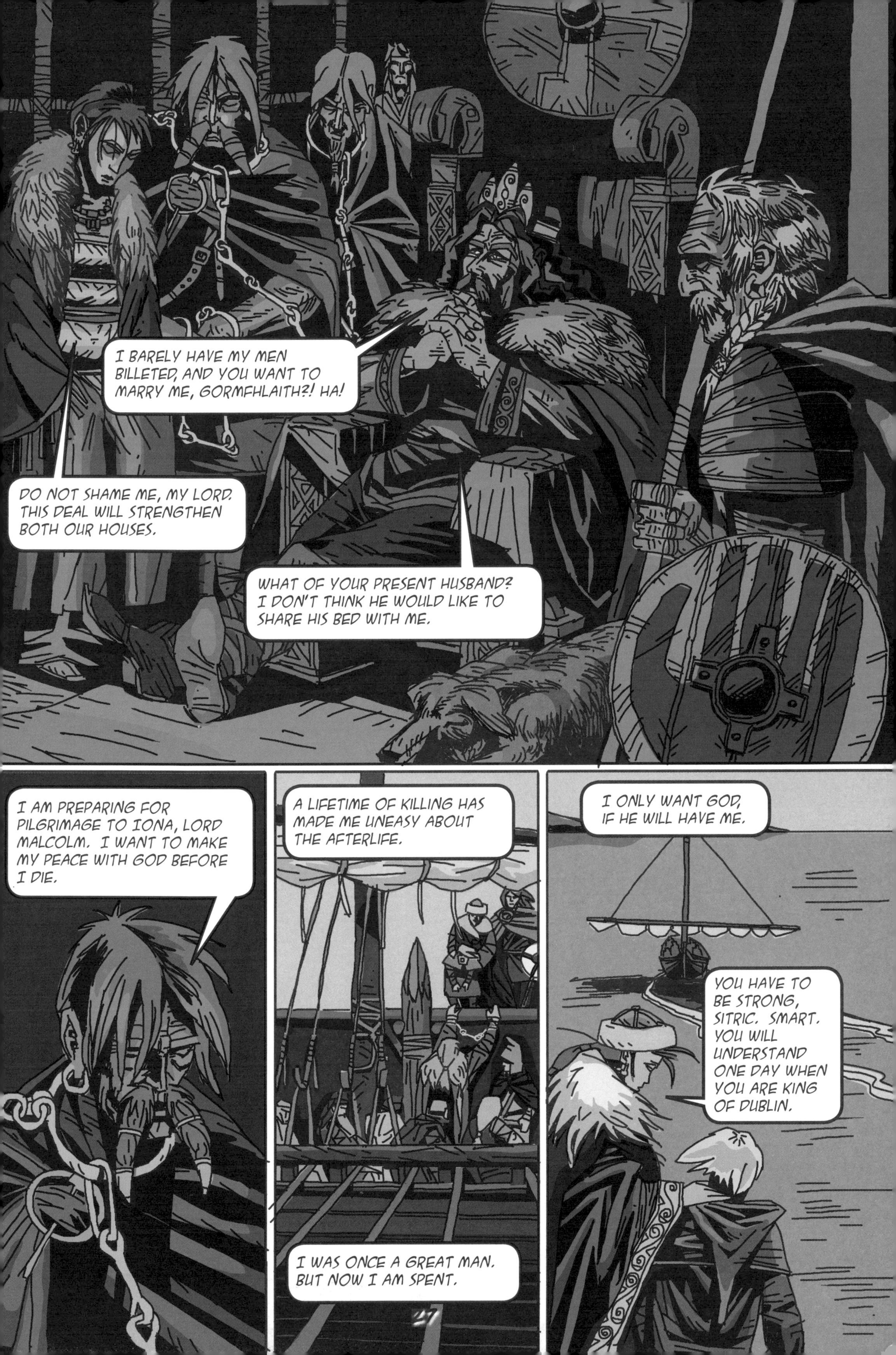
I BARELY HAVE MY MEN BILLETED, AND YOU WANT TO MARRY ME, GORMFHLAITH?! HA!
DO NOT SHAME ME, MY LORD. THIS DEAL WILL STRENGTHEN BOTH OUR HOUSES.
WHAT OF YOUR PRESENT HUSBAND? I DON'T THINK HE WOULD LIKE TO SHARE HIS BED WITH ME.
I AM PREPARING FOR PILGRIMAGE TO IONA, LORD MALCOLM. I WANT TO MAKE MY PEACE WITH GOD BEFORE I DIE.
A LIFETIME OF KILLING HAS MADE ME UNEASY ABOUT THE AFTERLIFE.
I WAS ONCE A GREAT MAN. BUT NOW I AM SPENT.
I ONLY WANT GOD, IF HE WILL HAVE ME.
YOU HAVE TO BE STRONG, SITRIC. SMART. YOU WILL UNDERSTAND ONE DAY WHEN YOU ARE KING OF DUBLIN.

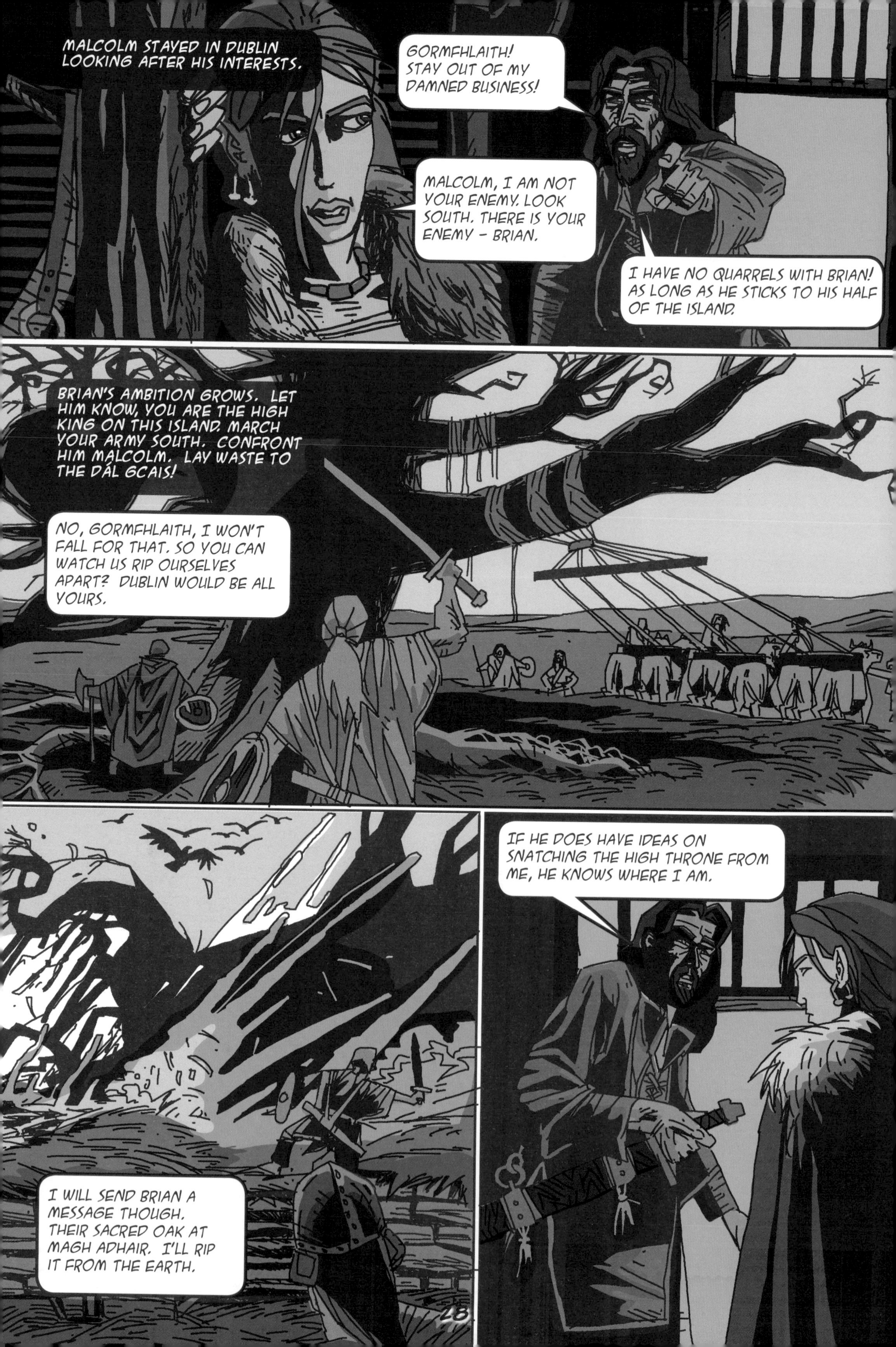
MALCOLM STAYED IN DUBLIN LOOKING AFTER HIS INTERESTS.
GORMFHLAITH! STAY OUT OF MY DAMNED BUSINESS!
MALCOLM, I AM NOT YOUR ENEMY. LOOK SOUTH. THERE IS YOUR ENEMY – BRIAN.
I HAVE NO QUARRELS WITH BRIAN! AS LONG AS HE STICKS TO HIS HALF OF THE ISLAND.
BRIAN'S AMBITION GROWS. LET HIM KNOW, YOU ARE THE HIGH KING ON THIS ISLAND. MARCH YOUR ARMY SOUTH. CONFRONT HIM MALCOLM. LAY WASTE TO THE DÁL GCAIS!
NO, GORMFHLAITH, I WON'T FALL FOR THAT. SO YOU CAN WATCH US RIP OURSELVES APART? DUBLIN WOULD BE ALL YOURS.
I WILL SEND BRIAN A MESSAGE THOUGH. THEIR SACRED OAK AT MAGH ADHAIR. I'LL RIP IT FROM THE EARTH.
IF HE DOES HAVE IDEAS ON SNATCHING THE HIGH THRONE FROM ME, HE KNOWS WHERE I AM.

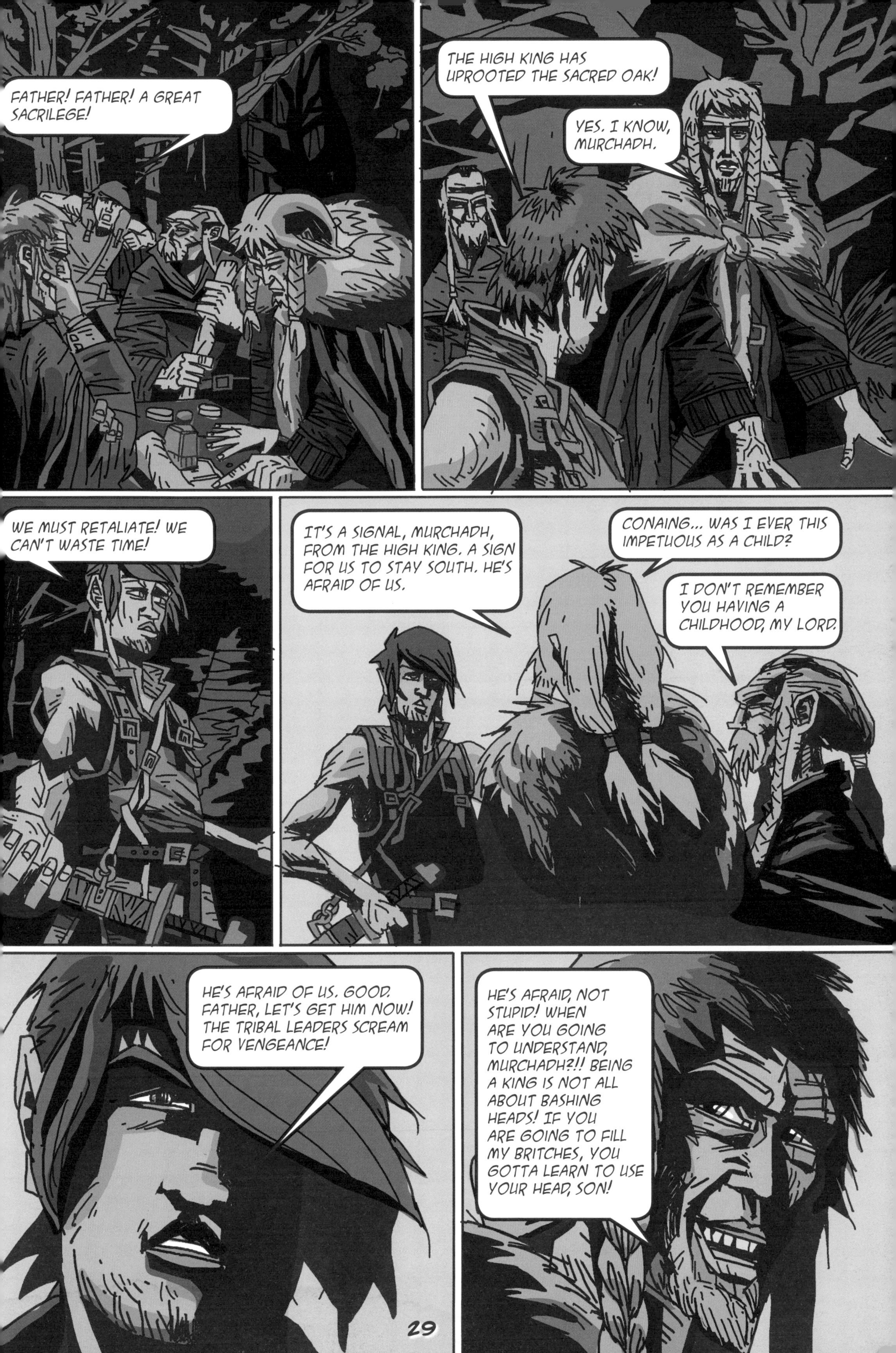
FATHER! FATHER! A GREAT SACRILEGE!
THE HIGH KING HAS UPROOTED THE SACRED OAK!
YES. I KNOW, MURCHADH.
WE MUST RETALIATE! WE CAN'T WASTE TIME!
IT'S A SIGNAL, MURCHADH, FROM THE HIGH KING. A SIGN FOR US TO STAY SOUTH. HE'S AFRAID OF US.
CONAING... WAS I EVER THIS IMPETUOUS AS A CHILD?
I DON'T REMEMBER YOU HAVING A CHILDHOOD, MY LORD.
HE'S AFRAID OF US. GOOD. FATHER, LET'S GET HIM NOW! THE TRIBAL LEADERS SCREAM FOR VENGEANCE!
HE'S AFRAID, NOT STUPID! WHEN ARE YOU GOING TO UNDERSTAND, MURCHADH?!! BEING A KING IS NOT ALL ABOUT BASHING HEADS! IF YOU ARE GOING TO FILL MY BRITCHES, YOU GOTTA LEARN TO USE YOUR HEAD, SON!

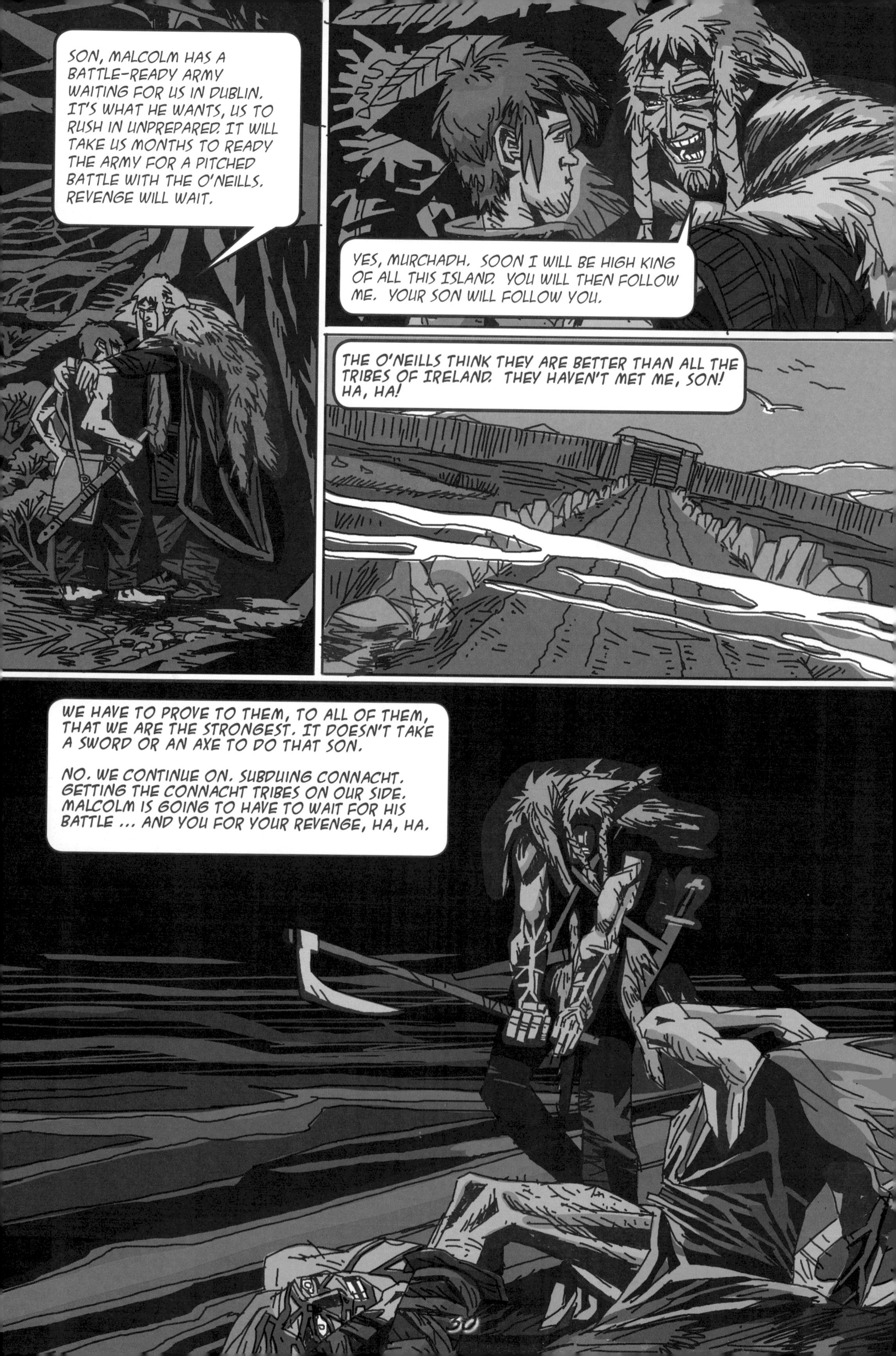
SON, MALCOLM HAS A BATTLE-READY ARMY WAITING FOR US IN DUBLIN. IT'S WHAT HE WANTS, US TO RUSH IN UNPREPARED. IT WILL TAKE US MONTHS TO READY THE ARMY FOR A PITCHED BATTLE WITH THE O'NEILLS. REVENGE WILL WAIT.
YES, MURCHADH. SOON I WILL BE HIGH KING OF ALL THIS ISLAND. YOU WILL THEN FOLLOW ME. YOUR SON WILL FOLLOW YOU.
THE O'NEILLS THINK THEY ARE BETTER THAN ALL THE TRIBES OF IRELAND. THEY HAVEN'T MET ME, SON! HA, HA!
WE HAVE TO PROVE TO THEM, TO ALL OF THEM, THAT WE ARE THE STRONGEST. IT DOESN'T TAKE A SWORD OR AN AXE TO DO THAT SON.
NO. WE CONTINUE ON. SUBDUING CONNACHT. GETTING THE CONNACHT TRIBES ON OUR SIDE. MALCOLM IS GOING TO HAVE TO WAIT FOR HIS BATTLE ... AND YOU FOR YOUR REVENGE, HA, HA.

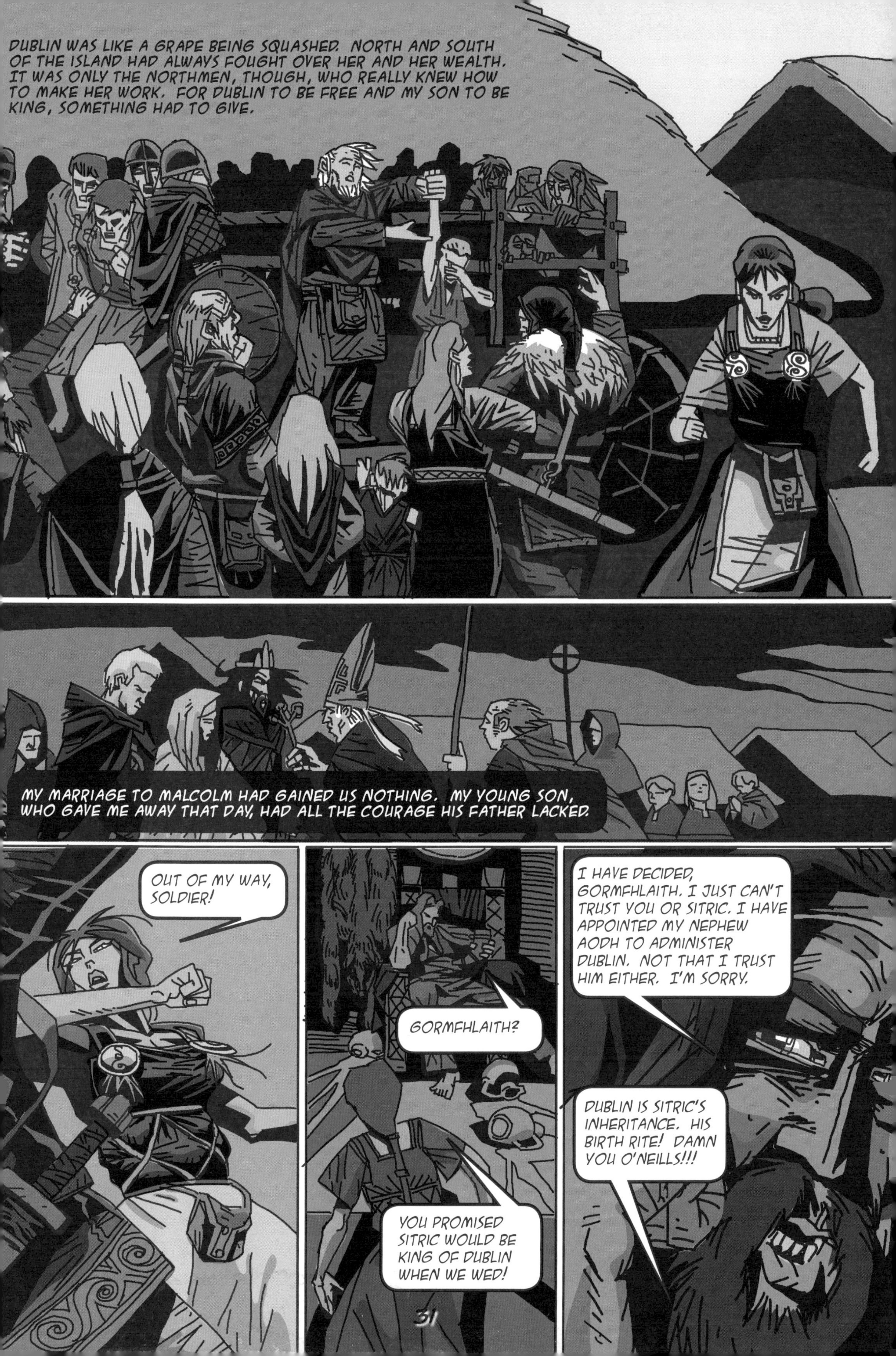

DUBLIN WAS LIKE A GRAPE BEING SQUASHED. NORTH AND SOUTH OF THE ISLAND HAD ALWAYS FOUGHT OVER HER AND HER WEALTH. IT WAS ONLY THE NORTHMEN, THOUGH, WHO REALLY KNEW HOW TO MAKE HER WORK. FOR DUBLIN TO BE FREE AND MY SON TO BE KING, SOMETHING HAD TO GIVE.
MY MARRIAGE TO MALCOLM HAD GAINED US NOTHING. MY YOUNG SON, WHO GAVE ME AWAY THAT DAY, HAD ALL THE COURAGE HIS FATHER LACKED.
OUT OF MY WAY, SOLDIER!
GORMFHLAITH?
YOU PROMISED SITRIC WOULD BE KING OF DUBLIN WHEN WE WED!
I HAVE DECIDED, GORMFHLAITH. I JUST CAN'T TRUST YOU OR SITRIC. I HAVE APPOINTED MY NEPHEW AODH TO ADMINISTER DUBLIN. NOT THAT I TRUST HIM EITHER. I'M SORRY.
DUBLIN IS SITRIC'S INHERITANCE. HIS BIRTH RITE! DAMN YOU O'NEILLS!!!

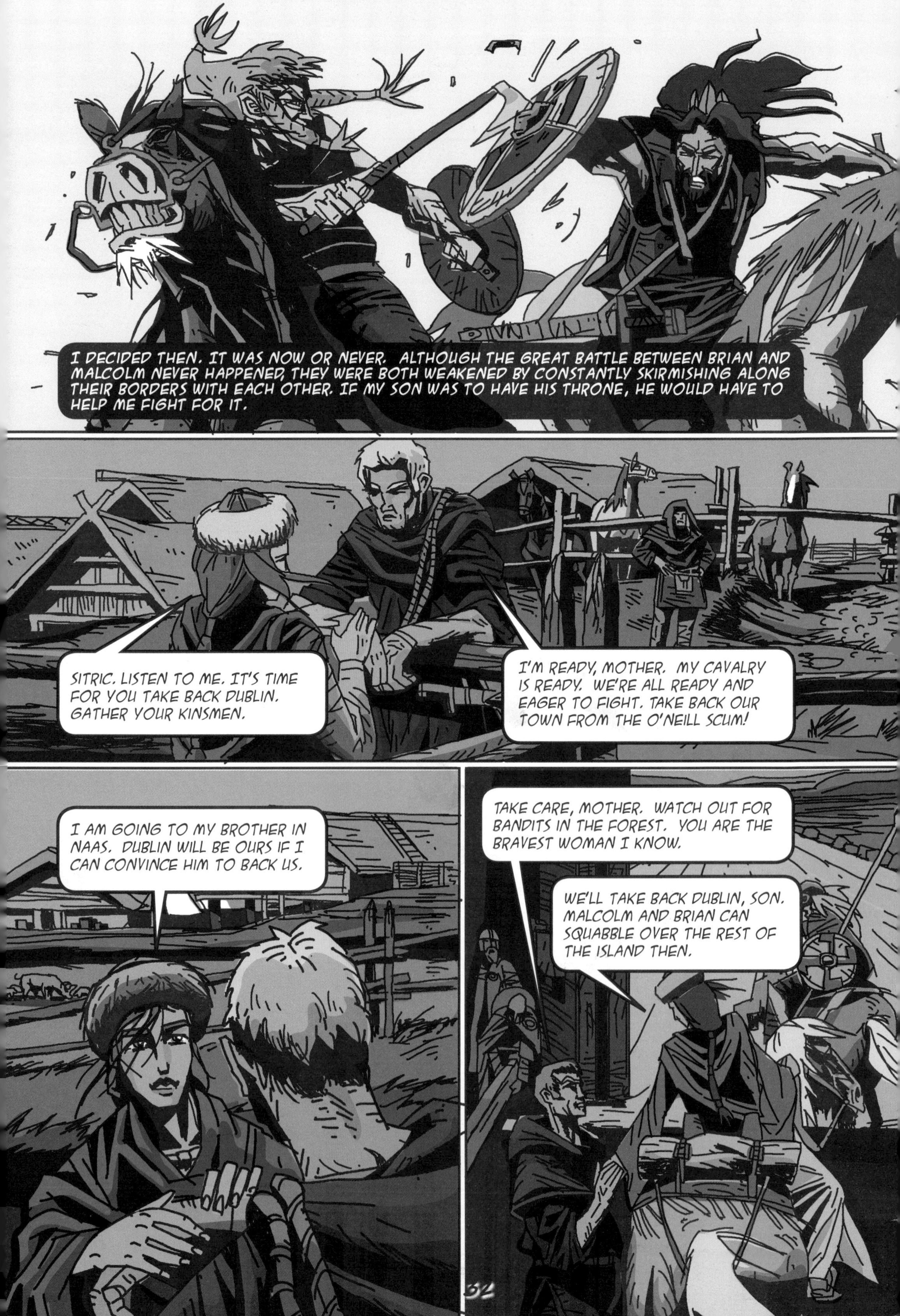

I DECIDED THEN. IT WAS NOW OR NEVER. ALTHOUGH THE GREAT BATTLE BETWEEN BRIAN AND MALCOLM NEVER HAPPENED, THEY WERE BOTH WEAKENED BY CONSTANTLY SKIRMISHING ALONG THEIR BORDERS WITH EACH OTHER. IF MY SON WAS TO HAVE HIS THRONE, HE WOULD HAVE TO HELP ME FIGHT FOR IT.
SITRIC. LISTEN TO ME. IT'S TIME FOR YOU TAKE BACK DUBLIN. GATHER YOUR KINSMEN.
I'M READY, MOTHER. MY CAVALRY IS READY. WE'RE ALL READY AND EAGER TO FIGHT. TAKE BACK OUR TOWN FROM THE O'NEILL SCUM!
I AM GOING TO MY BROTHER IN NAAS. DUBLIN WILL BE OURS IF I CAN CONVINCE HIM TO BACK US.
TAKE CARE, MOTHER. WATCH OUT FOR BANDITS IN THE FOREST. YOU ARE THE BRAVEST WOMAN I KNOW.
WE'LL TAKE BACK DUBLIN, SON. MALCOLM AND BRIAN CAN SQUABBLE OVER THE REST OF THE ISLAND THEN.

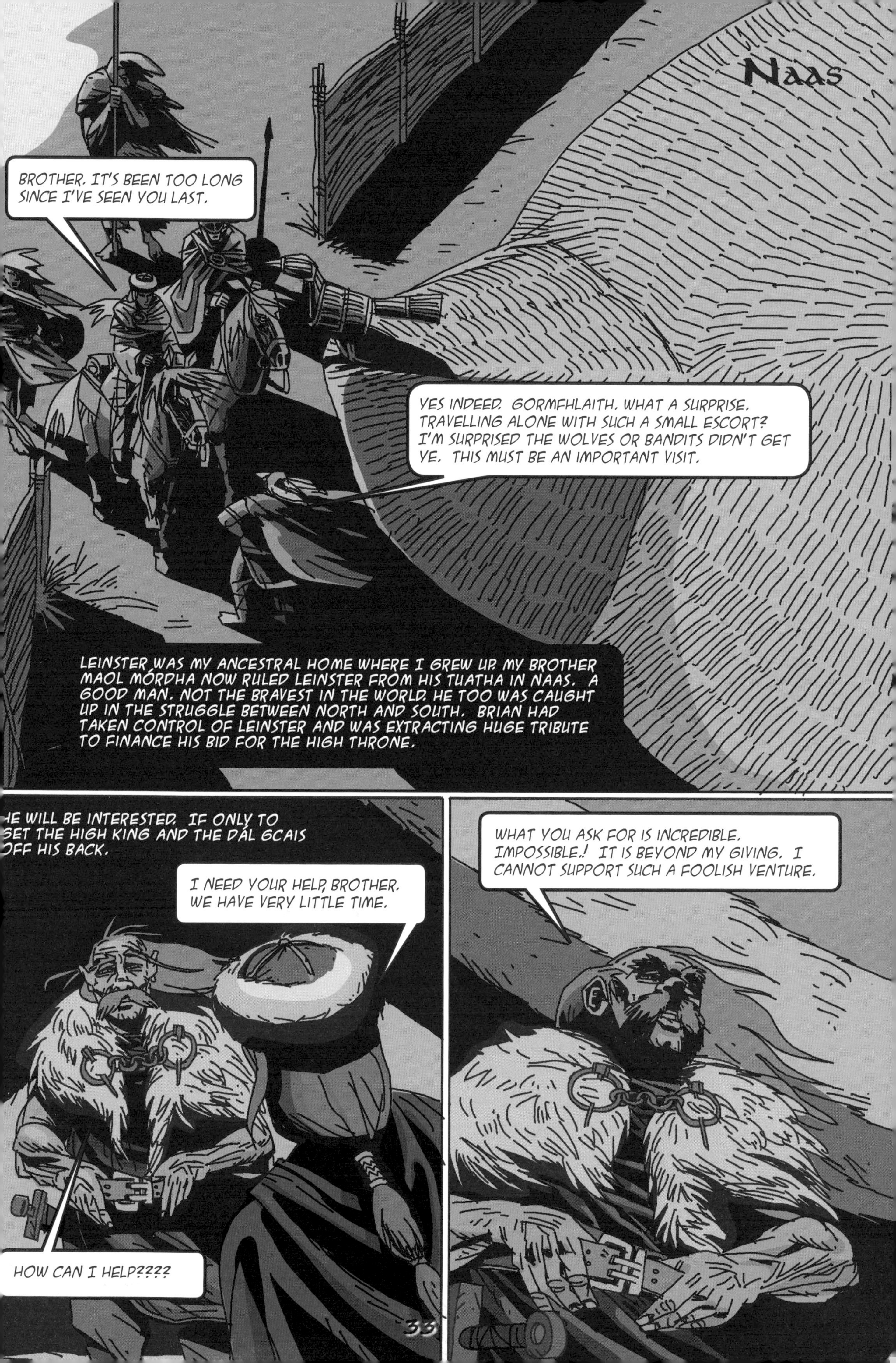
Naas
BROTHER. IT'S BEEN TOO LONG SINCE I'VE SEEN YOU LAST.
YES INDEED. GORMFHLAITH. WHAT A SURPRISE. TRAVELLING ALONE WITH SUCH A SMALL ESCORT? I'M SURPRISED THE WOLVES OR BANDITS DIDN'T GET YE. THIS MUST BE AN IMPORTANT VISIT.
LEINSTER WAS MY ANCESTRAL HOME WHERE I GREW UP. MY BROTHER MAOL MÓRDHA NOW RULED LEINSTER FROM HIS TUATHA IN NAAS. A GOOD MAN. NOT THE BRAVEST IN THE WORLD. HE TOO WAS CAUGHT UP IN THE STRUGGLE BETWEEN NORTH AND SOUTH. BRIAN HAD TAKEN CONTROL OF LEINSTER AND WAS EXTRACTING HUGE TRIBUTE TO FINANCE HIS BID FOR THE HIGH THRONE.
HE WILL BE INTERESTED. IF ONLY TO GET THE HIGH KING AND THE DÁL GCAIS OFF HIS BACK.
I NEED YOUR HELP, BROTHER. WE HAVE VERY LITTLE TIME.
HOW CAN I HELP????
WHAT YOU ASK FOR IS INCREDIBLE. IMPOSSIBLE.! IT IS BEYOND MY GIVING. I CANNOT SUPPORT SUCH A FOOLISH VENTURE.

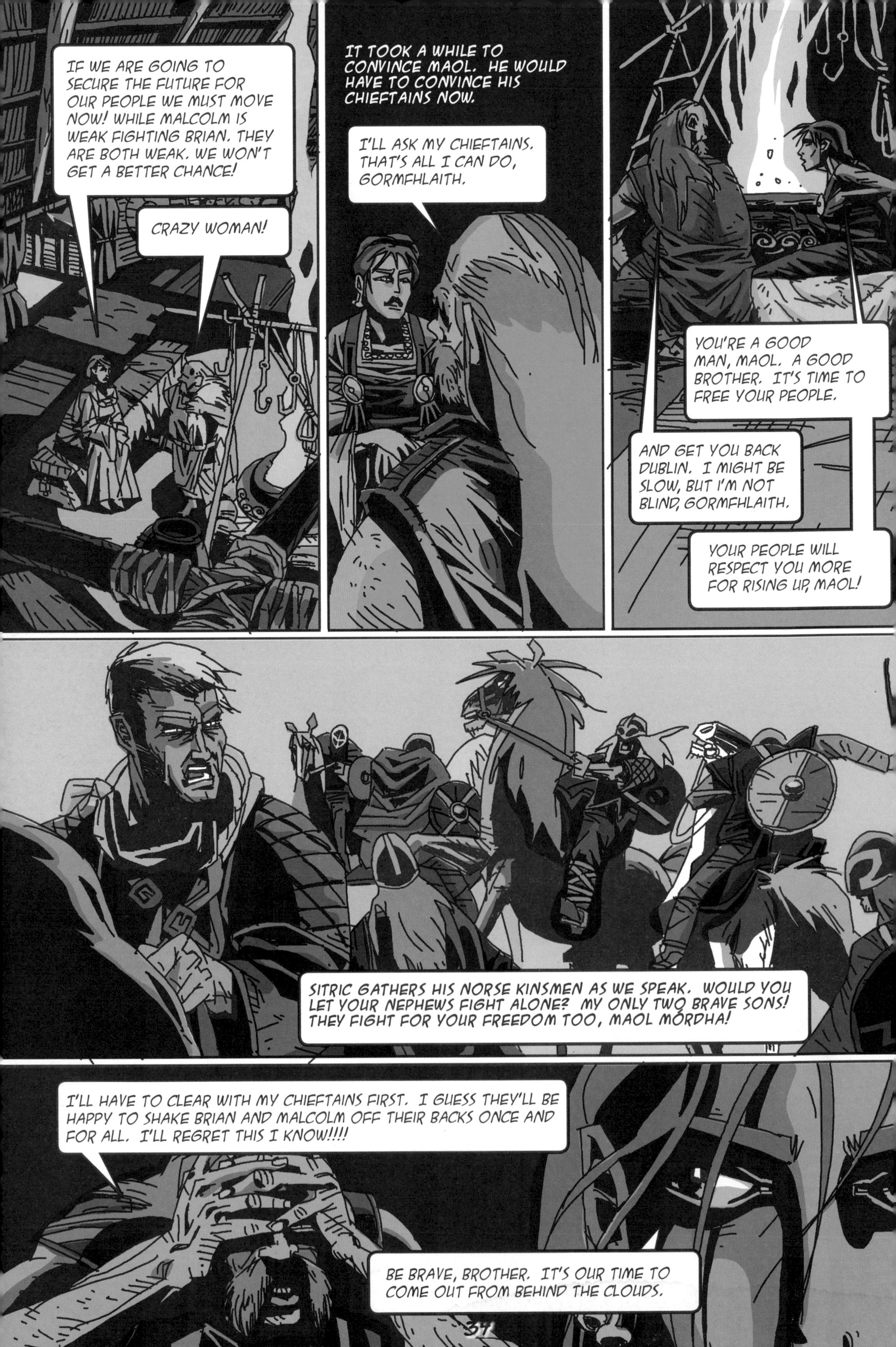
IF WE ARE GOING TO SECURE THE FUTURE FOR OUR PEOPLE WE MUST MOVE NOW! WHILE MALCOLM IS WEAK FIGHTING BRIAN. THEY ARE BOTH WEAK. WE WON'T GET A BETTER CHANCE!
CRAZY WOMAN!
IT TOOK A WHILE TO CONVINCE MAOL. HE WOULD HAVE TO CONVINCE HIS CHIEFTAINS NOW.
I'LL ASK MY CHIEFTAINS. THAT'S ALL I CAN DO, GORMFHLAITH.
YOU'RE A GOOD MAN, MAOL. A GOOD BROTHER. IT'S TIME TO FREE YOUR PEOPLE.
AND GET YOU BACK DUBLIN. I MIGHT BE SLOW, BUT I'M NOT BLIND, GORMFHLAITH.
YOUR PEOPLE WILL RESPECT YOU MORE FOR RISING UP, MAOL!
SITRIC GATHERS HIS NORSE KINSMEN AS WE SPEAK. WOULD YOU LET YOUR NEPHEWS FIGHT ALONE? MY ONLY TWO BRAVE SONS! THEY FIGHT FOR YOUR FREEDOM TOO, MAOL MÓRDHA!
I'LL HAVE TO CLEAR WITH MY CHIEFTAINS FIRST. I GUESS THEY'LL BE HAPPY TO SHAKE BRIAN AND MALCOLM OFF THEIR BACKS ONCE AND FOR ALL. I'LL REGRET THIS I KNOW!!!!
BE BRAVE, BROTHER. IT'S OUR TIME TO COME OUT FROM BEHIND THE CLOUDS.

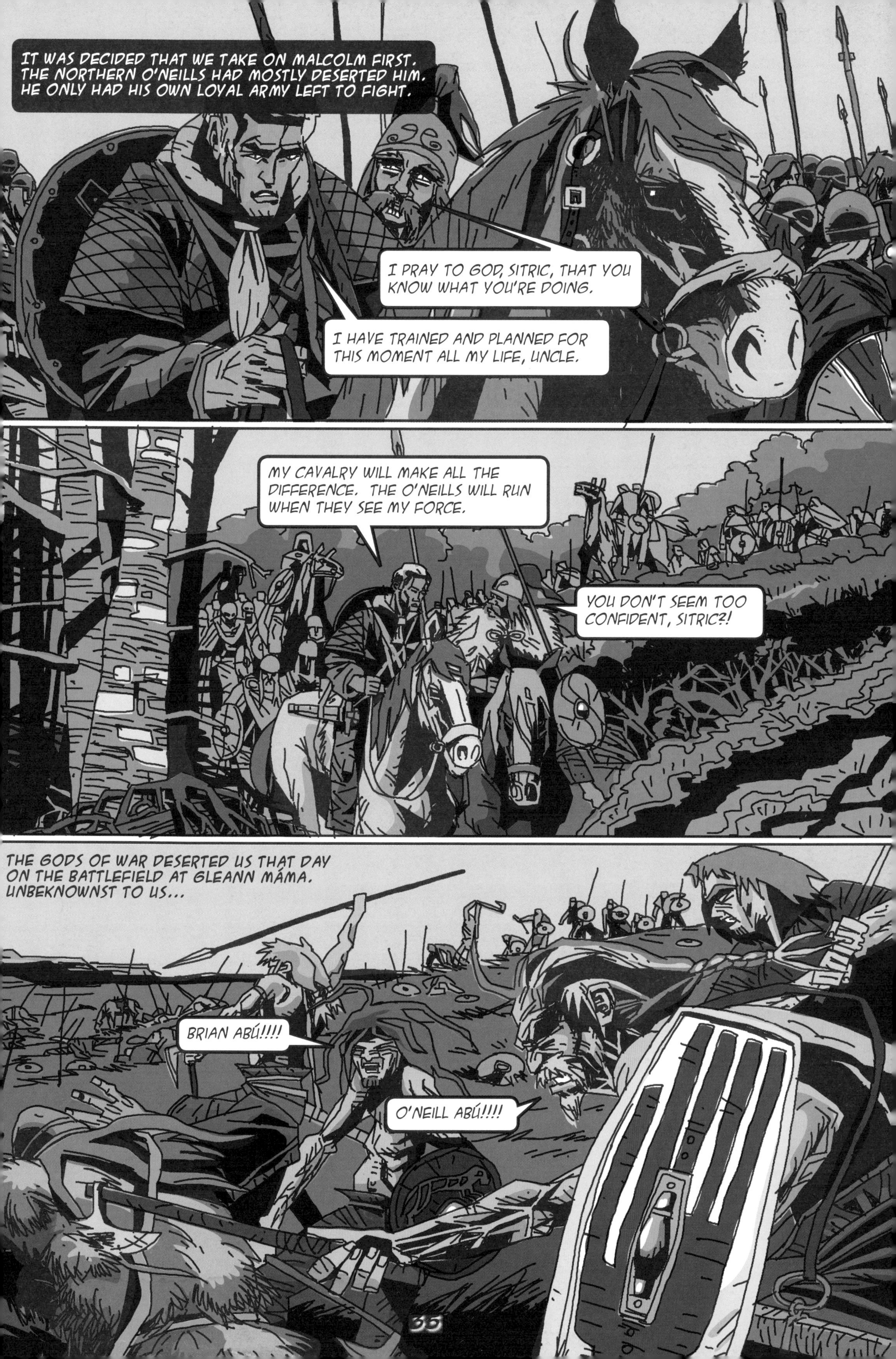
IT WAS DECIDED THAT WE TAKE ON MALCOLM FIRST. THE NORTHERN O'NEILLS HAD MOSTLY DESERTED HIM. HE ONLY HAD HIS OWN LOYAL ARMY LEFT TO FIGHT.
I PRAY TO GOD, SITRIC, THAT YOU KNOW WHAT YOU'RE DOING.
I HAVE TRAINED AND PLANNED FOR THIS MOMENT ALL MY LIFE, UNCLE.
MY CAVALRY WILL MAKE ALL THE DIFFERENCE. THE O'NEILLS WILL RUN WHEN THEY SEE MY FORCE.
YOU DON'T SEEM TOO CONFIDENT, SITRIC?!
THE GODS OF WAR DESERTED US THAT DAY ON THE BATTLEFIELD AT GLEANN MÁMA. UNBEKNOWNST TO US...
BRIAN ABÚ!!!!
O'NEILL ABÚ!!!!

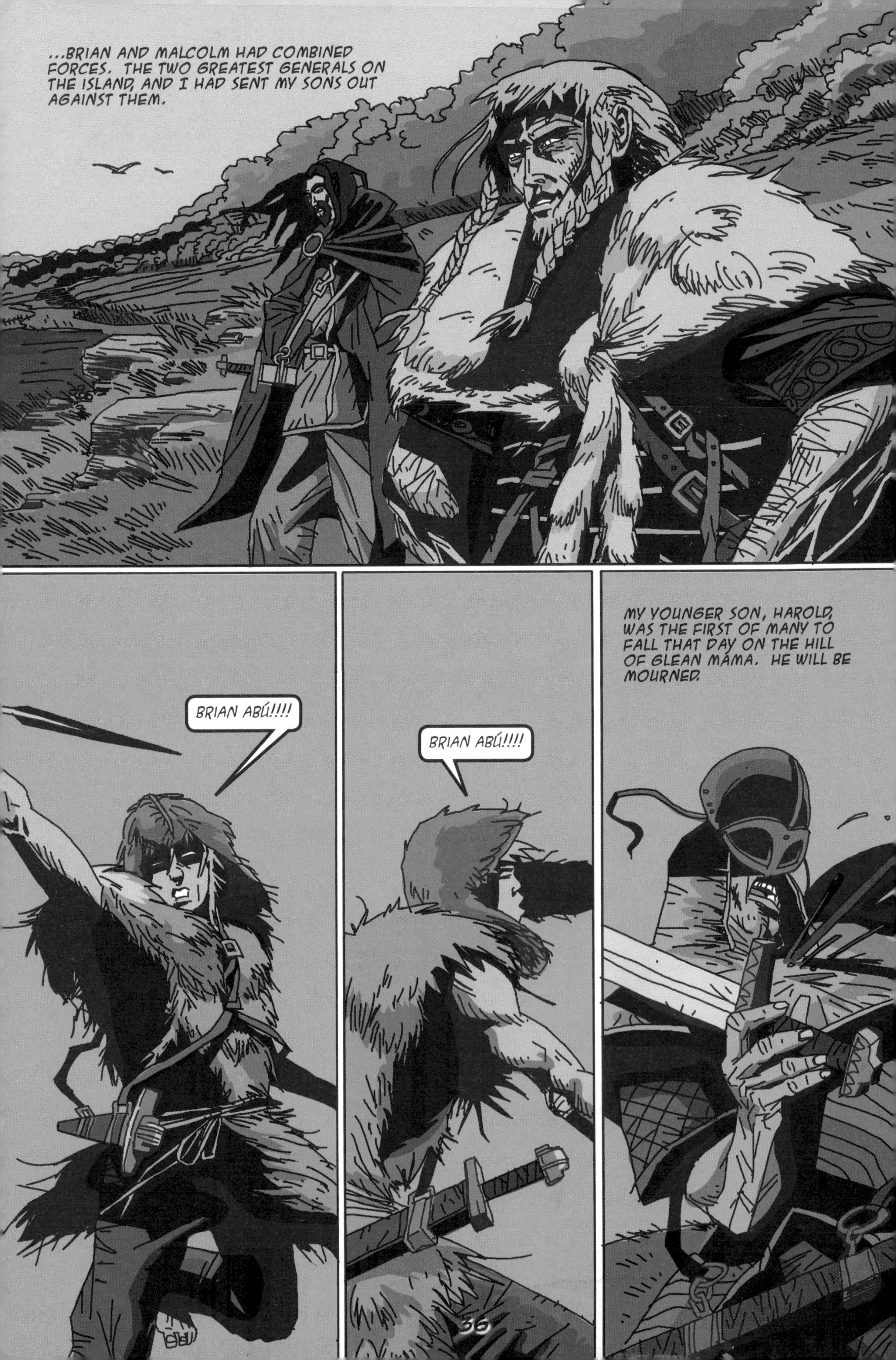
...BRIAN AND MALCOLM HAD COMBINED FORCES. THE TWO GREATEST GENERALS ON THE ISLAND, AND I HAD SENT MY SONS OUT AGAINST THEM.
BRIAN ABÚ!!!!
BRIAN ABÚ!!!!
MY YOUNGER SON, HAROLD, WAS THE FIRST OF MANY TO FALL THAT DAY ON THE HILL OF GLEAN MAMA. HE WILL BE MOURNED.

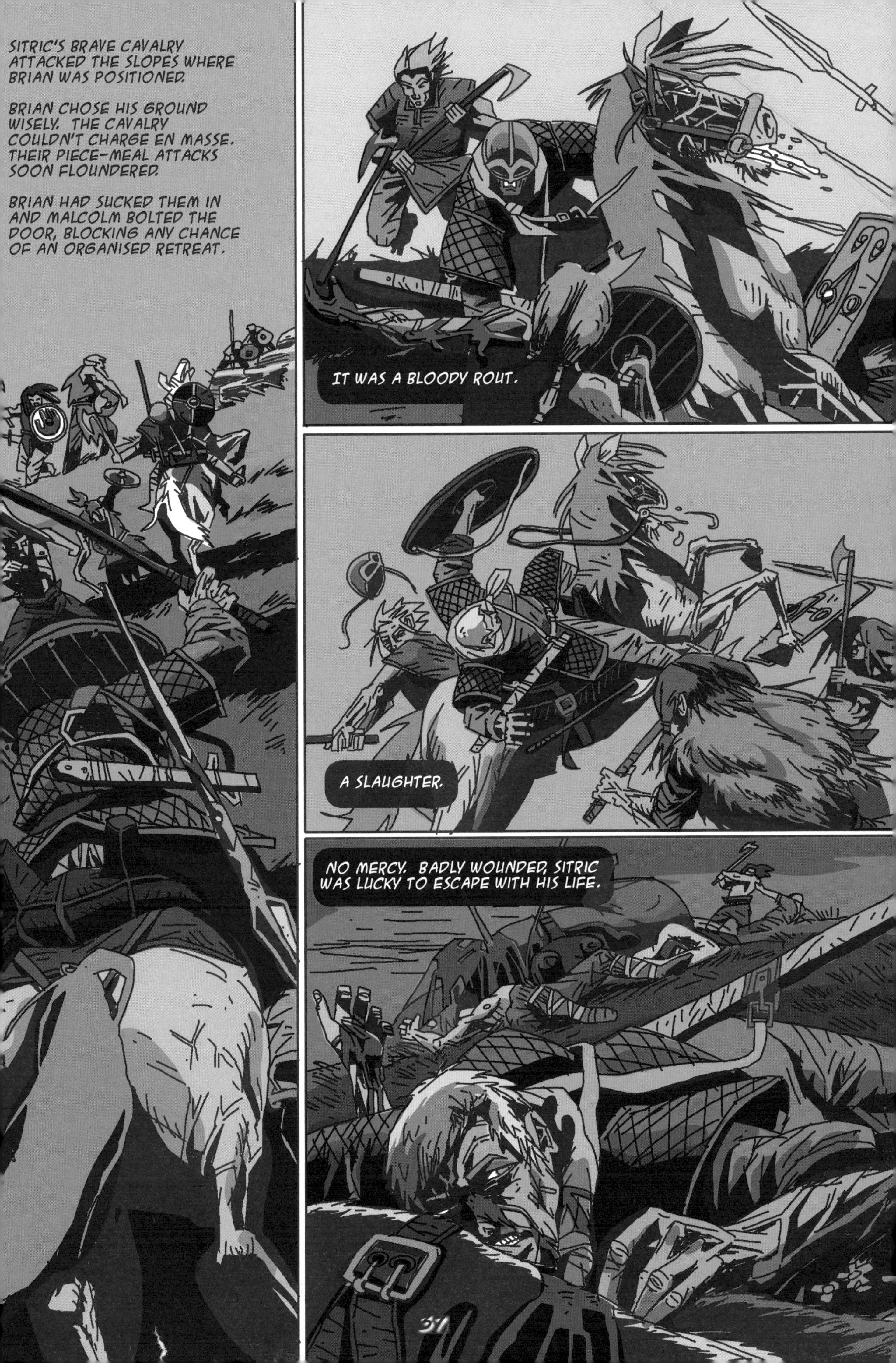
SITRIC'S BRAVE CAVALRY ATTACKED THE SLOPES WHERE BRIAN WAS POSITIONED.
BRIAN CHOSE HIS GROUND WISELY. THE CAVALRY COULDN'T CHARGE EN MASSE. THEIR PIECE-MEAL ATTACKS SOON FLOUNDERED.
BRIAN HAD SUCKED THEM IN AND MALCOLM BOLTED THE DOOR, BLOCKING ANY CHANCE OF AN ORGANISED RETREAT.
IT WAS A BLOODY ROUT.
A SLAUGHTER.
NO MERCY. BADLY WOUNDED, SITRIC WAS LUCKY TO ESCAPE WITH HIS LIFE.

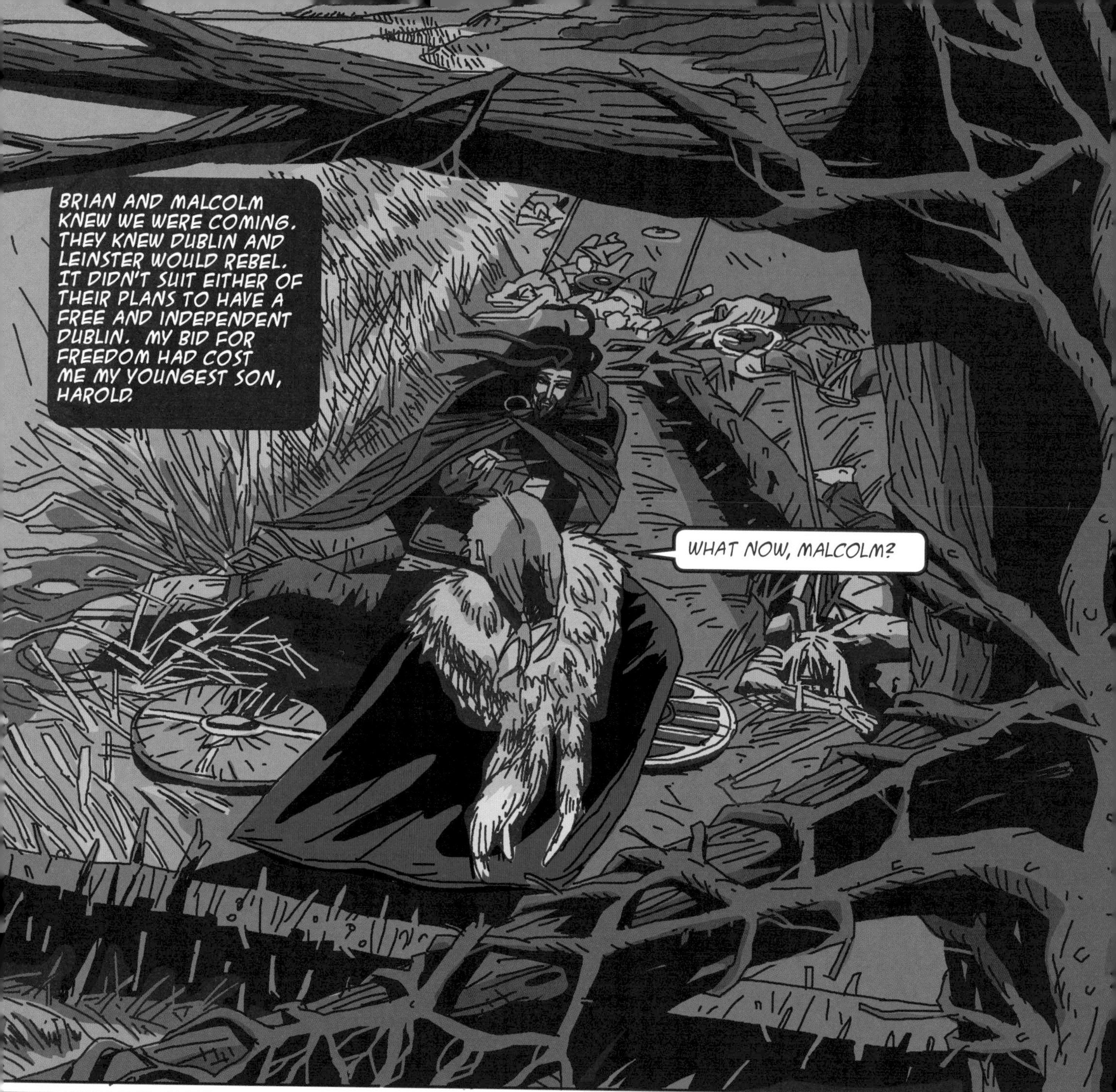
BRIAN AND MALCOLM KNEW WE WERE COMING. THEY KNEW DUBLIN AND LEINSTER WOULD REBEL. IT DIDN'T SUIT EITHER OF THEIR PLANS TO HAVE A FREE AND INDEPENDENT DUBLIN. MY BID FOR FREEDOM HAD COST ME MY YOUNGEST SON, HAROLD.
WHAT NOW, MALCOLM?
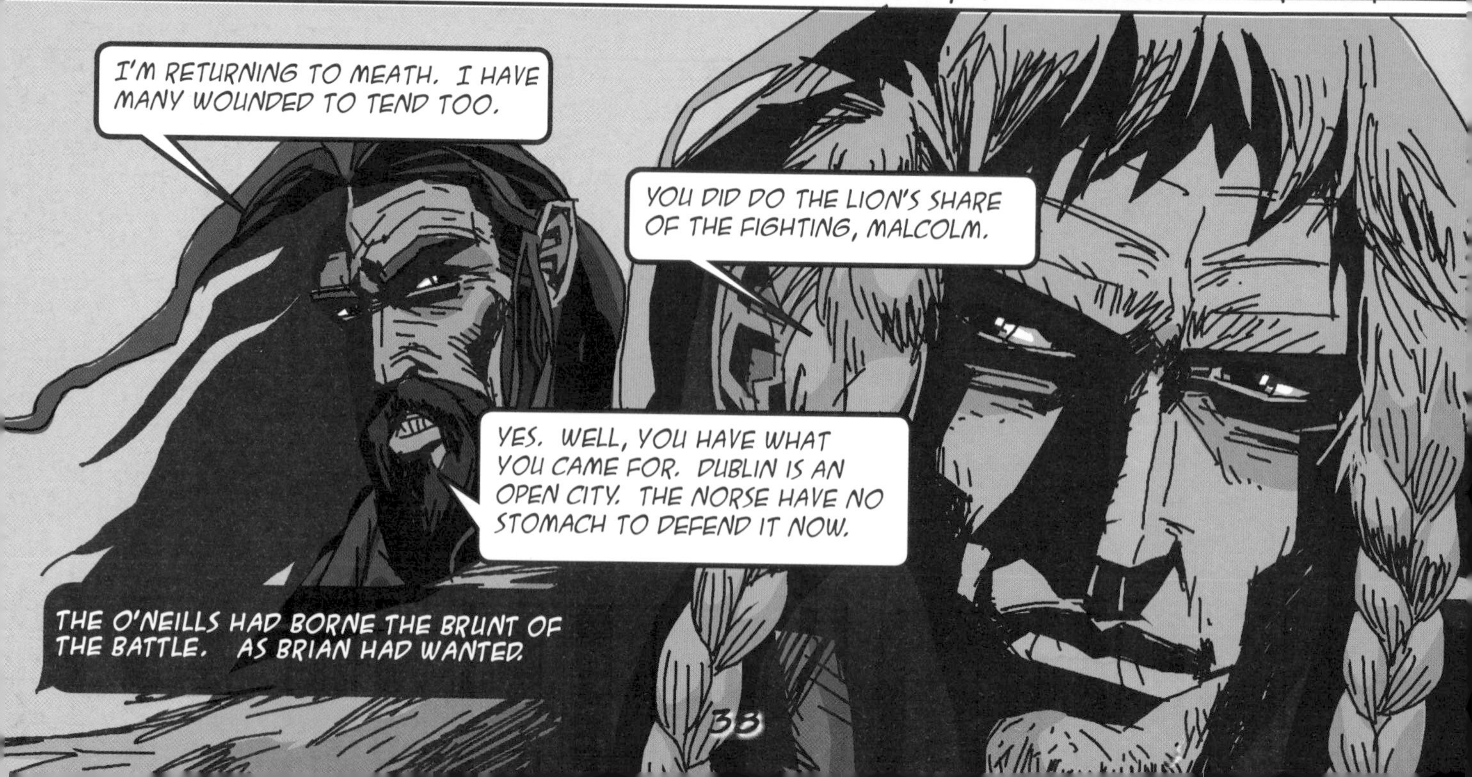
I'M RETURNING TO MEATH. I HAVE MANY WOUNDED TO TEND TOO.
YOU DID DO THE LION'S SHARE OF THE FIGHTING, MALCOLM.
YES. WELL, YOU HAVE WHAT YOU CAME FOR. DUBLIN IS AN OPEN CITY. THE NORSE HAVE NO STOMACH TO DEFEND IT NOW.
THE O'NEILLS HAD BORNE THE BRUNT OF THE BATTLE. AS BRIAN HAD WANTED.

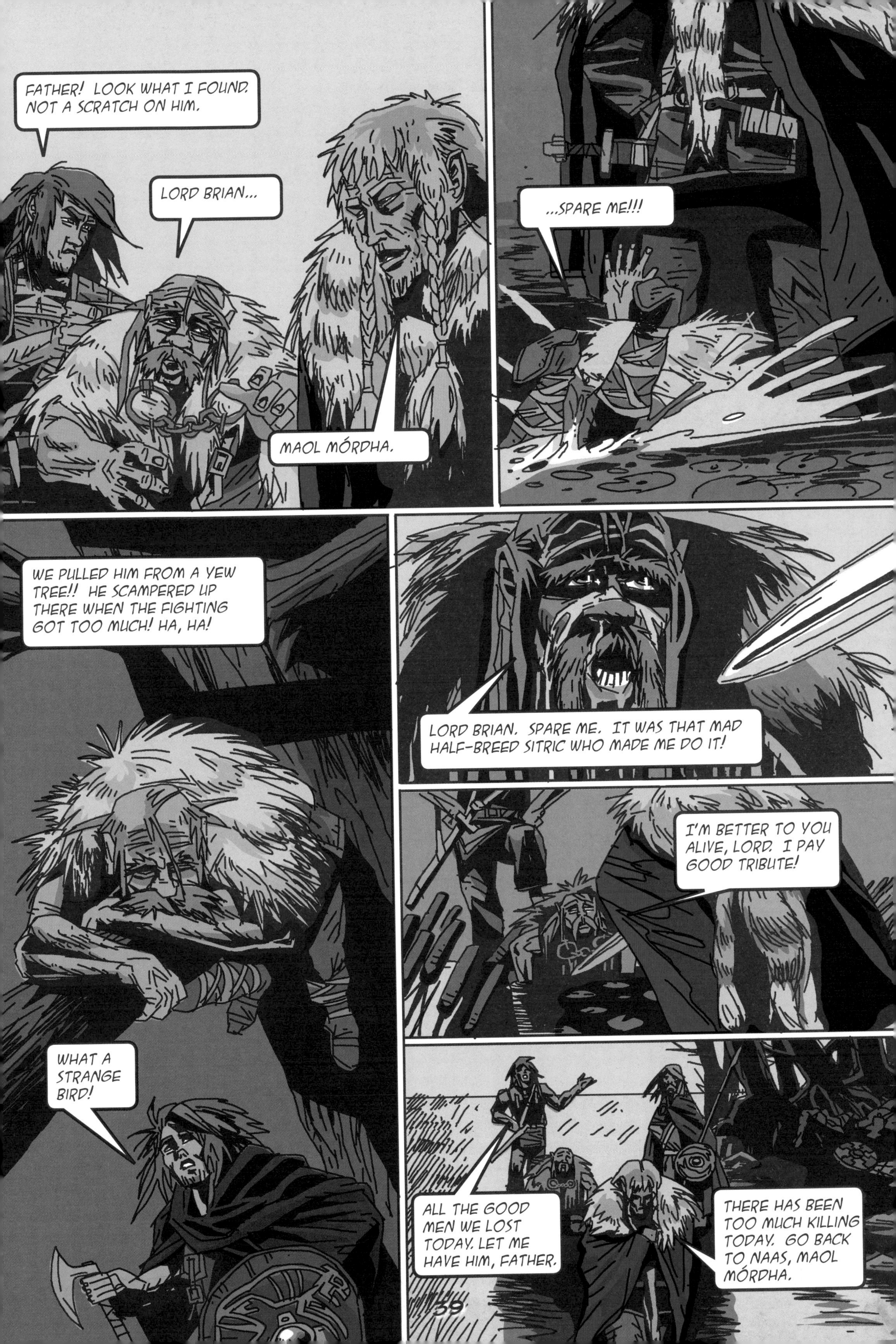

FATHER! LOOK WHAT I FOUND. NOT A SCRATCH ON HIM.
LORD BRIAN...
MAOL MÓRDHA.
...SPARE ME!!!
WE PULLED HIM FROM A YEW TREE!! HE SCAMPERED UP THERE WHEN THE FIGHTING GOT TOO MUCH! HA, HA!
WHAT A STRANGE BIRD!
LORD BRIAN. SPARE ME. IT WAS THAT MAD HALF-BREED SITRIC WHO MADE ME DO IT!
I'M BETTER TO YOU ALIVE, LORD. I PAY GOOD TRIBUTE!
ALL THE GOOD MEN WE LOST TODAY. LET ME HAVE HIM, FATHER.
THERE HAS BEEN TOO MUCH KILLING TODAY. GO BACK TO NAAS, MAOL MÓRDHA.

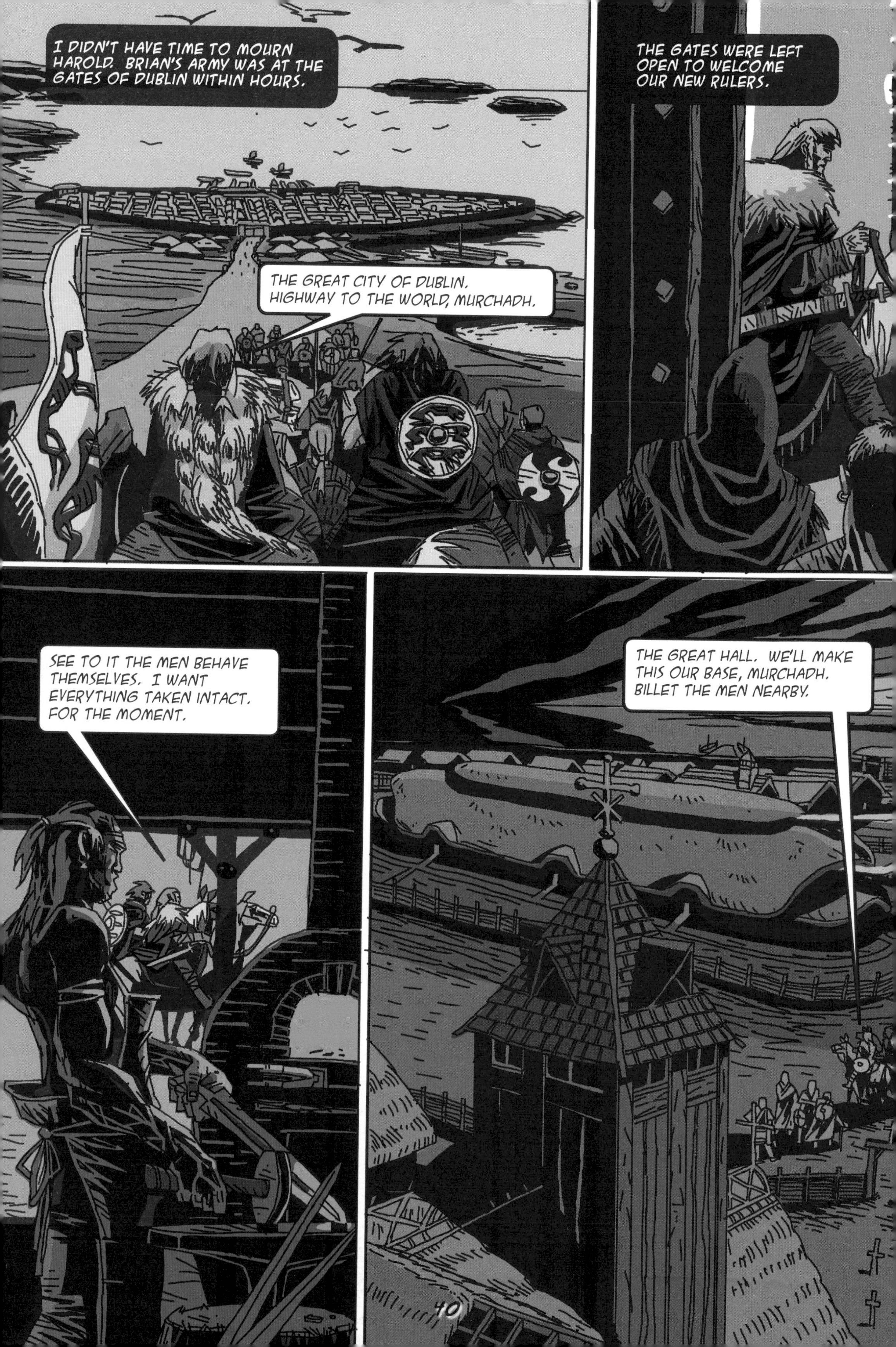

I DIDN'T HAVE TIME TO MOURN HAROLD. BRIAN'S ARMY WAS AT THE GATES OF DUBLIN WITHIN HOURS.
THE GREAT CITY OF DUBLIN. HIGHWAY TO THE WORLD, MURCHADH.
THE GATES WERE LEFT OPEN TO WELCOME OUR NEW RULERS.
SEE TO IT THE MEN BEHAVE THEMSELVES. I WANT EVERYTHING TAKEN INTACT. FOR THE MOMENT.
THE GREAT HALL. WE'LL MAKE THIS OUR BASE, MURCHADH. BILLET THE MEN NEARBY.

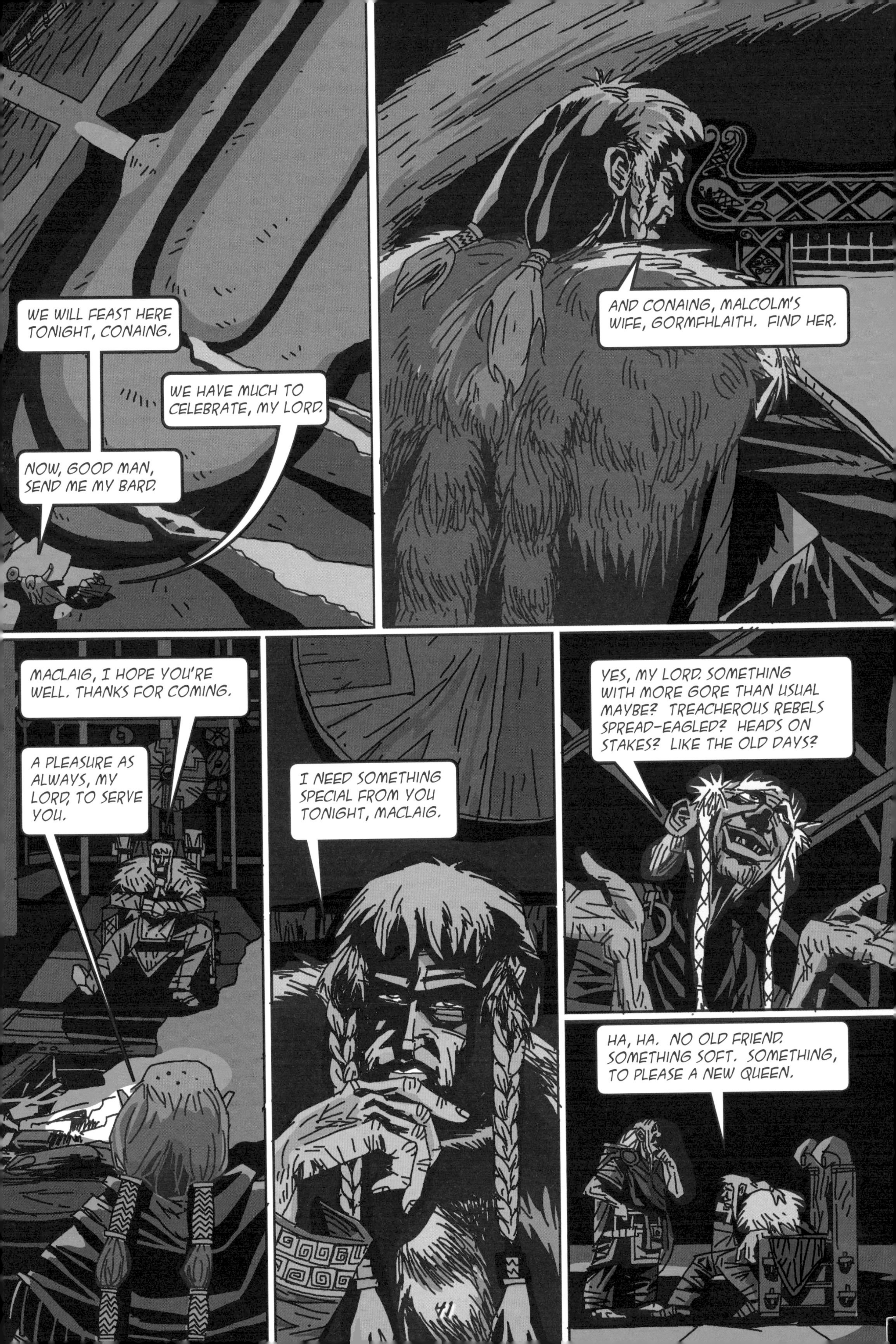

WE WILL FEAST HERE TONIGHT, CONAING.
WE HAVE MUCH TO CELEBRATE, MY LORD.
NOW, GOOD MAN, SEND ME MY BARD.
AND CONAING, MALCOLM'S WIFE, GORMFHLAITH. FIND HER.
MACLAIG, I HOPE YOU'RE WELL. THANKS FOR COMING.
A PLEASURE AS ALWAYS, MY LORD, TO SERVE YOU.
I NEED SOMETHING SPECIAL FROM YOU TONIGHT, MACLAIG.
YES, MY LORD. SOMETHING WITH MORE GORE THAN USUAL MAYBE? TREACHEROUS REBELS SPREAD-EAGLED? HEADS ON STAKES? LIKE THE OLD DAYS?
HA, HA. NO OLD FRIEND. SOMETHING SOFT. SOMETHING, TO PLEASE A NEW QUEEN.

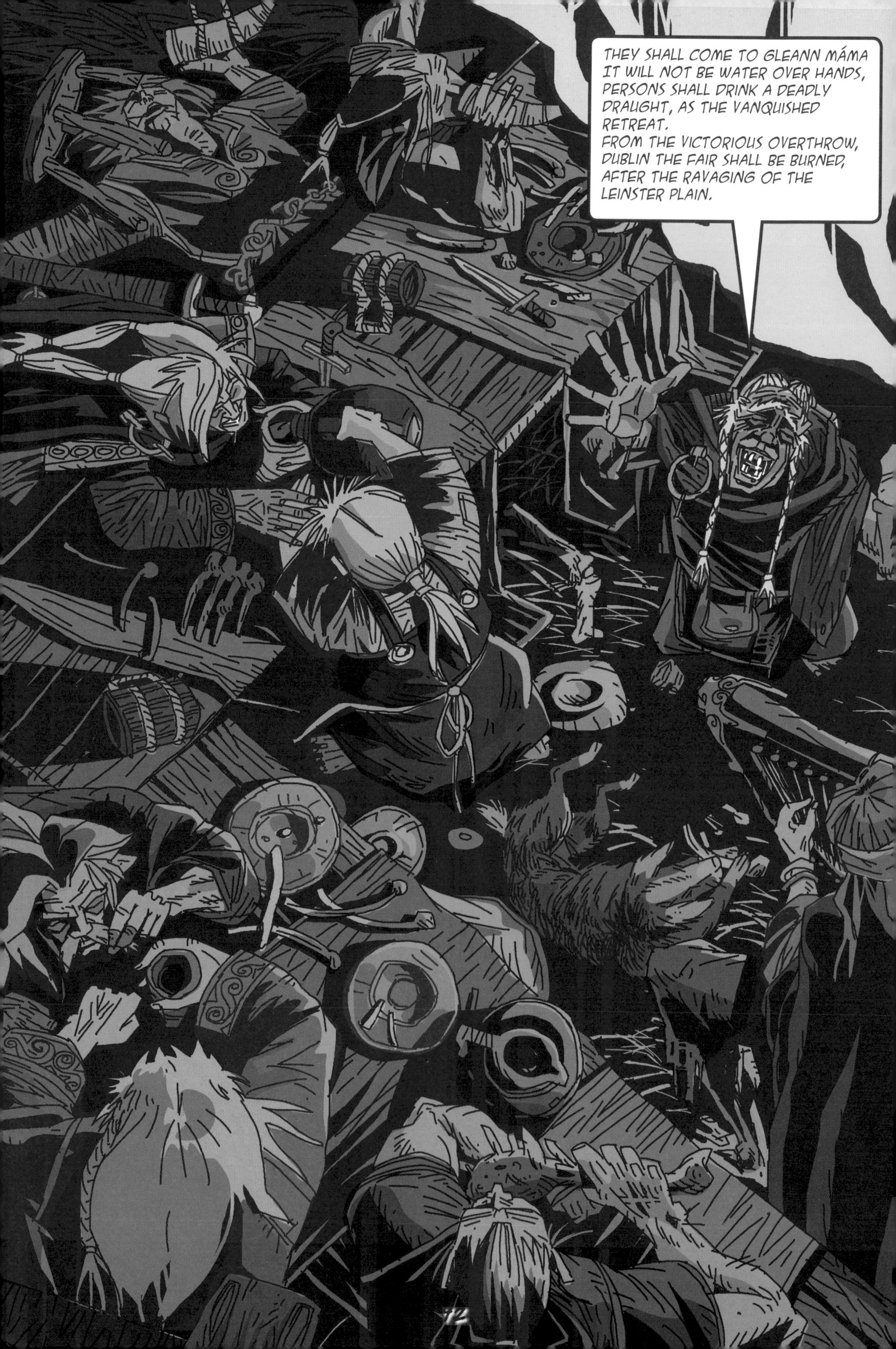
THEY SHALL COME TO GLEANN MÁMA IT WILL NOT BE WATER OVER HANDS, PERSONS SHALL DRINK A DEADLY DRAUGHT, AS THE VANQUISHED RETREAT. FROM THE VICTORIOUS OVERTHROW, DUBLIN THE FAIR SHALL BE BURNED, AFTER THE RAVAGING OF THE LEINSTER PLAIN.

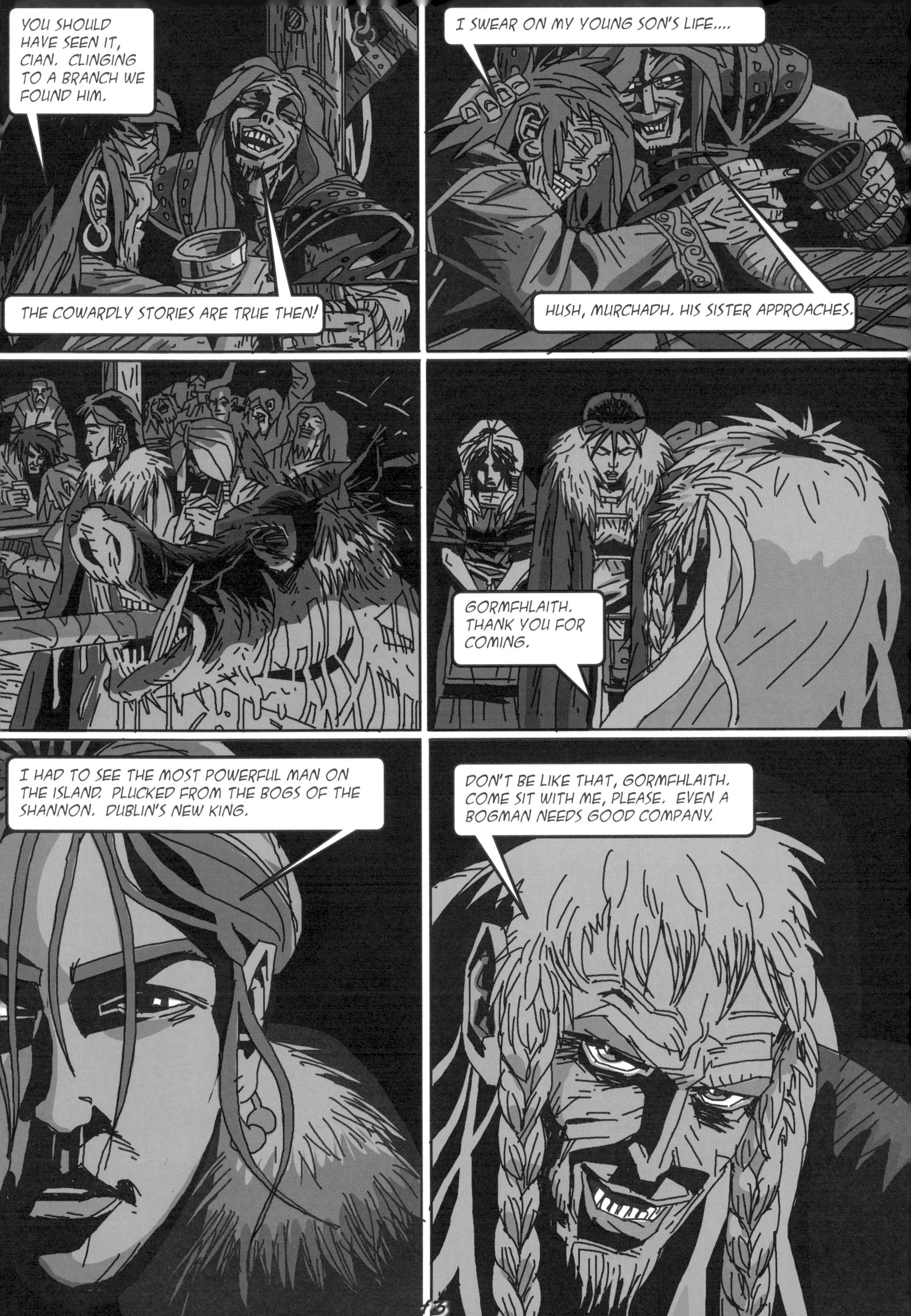
YOU SHOULD HAVE SEEN IT, CIAN. CLINGING TO A BRANCH WE FOUND HIM.
THE COWARDLY STORIES ARE TRUE THEN!
I SWEAR ON MY YOUNG SON'S LIFE....
HUSH, MURCHADH. HIS SISTER APPROACHES.
GORMFHLAITH. THANK YOU FOR COMING.
I HAD TO SEE THE MOST POWERFUL MAN ON THE ISLAND. PLUCKED FROM THE BOGS OF THE SHANNON. DUBLIN'S NEW KING.
DON'T BE LIKE THAT, GORMFHLAITH. COME SIT WITH ME, PLEASE. EVEN A BOGMAN NEEDS GOOD COMPANY.

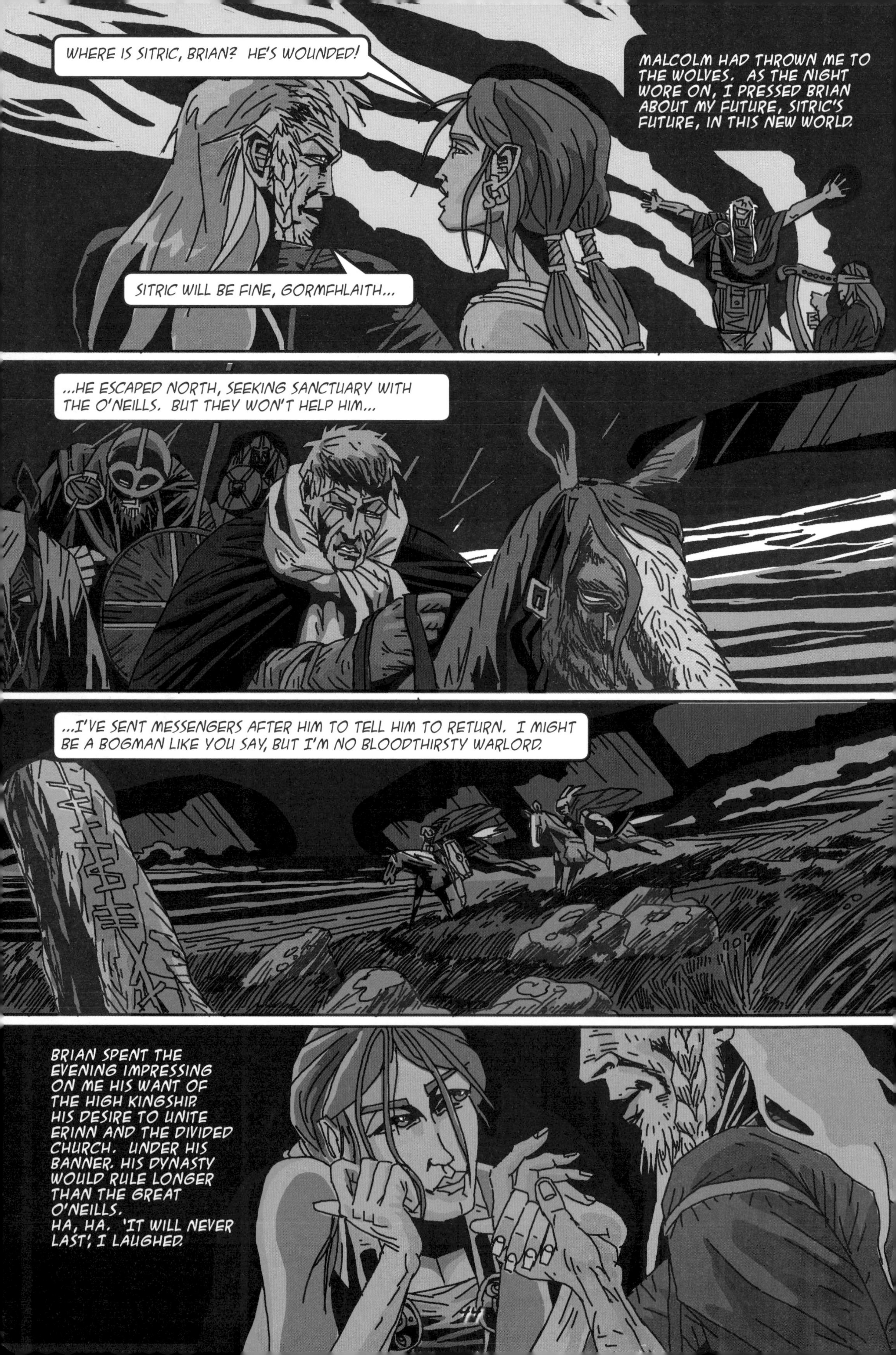
WHERE IS SITRIC, BRIAN? HE'S WOUNDED!
MALCOLM HAD THROWN ME TO THE WOLVES. AS THE NIGHT WORE ON, I PRESSED BRIAN ABOUT MY FUTURE, SITRIC'S FUTURE, IN THIS NEW WORLD.
SITRIC WILL BE FINE, GORMFHLAITH...
...HE ESCAPED NORTH, SEEKING SANCTUARY WITH THE O'NEILLS. BUT THEY WON'T HELP HIM...
...I'VE SENT MESSENGERS AFTER HIM TO TELL HIM TO RETURN. I MIGHT BE A BOGMAN LIKE YOU SAY, BUT I'M NO BLOODTHIRSTY WARLORD.
BRIAN SPENT THE EVENING IMPRESSING ON ME HIS WANT OF THE HIGH KINGSHIP. HIS DESIRE TO UNITE ERINN AND THE DIVIDED CHURCH. UNDER HIS BANNER. HIS DYNASTY WOULD RULE LONGER THAN THE GREAT O'NEILLS. HA, HA. 'IT WILL NEVER LAST', I LAUGHED.

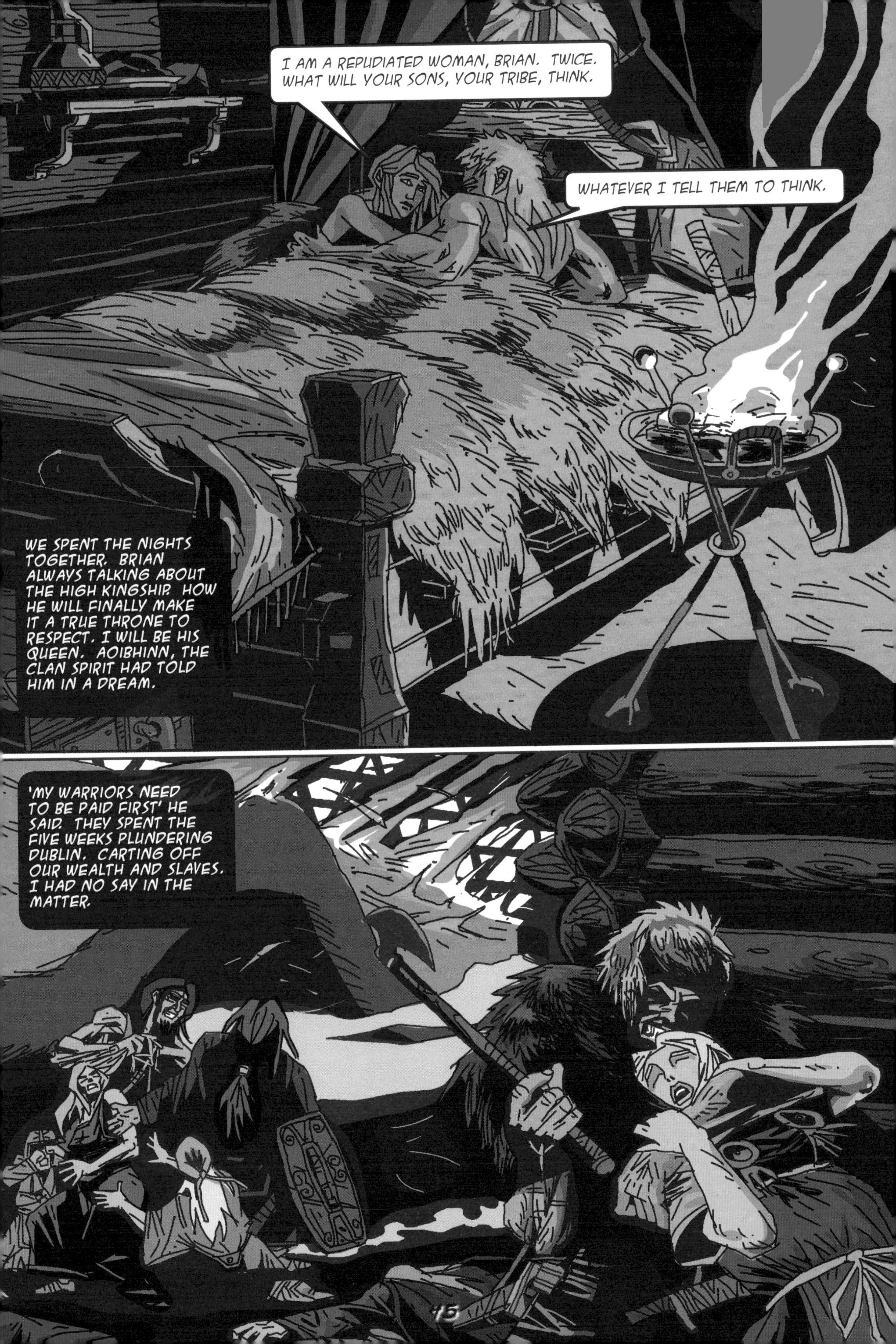
I AM A REPUDIATED WOMAN, BRIAN. TWICE. WHAT WILL YOUR SONS, YOUR TRIBE, THINK.
WHATEVER I TELL THEM TO THINK.
WE SPENT THE NIGHTS TOGETHER. BRIAN ALWAYS TALKING ABOUT THE HIGH KINGSHIP. HOW HE WILL FINALLY MAKE IT A TRUE THRONE TO RESPECT. I WILL BE HIS QUEEN. AOIBHINN, THE CLAN SPIRIT HAD TOLD HIM IN A DREAM.
'MY WARRIORS NEED TO BE PAID FIRST' HE SAID. THEY SPENT THE FIVE WEEKS PLUNDERING DUBLIN. CARTING OFF OUR WEALTH AND SLAVES. I HAD NO SAY IN THE MATTER.

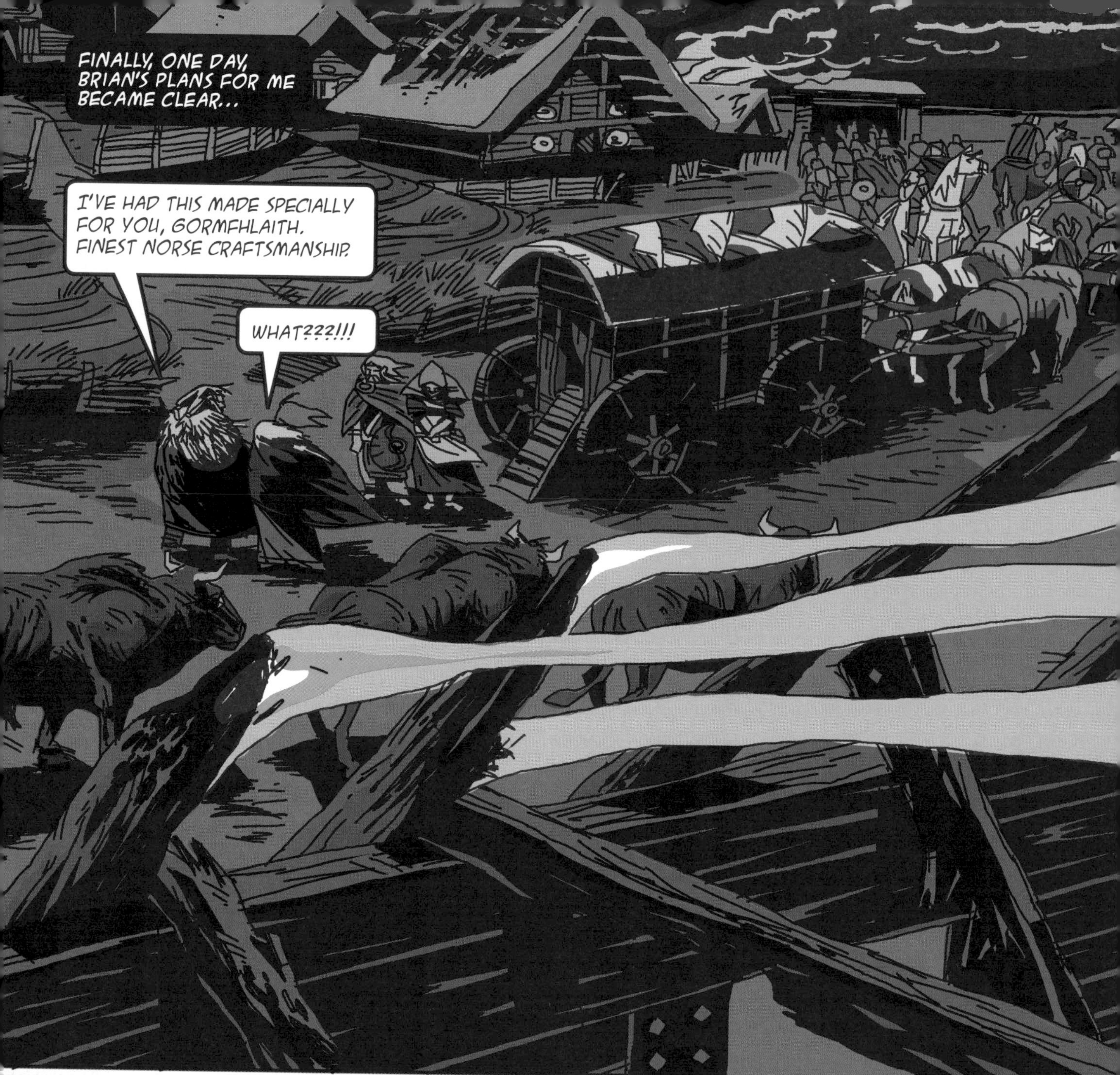
FINALLY, ONE DAY, BRIAN'S PLANS FOR ME BECAME CLEAR...
I'VE HAD THIS MADE SPECIALLY FOR YOU, GORMFHLAITH. FINEST NORSE CRAFTSMANSHIP.
WHAT???!!!
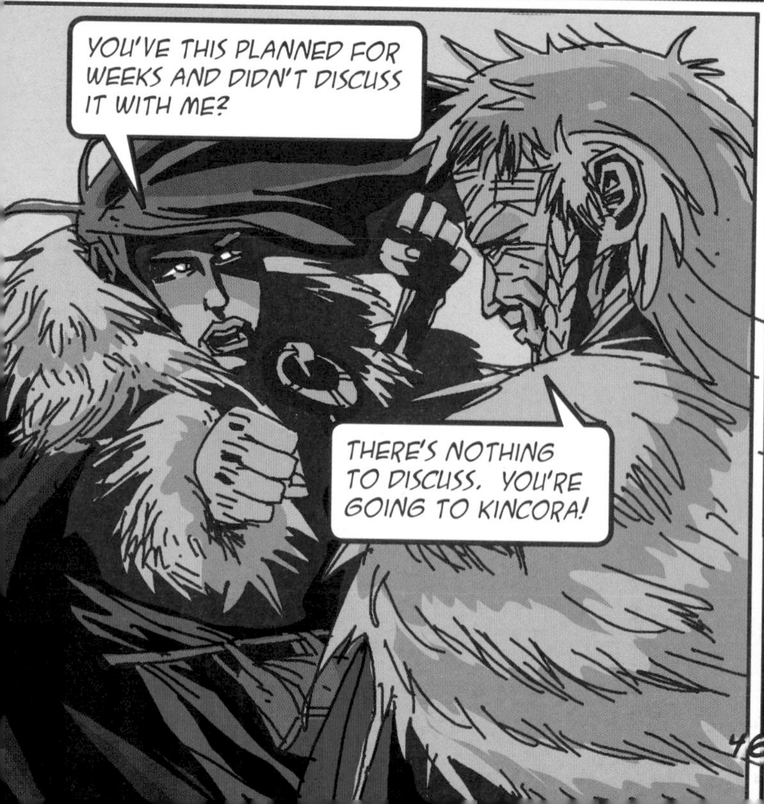
YOU'VE THIS PLANNED FOR WEEKS AND DIDN'T DISCUSS IT WITH ME?
THERE'S NOTHING TO DISCUSS. YOU'RE GOING TO KINCORA!
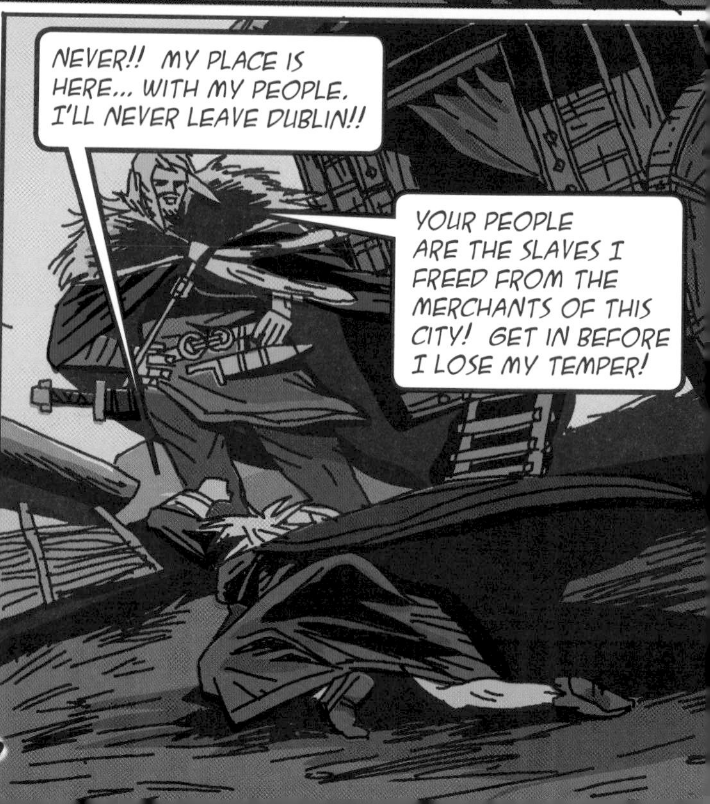
NEVER!! MY PLACE IS HERE... WITH MY PEOPLE. I'LL NEVER LEAVE DUBLIN!!
YOUR PEOPLE ARE THE SLAVES I FREED FROM THE MERCHANTS OF THIS CITY! GET IN BEFORE I LOSE MY TEMPER!

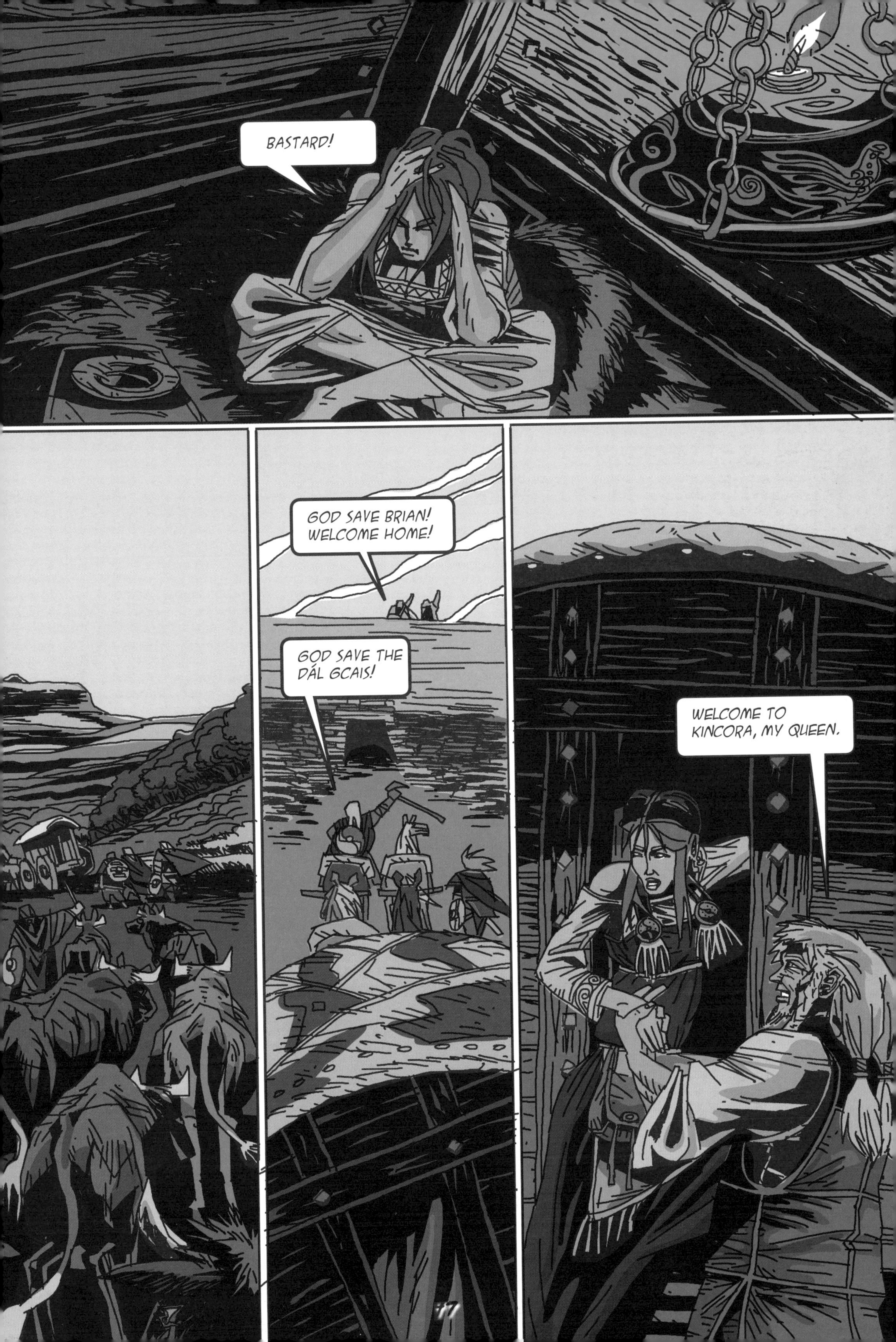
BASTARD!
GOD SAVE BRIAN! WELCOME HOME!
GOD SAVE THE DÁL GCAIS!
WELCOME TO KINCORA, MY QUEEN.

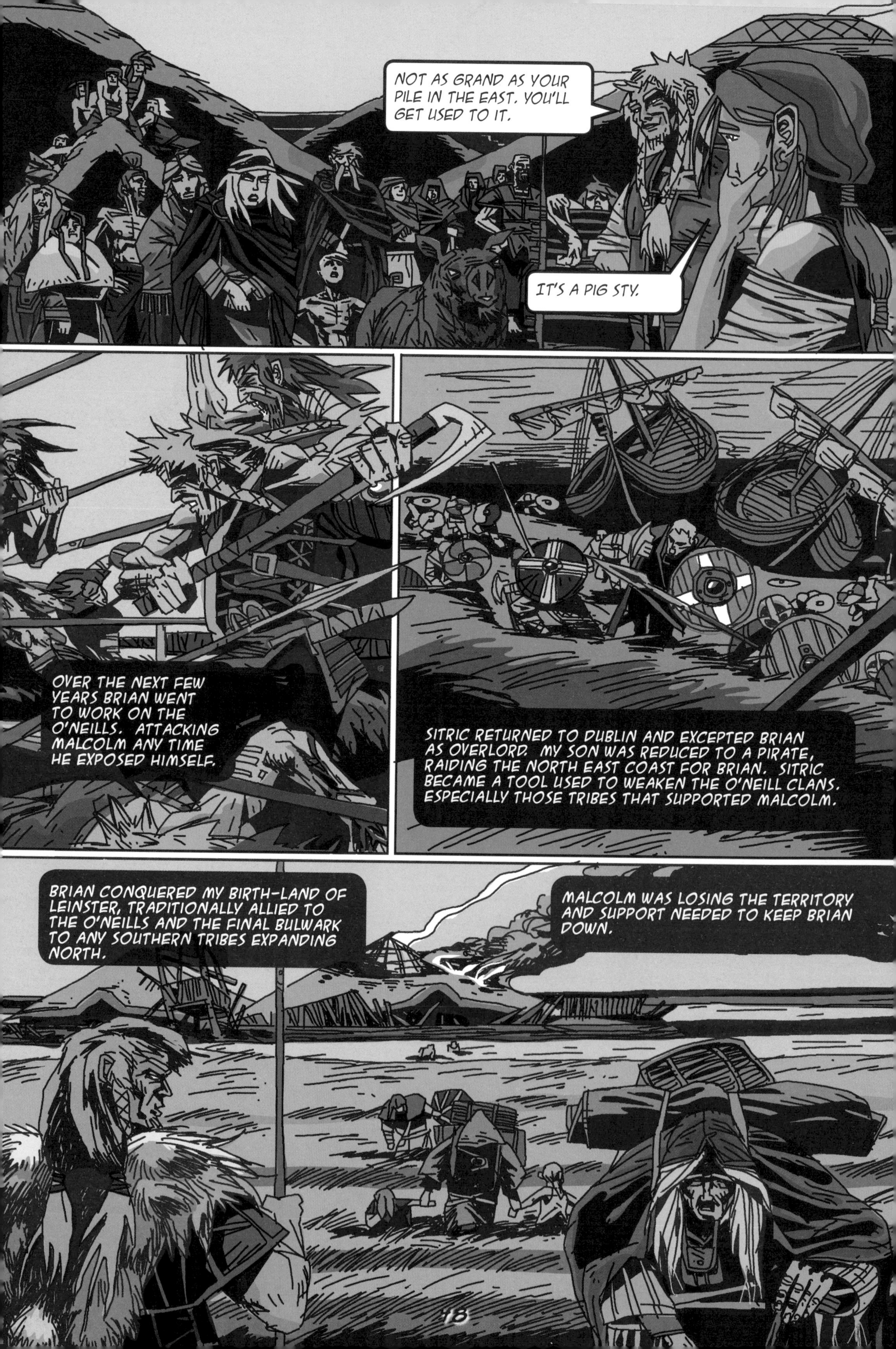
NOT AS GRAND AS YOUR PILE IN THE EAST. YOU'LL GET USED TO IT.
IT'S A PIG STY.
OVER THE NEXT FEW YEARS BRIAN WENT TO WORK ON THE O'NEILLS. ATTACKING MALCOLM ANY TIME HE EXPOSED HIMSELF.
SITRIC RETURNED TO DUBLIN AND EXCEPTED BRIAN AS OVERLORD. MY SON WAS REDUCED TO A PIRATE, RAIDING THE NORTH EAST COAST FOR BRIAN. SITRIC BECAME A TOOL USED TO WEAKEN THE O'NEILL CLANS. ESPECIALLY THOSE TRIBES THAT SUPPORTED MALCOLM.
BRIAN CONQUERED MY BIRTH-LAND OF LEINSTER, TRADITIONALLY ALLIED TO THE O'NEILLS AND THE FINAL BULWARK TO ANY SOUTHERN TRIBES EXPANDING NORTH.
MALCOLM WAS LOSING THE TERRITORY AND SUPPORT NEEDED TO KEEP BRIAN DOWN.

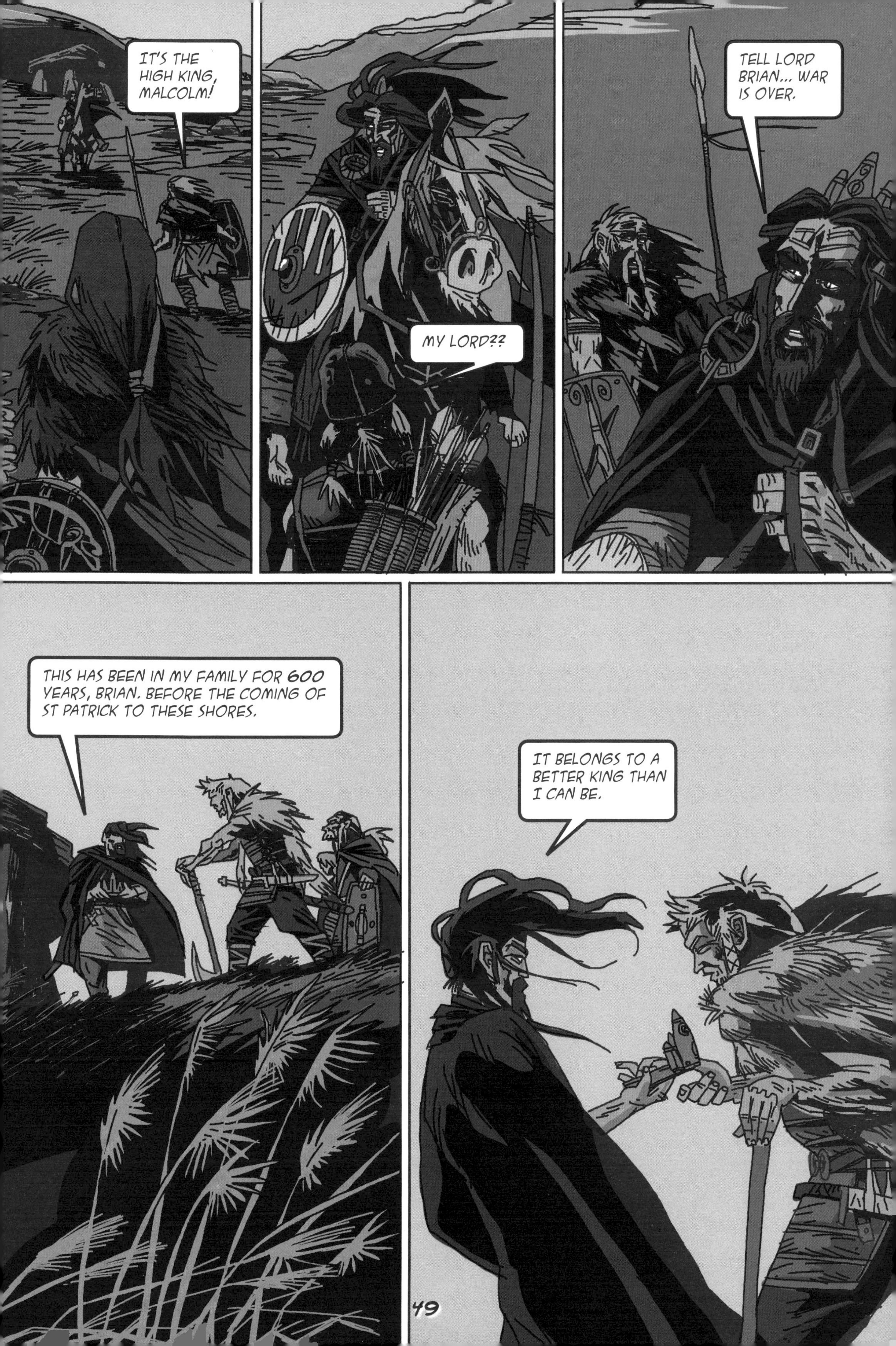
IT'S THE HIGH KING, MALCOLM!
MY LORD??
TELL LORD BRIAN... WAR IS OVER.
THIS HAS BEEN IN MY FAMILY FOR 600 YEARS, BRIAN. BEFORE THE COMING OF ST PATRICK TO THESE SHORES.
IT BELONGS TO A BETTER KING THAN I CAN BE.

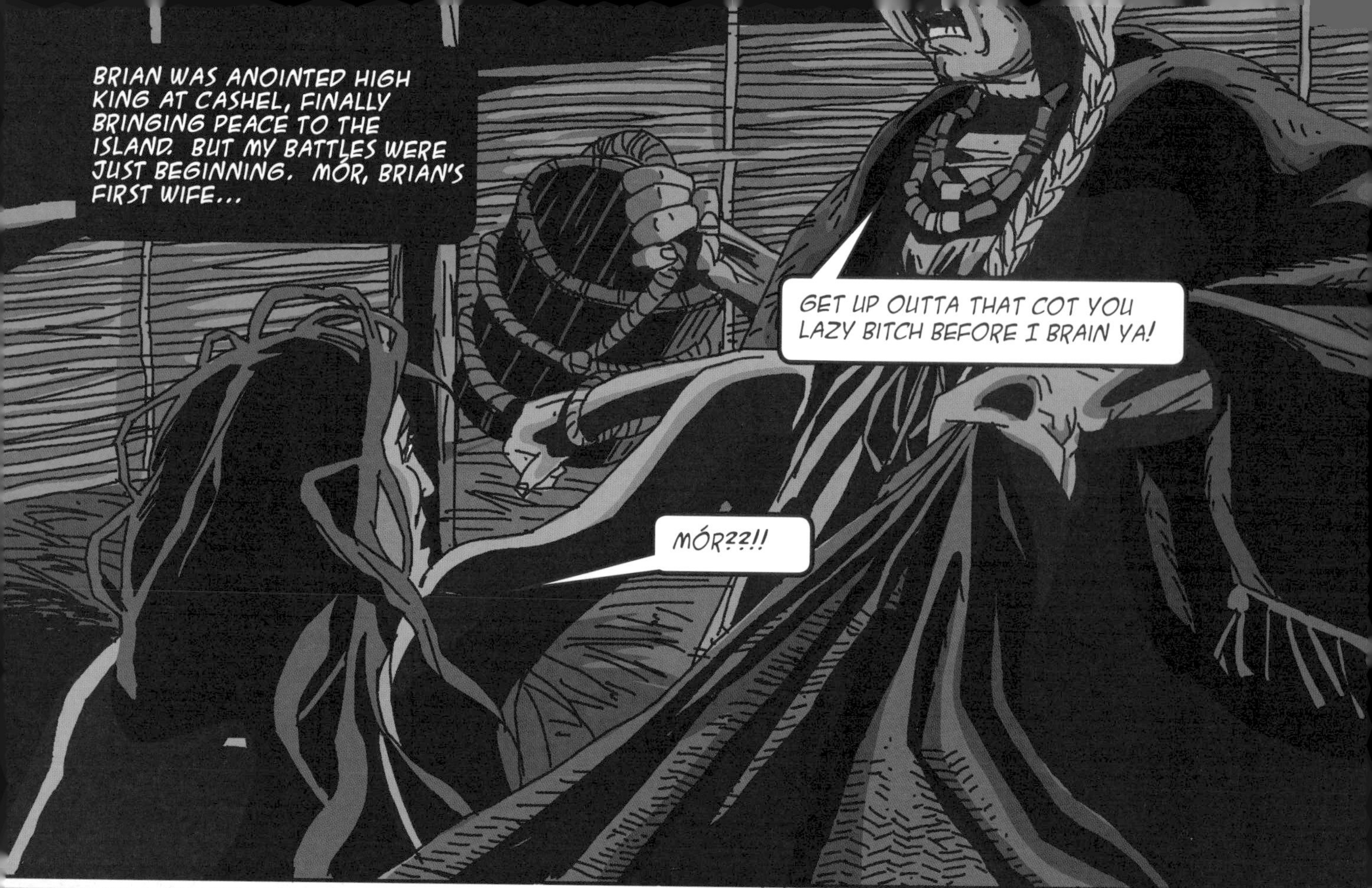
BRIAN WAS ANOINTED HIGH KING AT CASHEL, FINALLY BRINGING PEACE TO THE ISLAND. BUT MY BATTLES WERE JUST BEGINNING. MÓR, BRIAN'S FIRST WIFE...
GET UP OUTTA THAT COT YOU LAZY BITCH BEFORE I BRAIN YA!
MÓR??!!
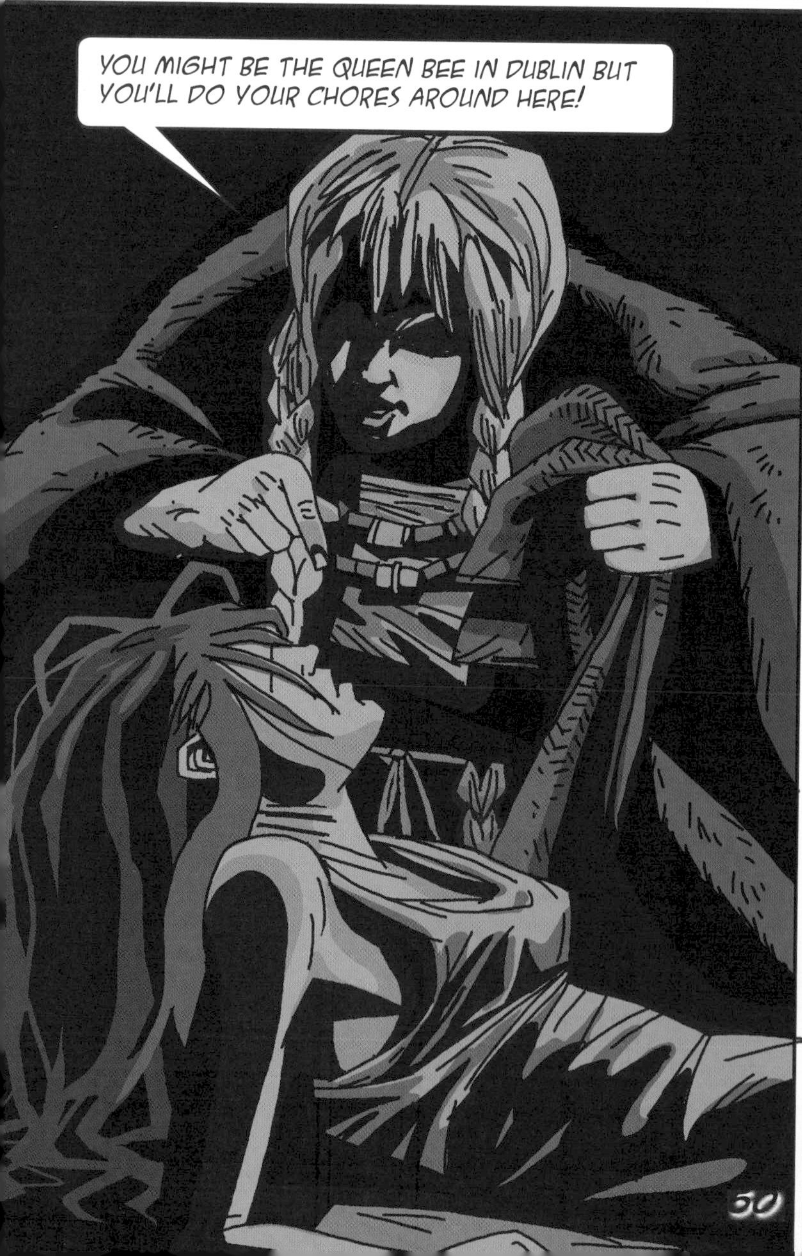
YOU MIGHT BE THE QUEEN BEE IN DUBLIN BUT YOU'LL DO YOUR CHORES AROUND HERE!
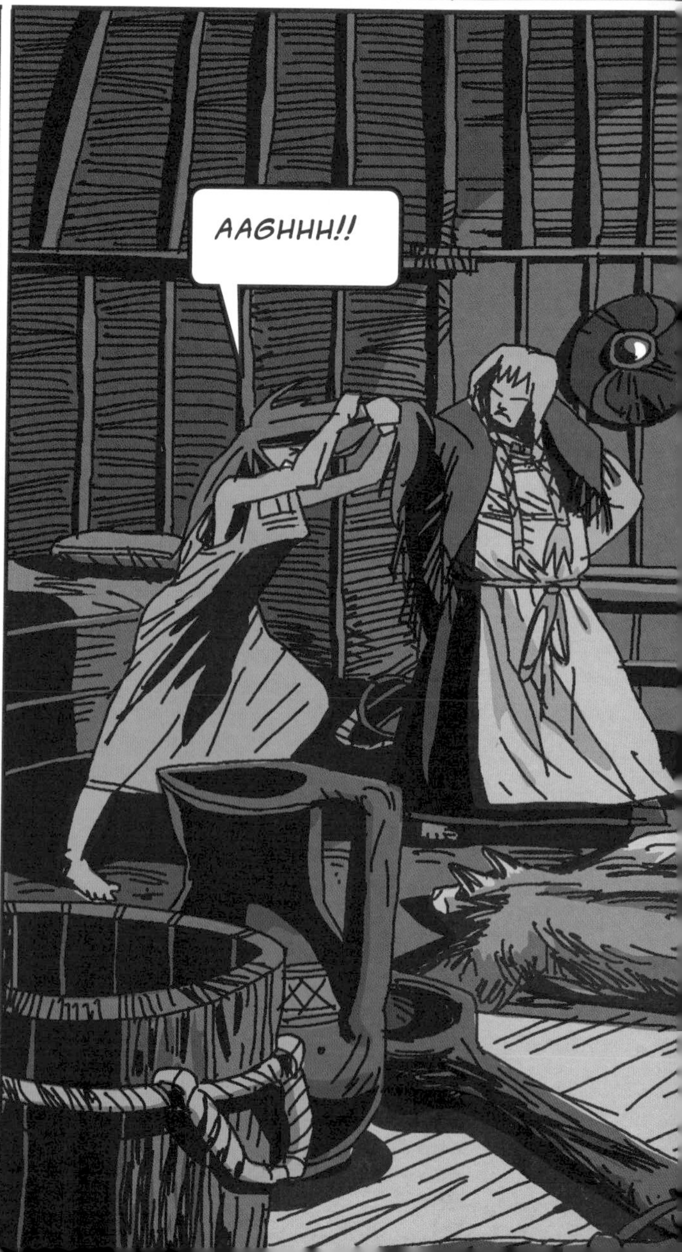
AAGHHH!!

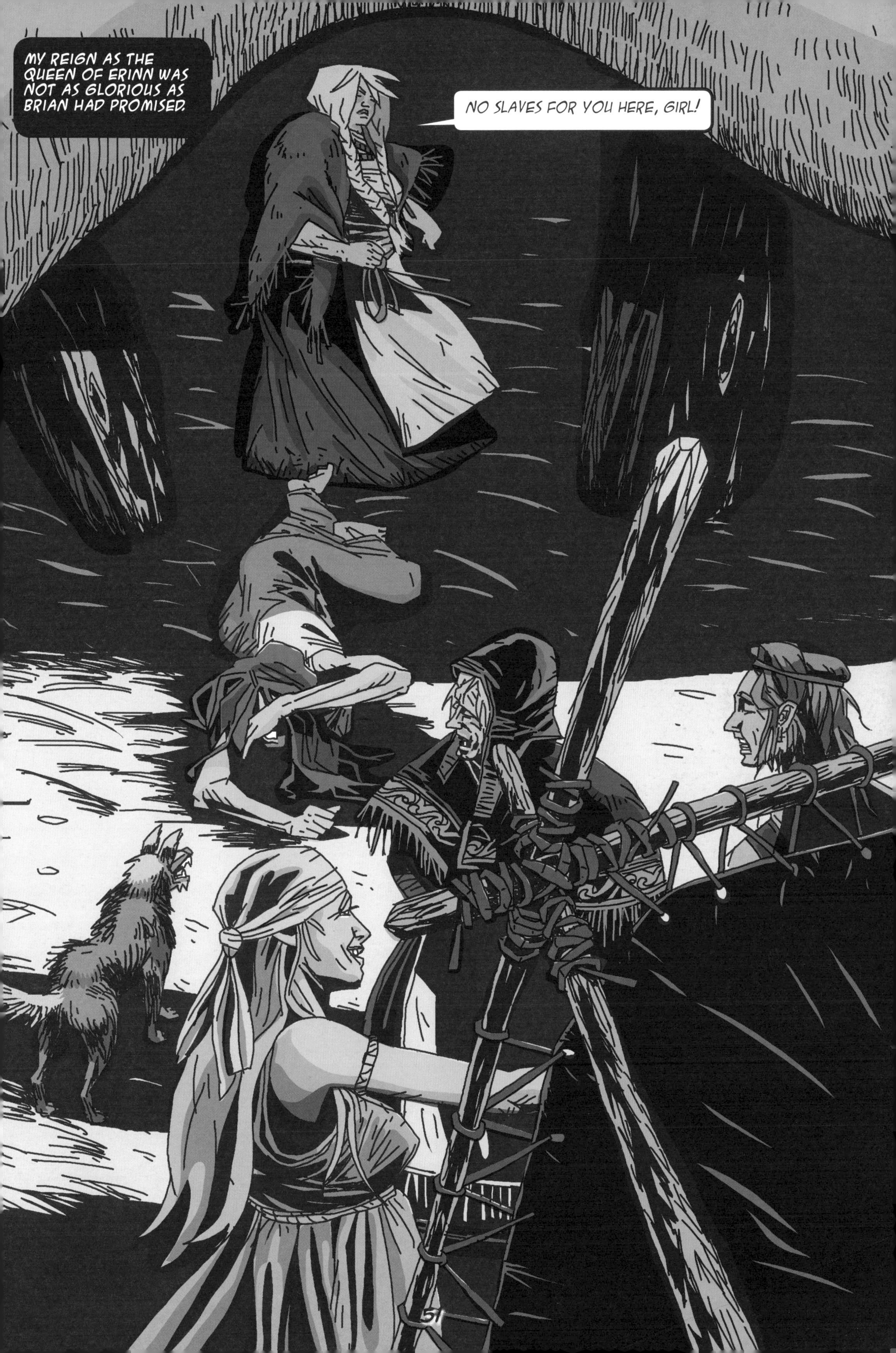
MY REIGN AS THE QUEEN OF ERINN WAS NOT AS GLORIOUS AS BRIAN HAD PROMISED.
NO SLAVES FOR YOU HERE, GIRL!

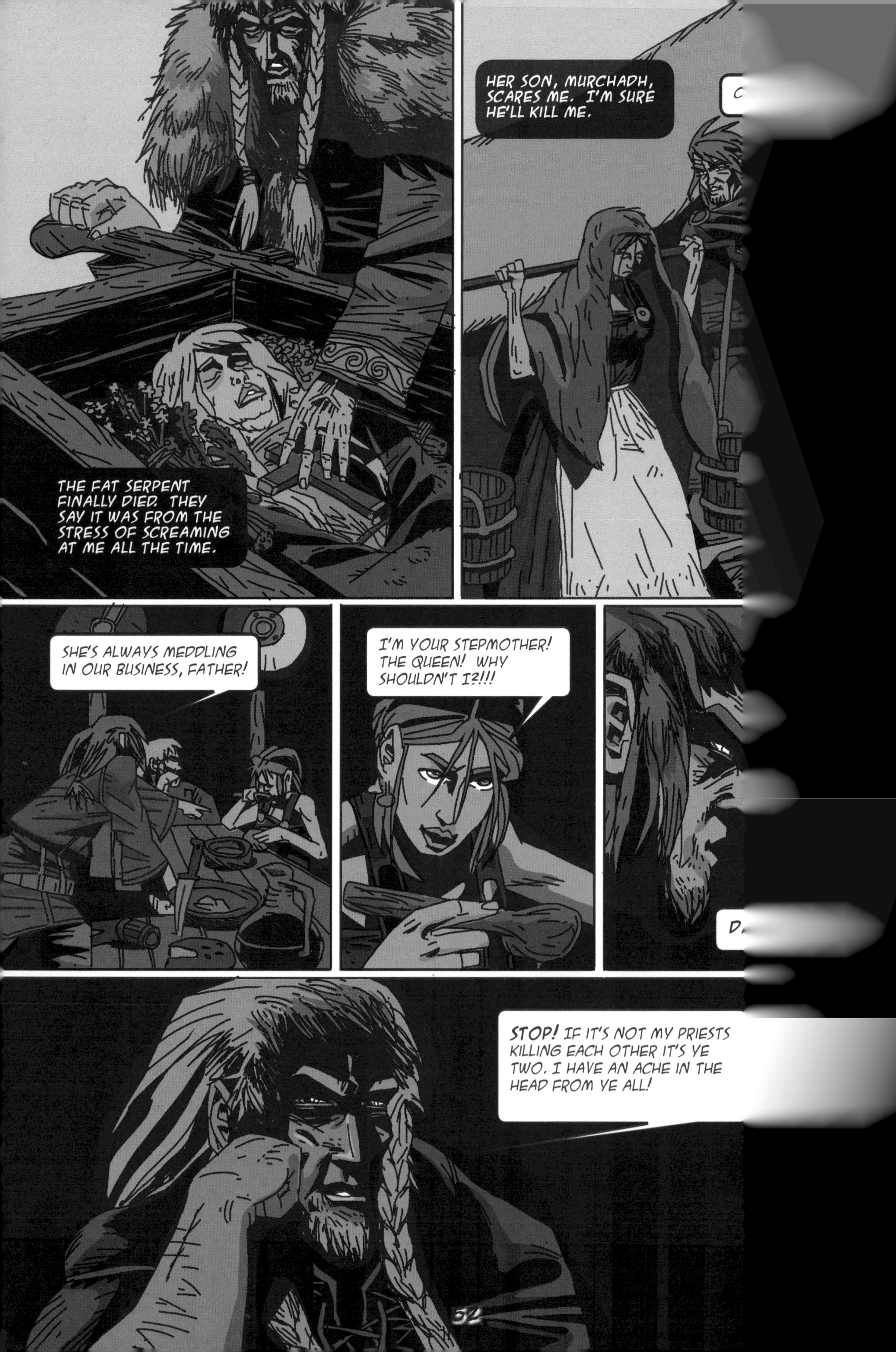
THE FAT SERPENT FINALLY DIED. THEY SAY IT WAS FROM THE STRESS OF SCREAMING AT ME ALL THE TIME.
HER SON, MURCHADH, SCARES ME. I'M SURE HE'LL KILL ME.
SHE'S ALWAYS MEDDLING IN OUR BUSINESS, FATHER!
I'M YOUR STEPMOTHER! THE QUEEN! WHY SHOULDN'T I?!!!
STOP! IF IT'S NOT MY PRIESTS KILLING EACH OTHER IT'S YE TWO. I HAVE AN ACHE IN THE HEAD FROM YE ALL!

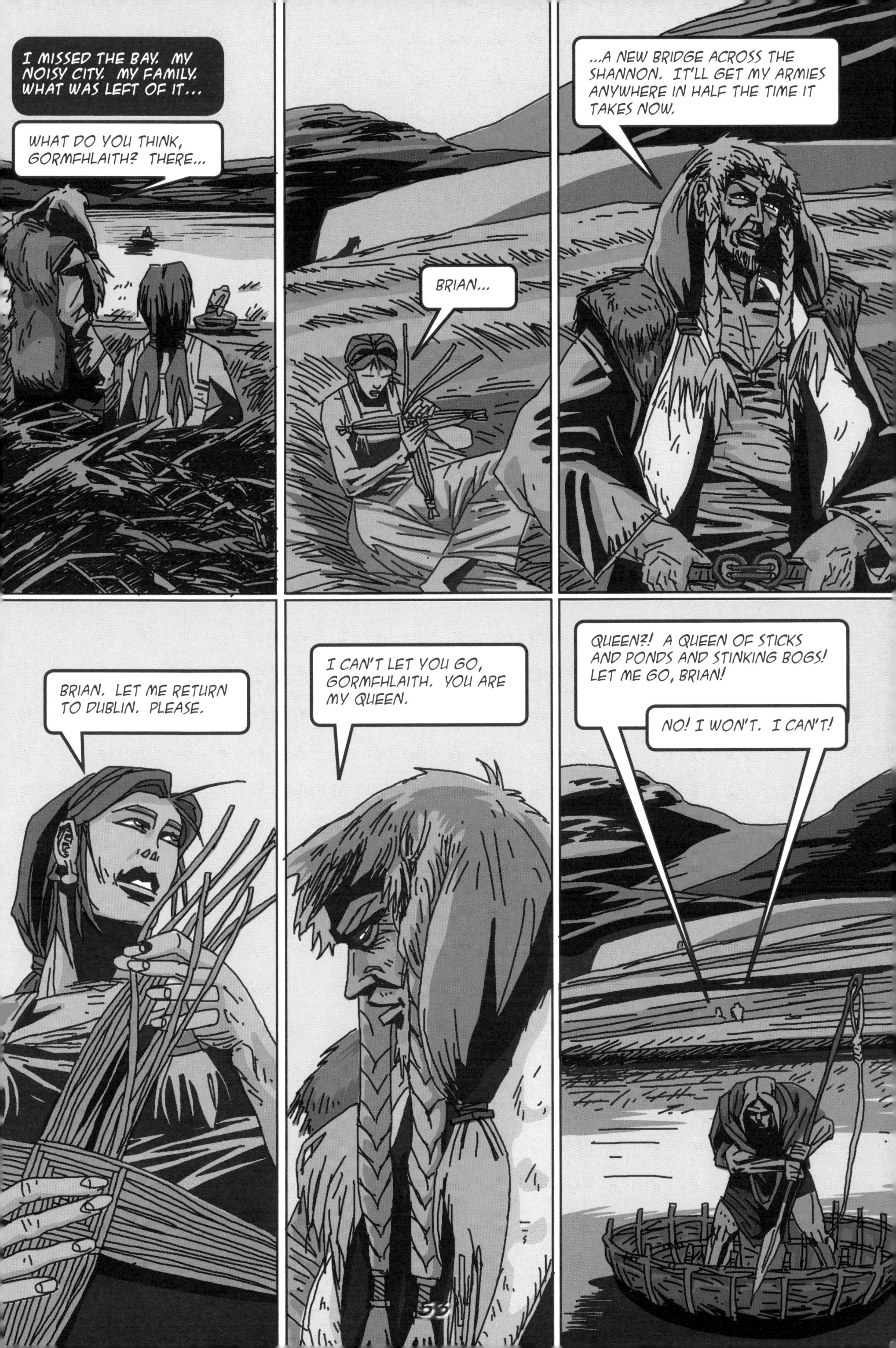
I MISSED THE BAY. MY NOISY CITY. MY FAMILY. WHAT WAS LEFT OF IT...
WHAT DO YOU THINK, GORMFHLAITH? THERE...
BRIAN...
...A NEW BRIDGE ACROSS THE SHANNON. IT'LL GET MY ARMIES ANYWHERE IN HALF THE TIME IT TAKES NOW.
BRIAN. LET ME RETURN TO DUBLIN. PLEASE.
I CAN'T LET YOU GO, GORMFHLAITH. YOU ARE MY QUEEN.
QUEEN?! A QUEEN OF STICKS AND PONDS AND STINKING BOGS! LET ME GO, BRIAN!
NO! I WON'T. I CAN'T!

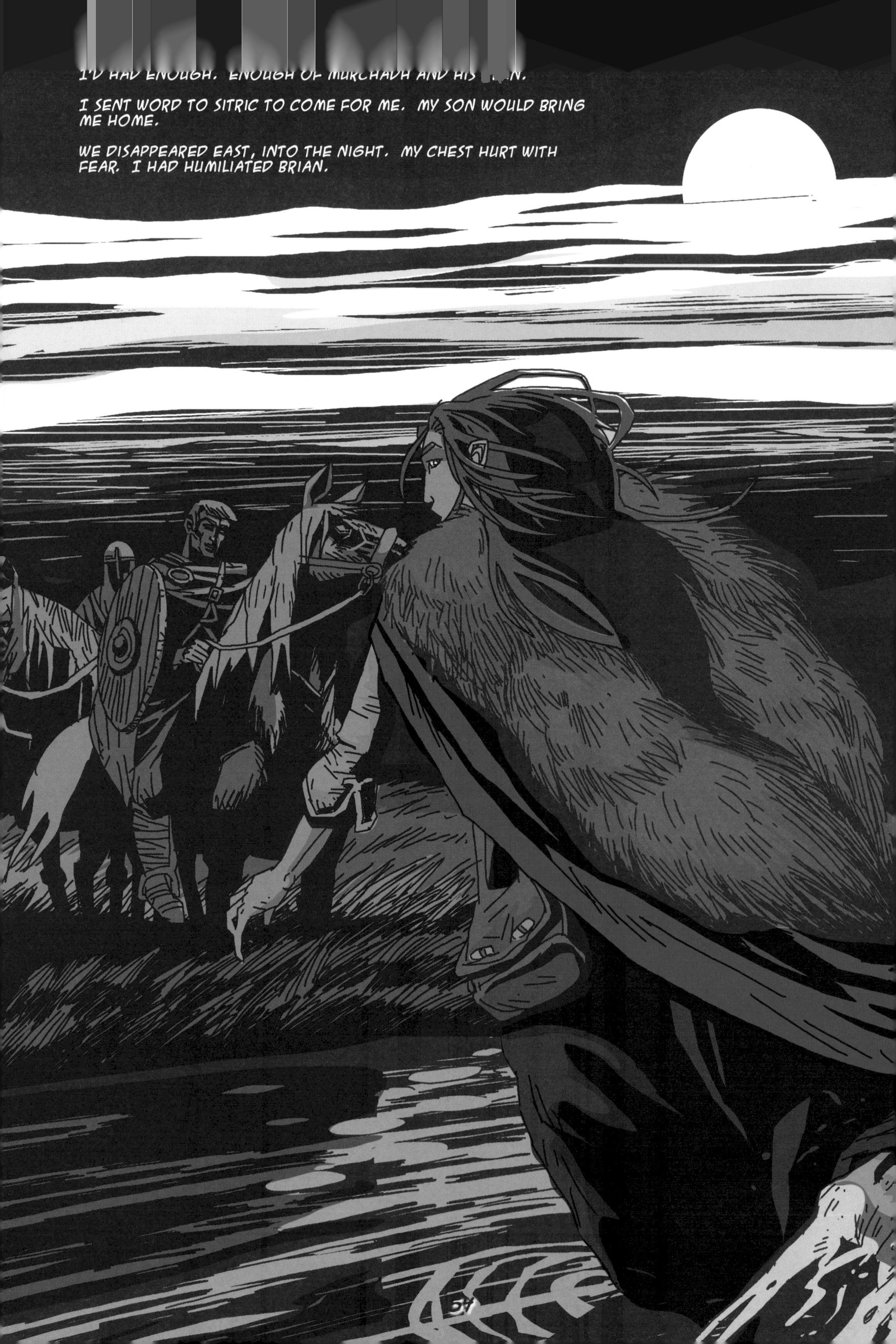
I'D HAD ENOUGH. ENOUGH OF MURCHADH AND HIS [redacted]
I SENT WORD TO SITRIC TO COME FOR ME. MY SON WOULD BRING ME HOME.
WE DISAPPEARED EAST, INTO THE NIGHT. MY CHEST HURT WITH FEAR. I HAD HUMILIATED BRIAN.

BRIAN THOUGHT HE COULD REPAIR WHAT HAD TAKEN CENTURIES TO BREAK. AN ISLAND MUTILATED BY CONSTANT CONFLICT. HE WOULD BUILD A NATION, MAKE HIS ANCESTORS PROUD. HE WAS TOO BUSY REBUILDING THE IRELAND OF HIS DREAMS TO CARE ABOUT ME.

IT ALL WORKED WELL WITH THE PEOPLE. THEY TOOK HIM TO THEIR HEARTS.

I WAS HAPPY TO BE BACK IN DUBLIN.

YOU'RE HOME, MOTHER.

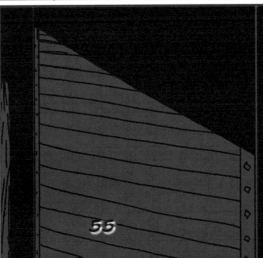

55

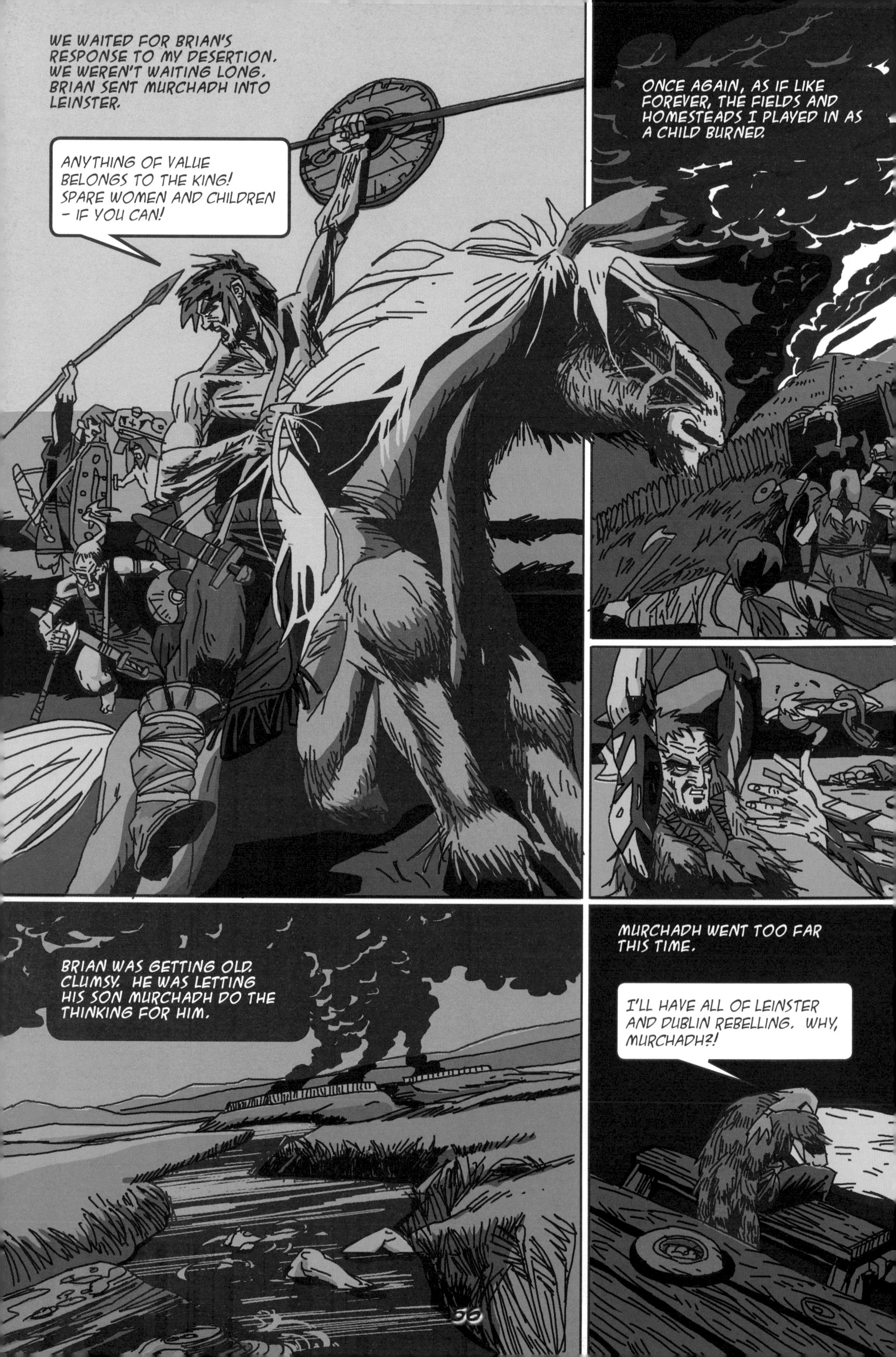
WE WAITED FOR BRIAN'S RESPONSE TO MY DESERTION. WE WEREN'T WAITING LONG. BRIAN SENT MURCHADH INTO LEINSTER.
ANYTHING OF VALUE BELONGS TO THE KING! SPARE WOMEN AND CHILDREN - IF YOU CAN!
ONCE AGAIN, AS IF LIKE FOREVER, THE FIELDS AND HOMESTEADS I PLAYED IN AS A CHILD BURNED.
BRIAN WAS GETTING OLD. CLUMSY. HE WAS LETTING HIS SON MURCHADH DO THE THINKING FOR HIM.
MURCHADH WENT TOO FAR THIS TIME.
I'LL HAVE ALL OF LEINSTER AND DUBLIN REBELLING. WHY, MURCHADH?!

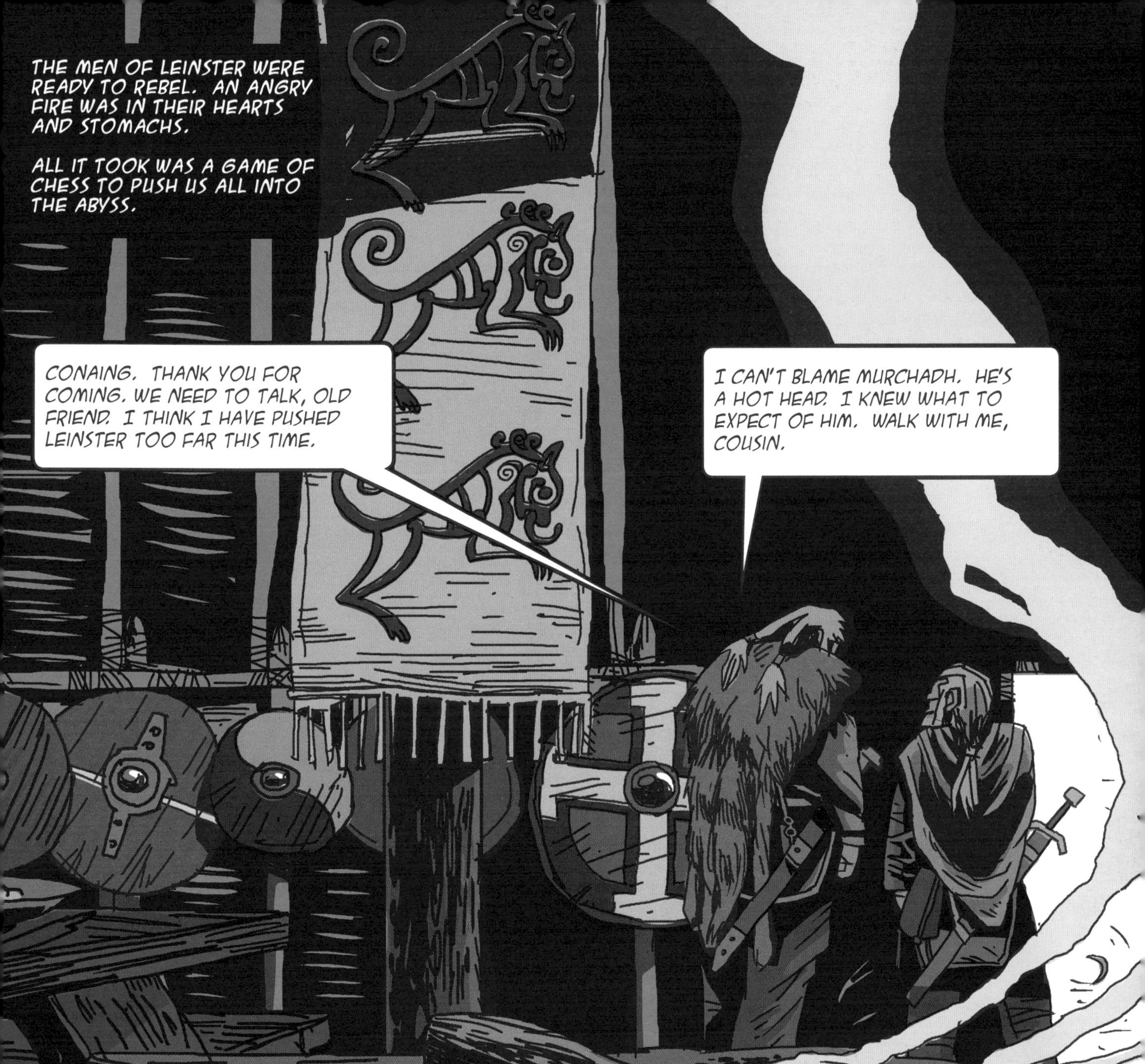
THE MEN OF LEINSTER WERE READY TO REBEL. AN ANGRY FIRE WAS IN THEIR HEARTS AND STOMACHS.
ALL IT TOOK WAS A GAME OF CHESS TO PUSH US ALL INTO THE ABYSS.
CONAING. THANK YOU FOR COMING. WE NEED TO TALK, OLD FRIEND. I THINK I HAVE PUSHED LEINSTER TOO FAR THIS TIME.
I CAN'T BLAME MURCHADH. HE'S A HOT HEAD. I KNEW WHAT TO EXPECT OF HIM. WALK WITH ME, COUSIN.

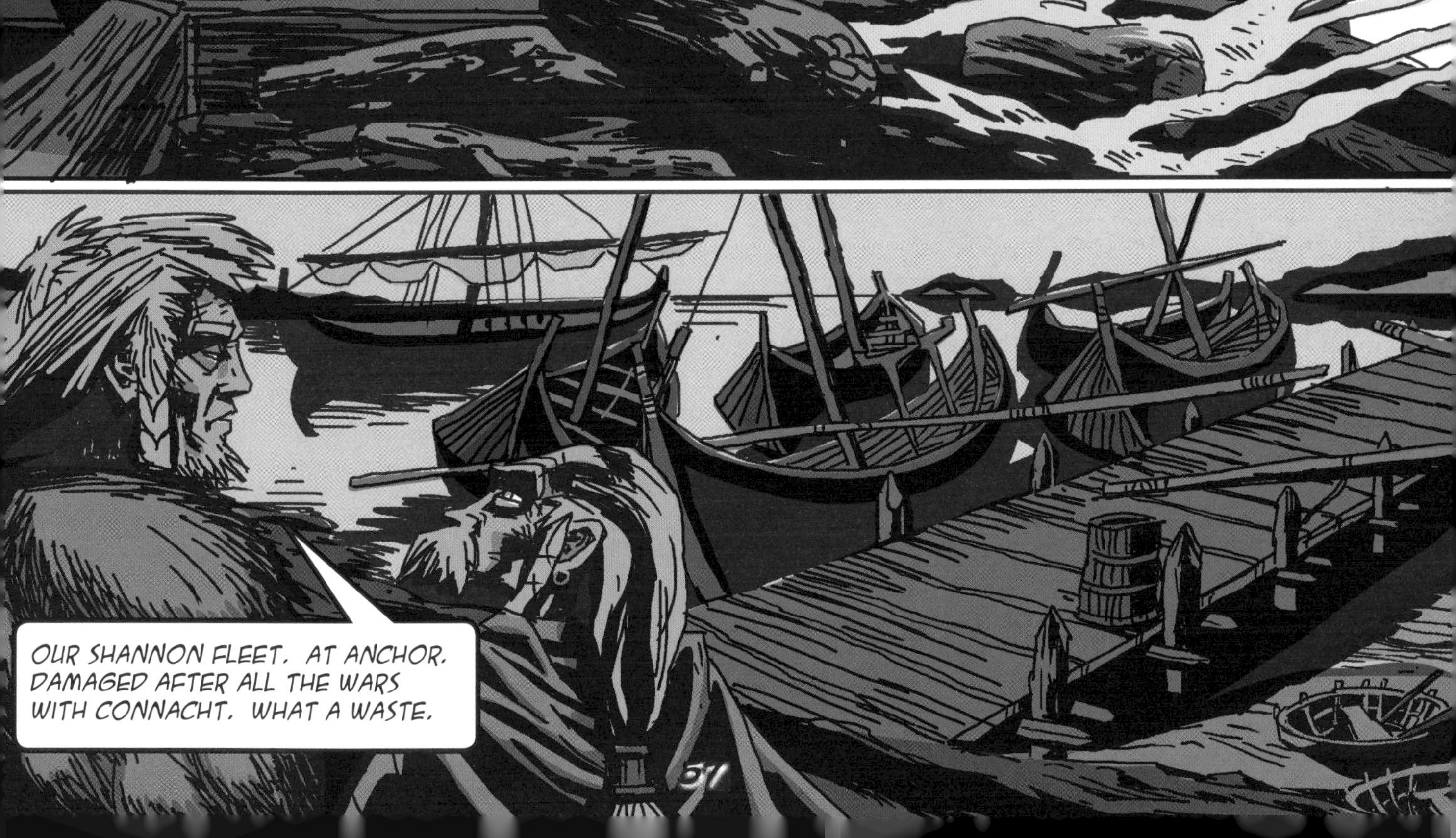
OUR SHANNON FLEET. AT ANCHOR. DAMAGED AFTER ALL THE WARS WITH CONNACHT. WHAT A WASTE.

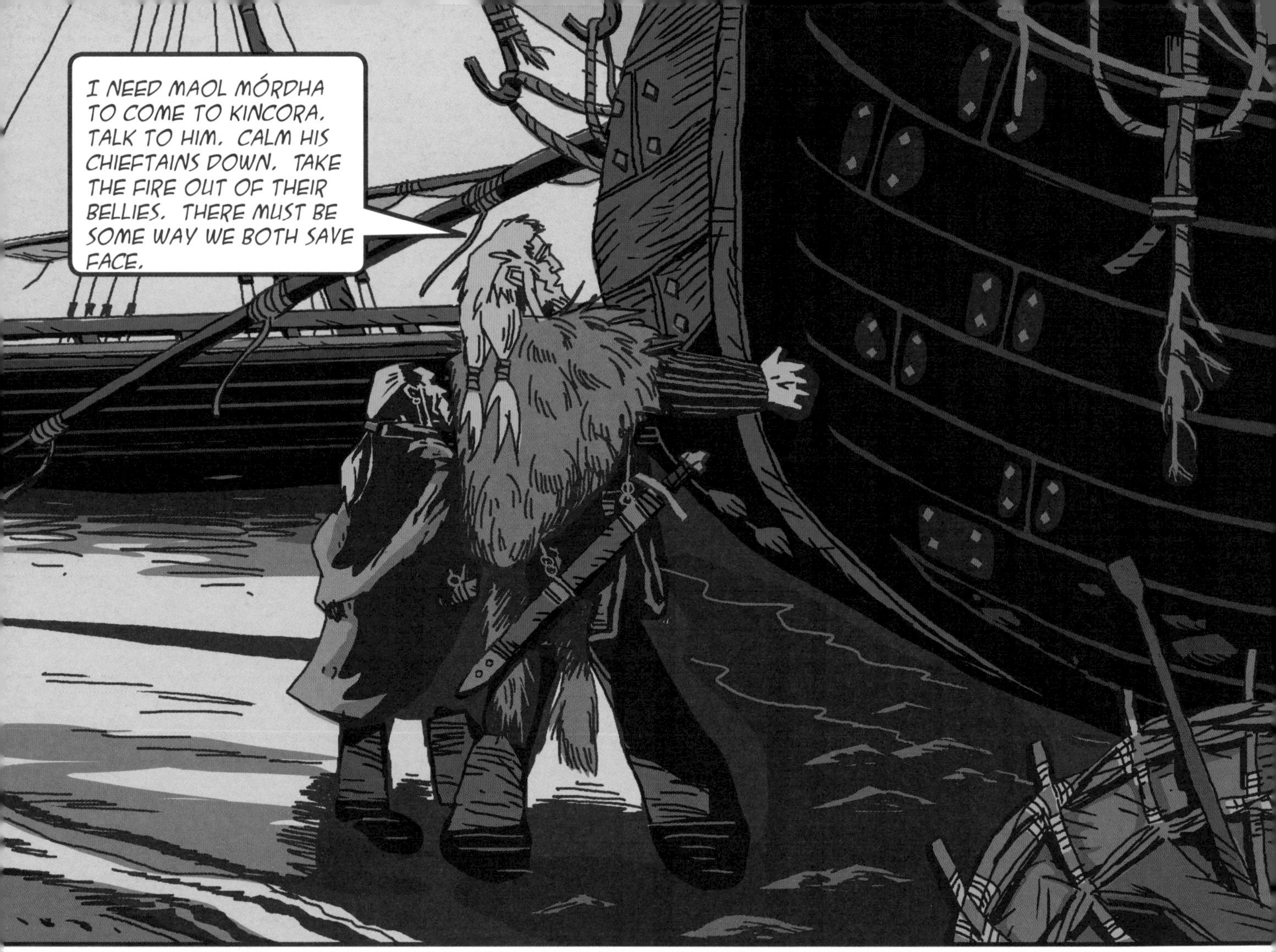
I NEED MAOL MÓRDHA TO COME TO KINCORA. TALK TO HIM. CALM HIS CHIEFTAINS DOWN. TAKE THE FIRE OUT OF THEIR BELLIES. THERE MUST BE SOME WAY WE BOTH SAVE FACE.
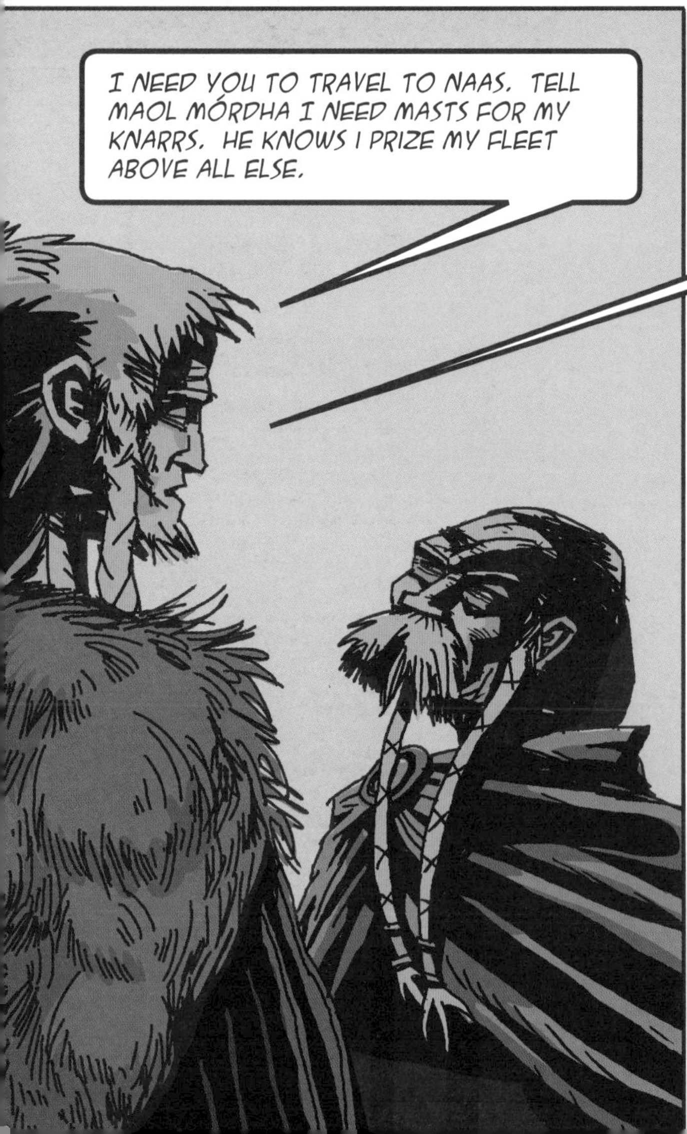
I NEED YOU TO TRAVEL TO NAAS. TELL MAOL MÓRDHA I NEED MASTS FOR MY KNARRS. HE KNOWS I PRIZE MY FLEET ABOVE ALL ELSE.
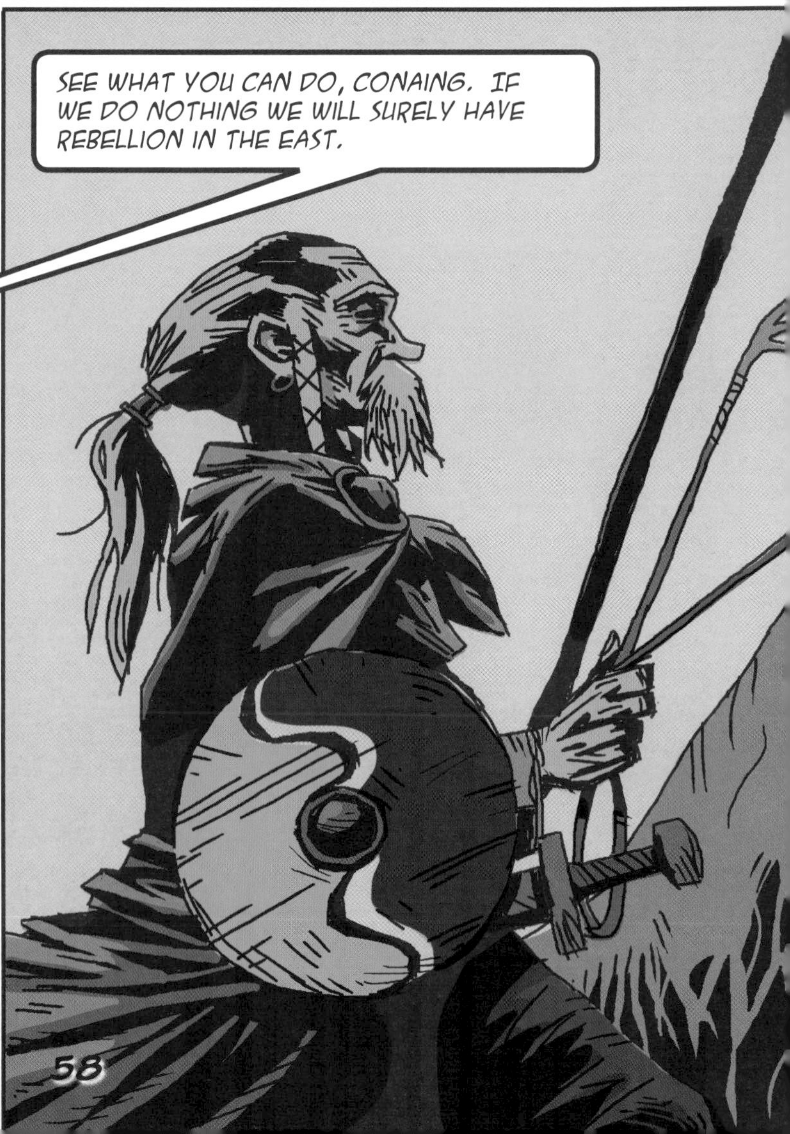
SEE WHAT YOU CAN DO, CONAING. IF WE DO NOTHING WE WILL SURELY HAVE REBELLION IN THE EAST.

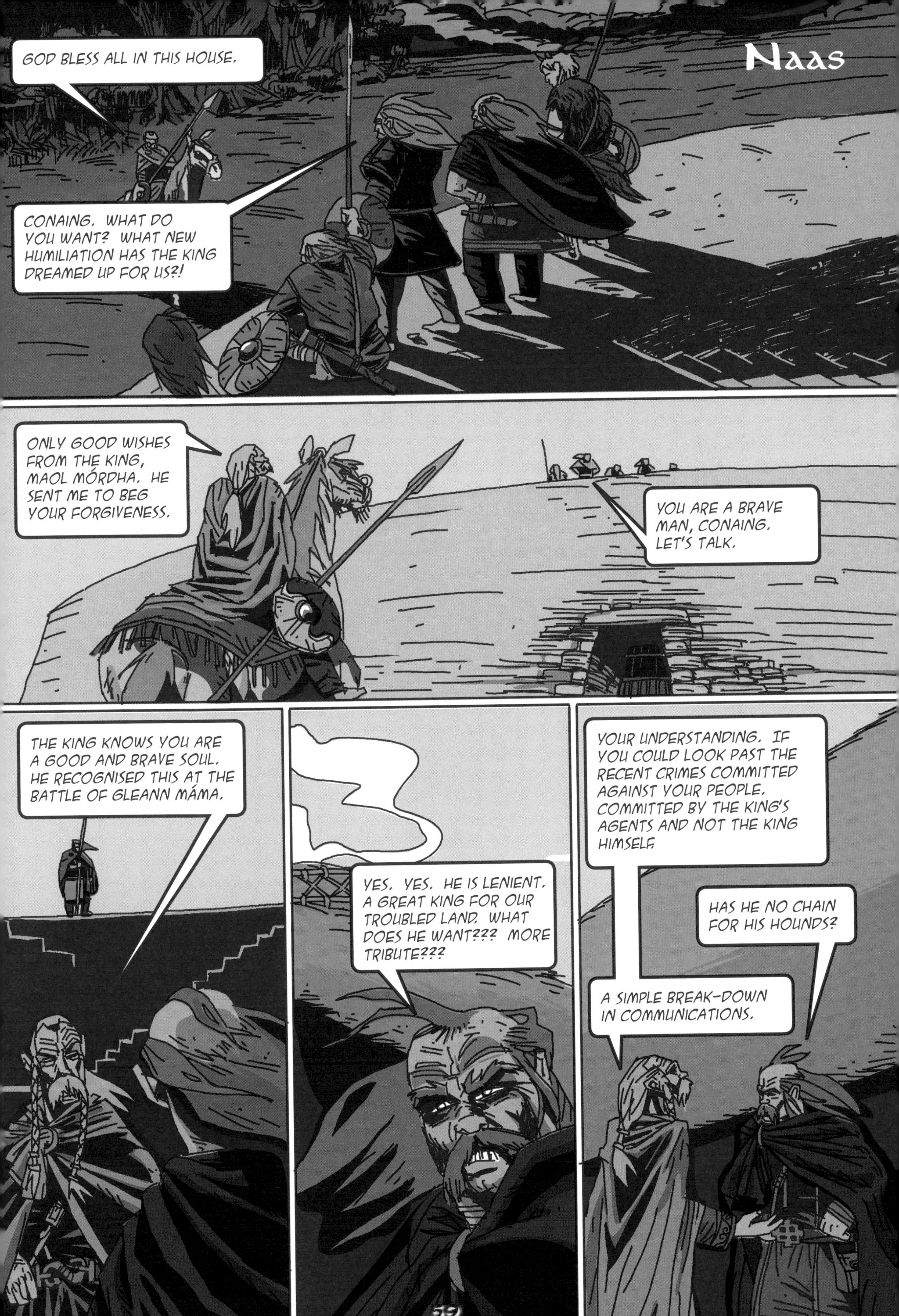
Naas
GOD BLESS ALL IN THIS HOUSE.
CONAING. WHAT DO YOU WANT? WHAT NEW HUMILIATION HAS THE KING DREAMED UP FOR US?!
ONLY GOOD WISHES FROM THE KING, MAOL MÓRDHA. HE SENT ME TO BEG YOUR FORGIVENESS.
YOU ARE A BRAVE MAN, CONAING. LET'S TALK.
THE KING KNOWS YOU ARE A GOOD AND BRAVE SOUL. HE RECOGNISED THIS AT THE BATTLE OF GLEANN MÁMA.
YES. YES. HE IS LENIENT. A GREAT KING FOR OUR TROUBLED LAND. WHAT DOES HE WANT??? MORE TRIBUTE???
YOUR UNDERSTANDING. IF YOU COULD LOOK PAST THE RECENT CRIMES COMMITTED AGAINST YOUR PEOPLE. COMMITTED BY THE KING'S AGENTS AND NOT THE KING HIMSELF.
HAS HE NO CHAIN FOR HIS HOUNDS?
A SIMPLE BREAK-DOWN IN COMMUNICATIONS.

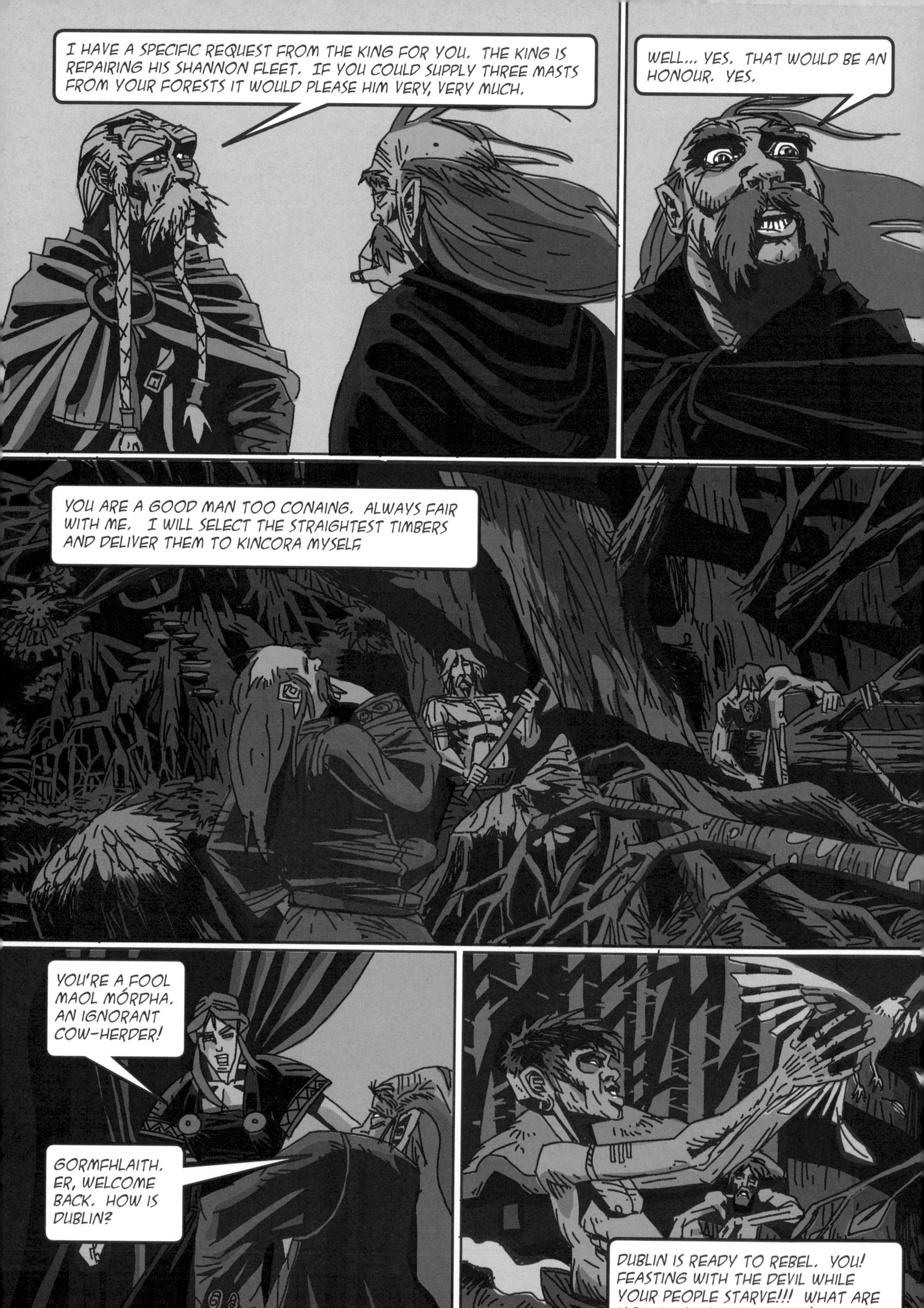
I HAVE A SPECIFIC REQUEST FROM THE KING FOR YOU. THE KING IS REPAIRING HIS SHANNON FLEET. IF YOU COULD SUPPLY THREE MASTS FROM YOUR FORESTS IT WOULD PLEASE HIM VERY, VERY MUCH.
WELL... YES. THAT WOULD BE AN HONOUR. YES.
YOU ARE A GOOD MAN TOO CONAING. ALWAYS FAIR WITH ME. I WILL SELECT THE STRAIGHTEST TIMBERS AND DELIVER THEM TO KINCORA MYSELF.
YOU'RE A FOOL MAOL MÓRDHA. AN IGNORANT COW-HERDER!
GORMFHLAITH. ER, WELCOME BACK. HOW IS DUBLIN?
DUBLIN IS READY TO REBEL. YOU! FEASTING WITH THE DEVIL WHILE YOUR PEOPLE STARVE!!! WHAT ARE YOU THINKING OF, MAOL?!

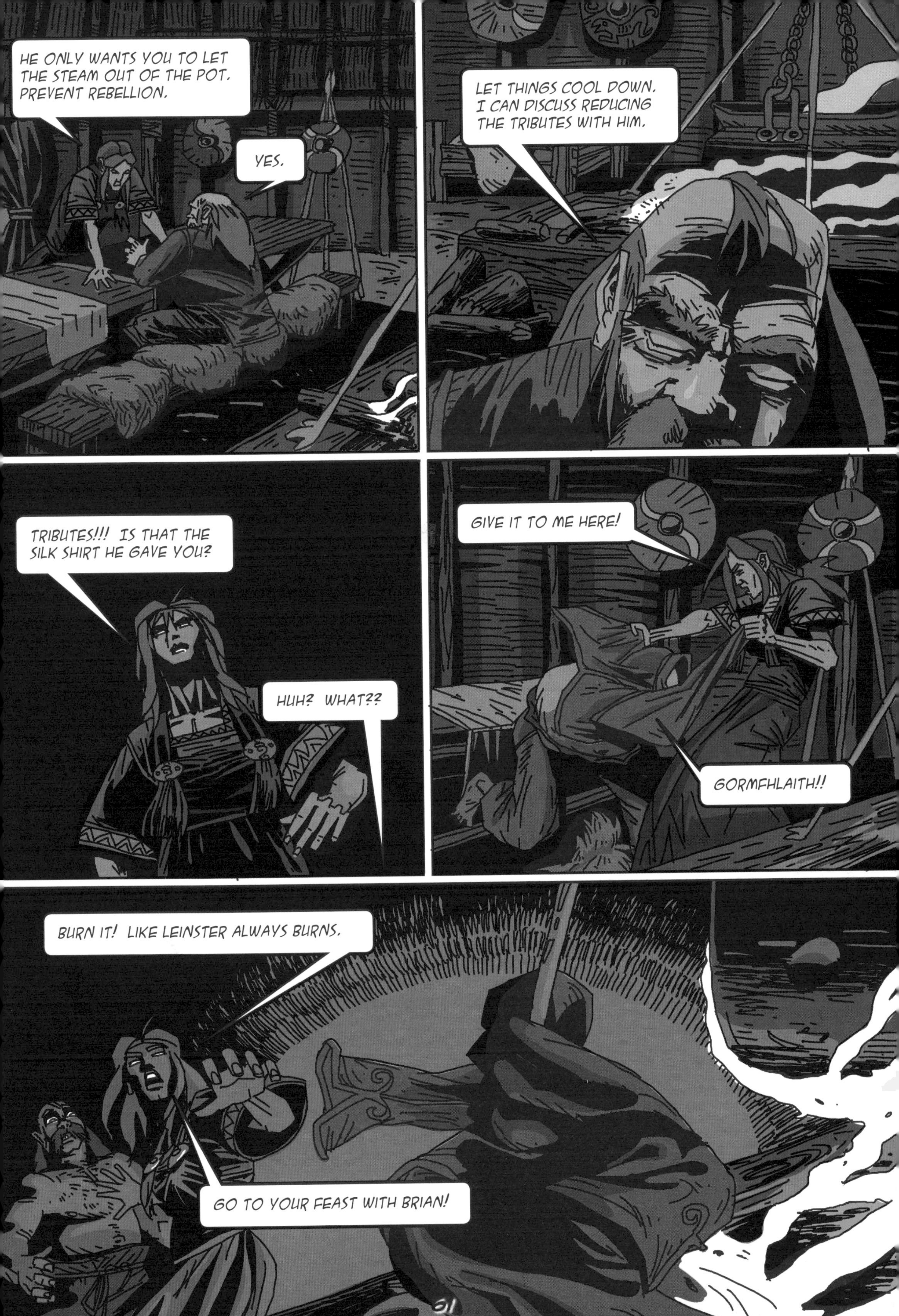
HE ONLY WANTS YOU TO LET THE STEAM OUT OF THE POT. PREVENT REBELLION.
YES.
LET THINGS COOL DOWN. I CAN DISCUSS REDUCING THE TRIBUTES WITH HIM.
TRIBUTES!!! IS THAT THE SILK SHIRT HE GAVE YOU?
HUH? WHAT??
GIVE IT TO ME HERE!
GORMFHLAITH!!
BURN IT! LIKE LEINSTER ALWAYS BURNS.
GO TO YOUR FEAST WITH BRIAN!

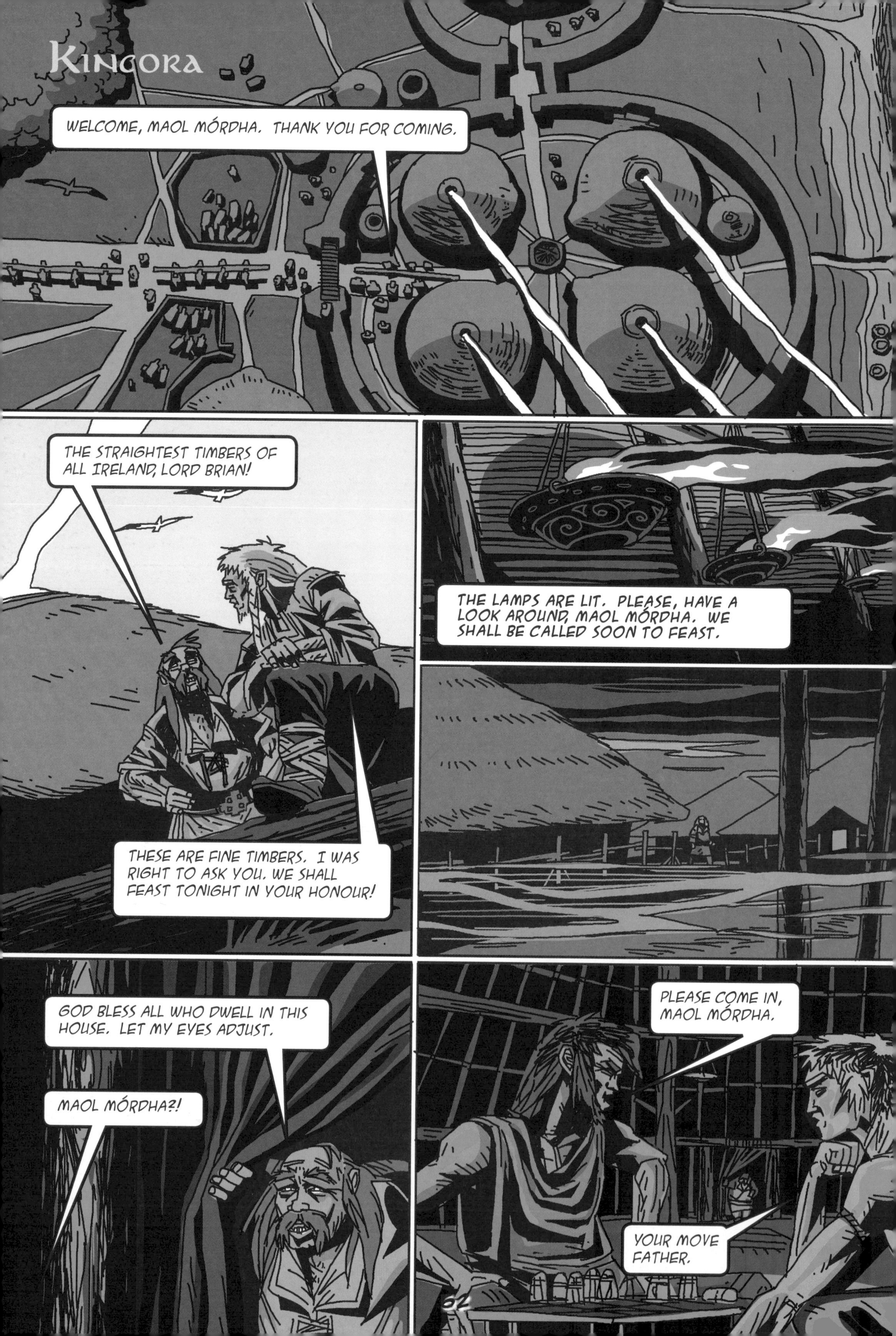
WELCOME, MAOL MÓRDHA. THANK YOU FOR COMING.
THE STRAIGHTEST TIMBERS OF ALL IRELAND, LORD BRIAN!
THESE ARE FINE TIMBERS. I WAS RIGHT TO ASK YOU. WE SHALL FEAST TONIGHT IN YOUR HONOUR!
THE LAMPS ARE LIT. PLEASE, HAVE A LOOK AROUND, MAOL MÓRDHA. WE SHALL BE CALLED SOON TO FEAST.
GOD BLESS ALL WHO DWELL IN THIS HOUSE. LET MY EYES ADJUST.
MAOL MÓRDHA?!
PLEASE COME IN, MAOL MÓRDHA.
YOUR MOVE FATHER.

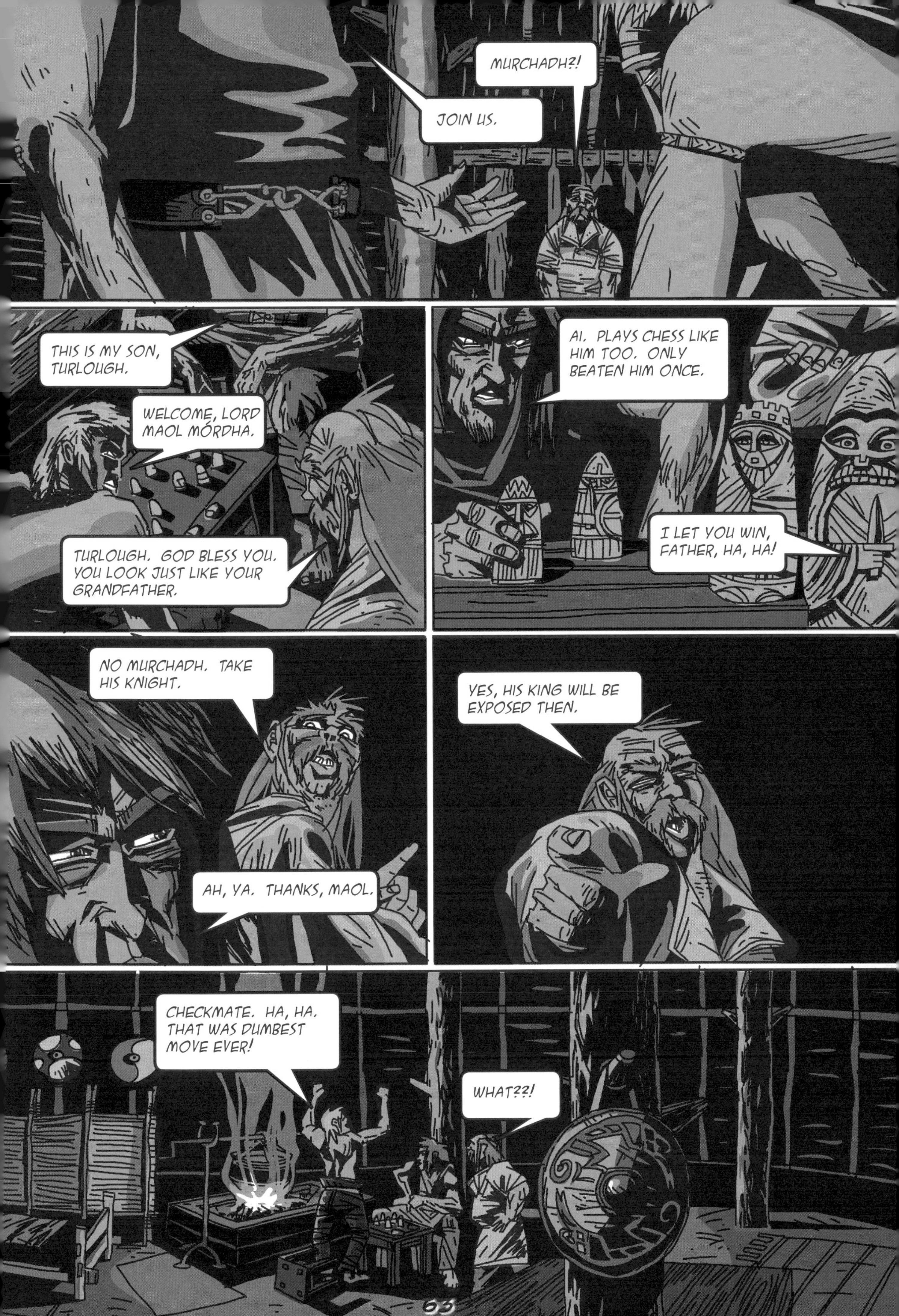
MURCHADH?!
JOIN US.
THIS IS MY SON, TURLOUGH.
WELCOME, LORD MAOL MÓRDHA.
TURLOUGH. GOD BLESS YOU. YOU LOOK JUST LIKE YOUR GRANDFATHER.
AI. PLAYS CHESS LIKE HIM TOO. ONLY BEATEN HIM ONCE.
I LET YOU WIN, FATHER, HA, HA!
NO MURCHADH. TAKE HIS KNIGHT.
AH, YA. THANKS, MAOL.
YES, HIS KING WILL BE EXPOSED THEN.
CHECKMATE. HA, HA. THAT WAS DUMBEST MOVE EVER!
WHAT??!

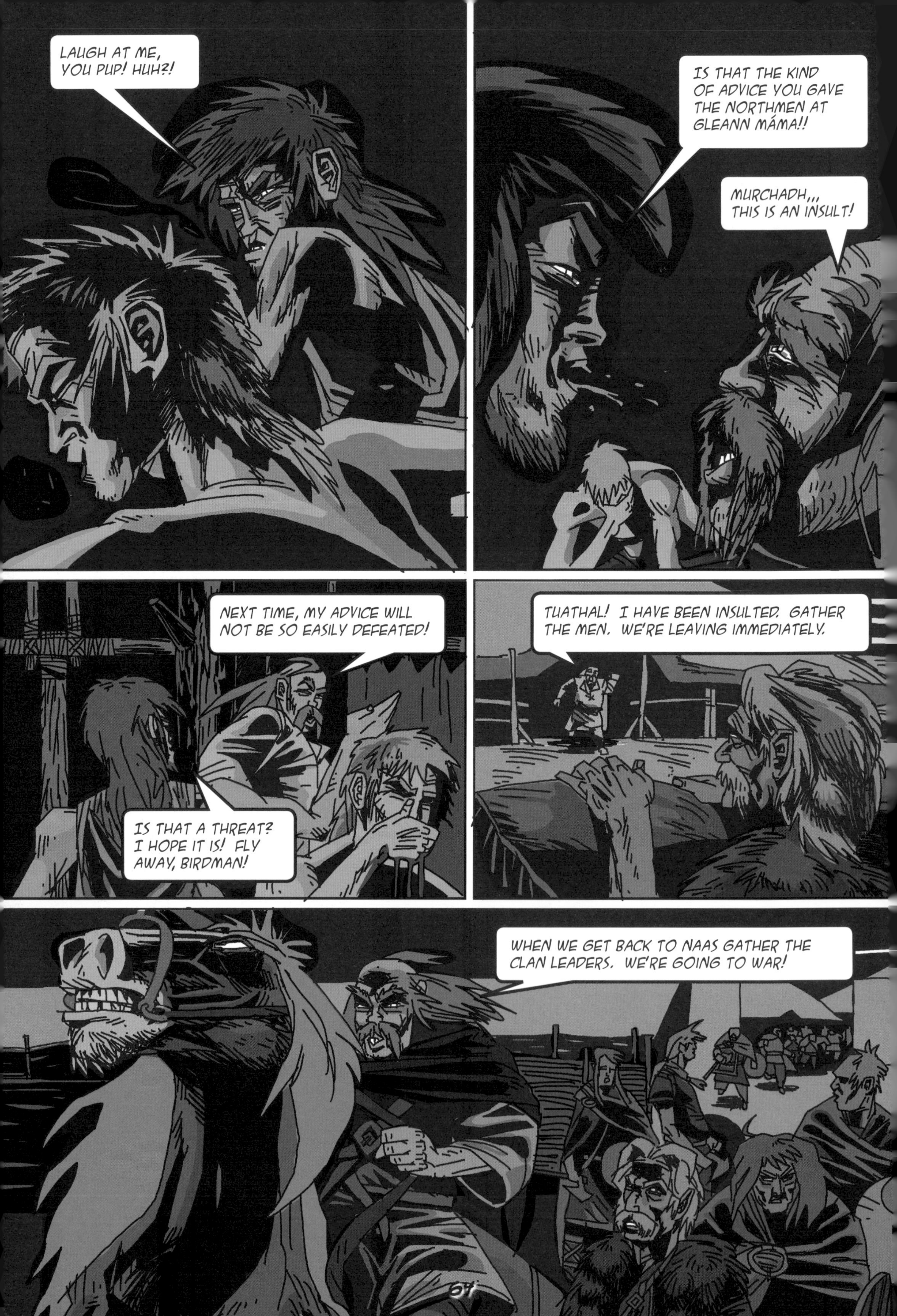
LAUGH AT ME, YOU PUP! HUH?!
IS THAT THE KIND OF ADVICE YOU GAVE THE NORTHMEN AT GLEANN MÁMA!!
MURCHADH,,, THIS IS AN INSULT!
NEXT TIME, MY ADVICE WILL NOT BE SO EASILY DEFEATED!
IS THAT A THREAT? I HOPE IT IS! FLY AWAY, BIRDMAN!
TUATHAL! I HAVE BEEN INSULTED. GATHER THE MEN. WE'RE LEAVING IMMEDIATELY.
WHEN WE GET BACK TO NAAS GATHER THE CLAN LEADERS. WE'RE GOING TO WAR!

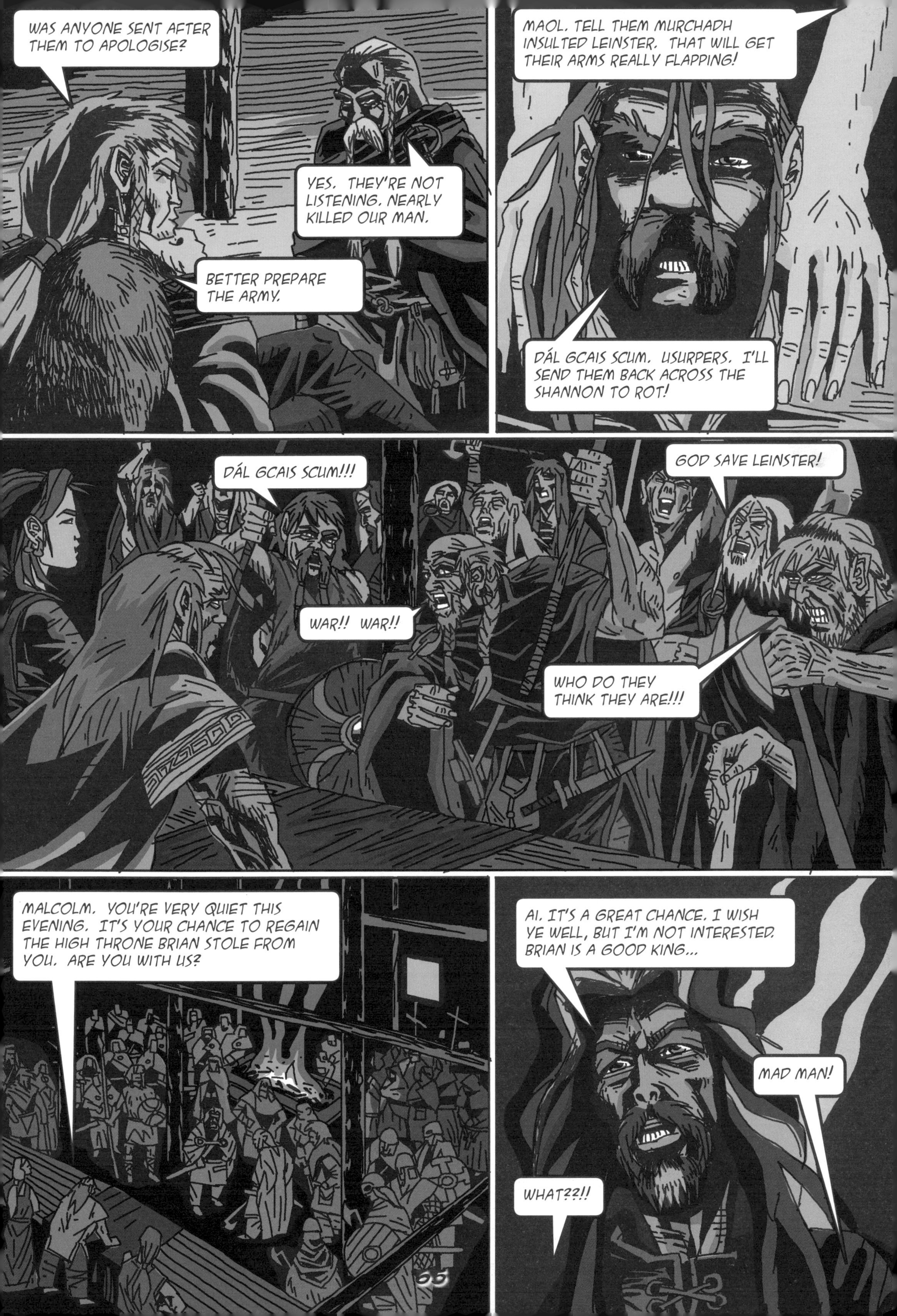
WAS ANYONE SENT AFTER THEM TO APOLOGISE?
YES. THEY'RE NOT LISTENING. NEARLY KILLED OUR MAN.
BETTER PREPARE THE ARMY.
MAOL. TELL THEM MURCHADH INSULTED LEINSTER. THAT WILL GET THEIR ARMS REALLY FLAPPING!
DÁL GCAIS SCUM. USURPERS. I'LL SEND THEM BACK ACROSS THE SHANNON TO ROT!
DÁL GCAIS SCUM!!!
GOD SAVE LEINSTER!
WAR!! WAR!!
WHO DO THEY THINK THEY ARE!!!
MALCOLM. YOU'RE VERY QUIET THIS EVENING. IT'S YOUR CHANCE TO REGAIN THE HIGH THRONE BRIAN STOLE FROM YOU. ARE YOU WITH US?
AI. IT'S A GREAT CHANCE. I WISH YE WELL, BUT I'M NOT INTERESTED. BRIAN IS A GOOD KING...
MAD MAN!
WHAT??!!

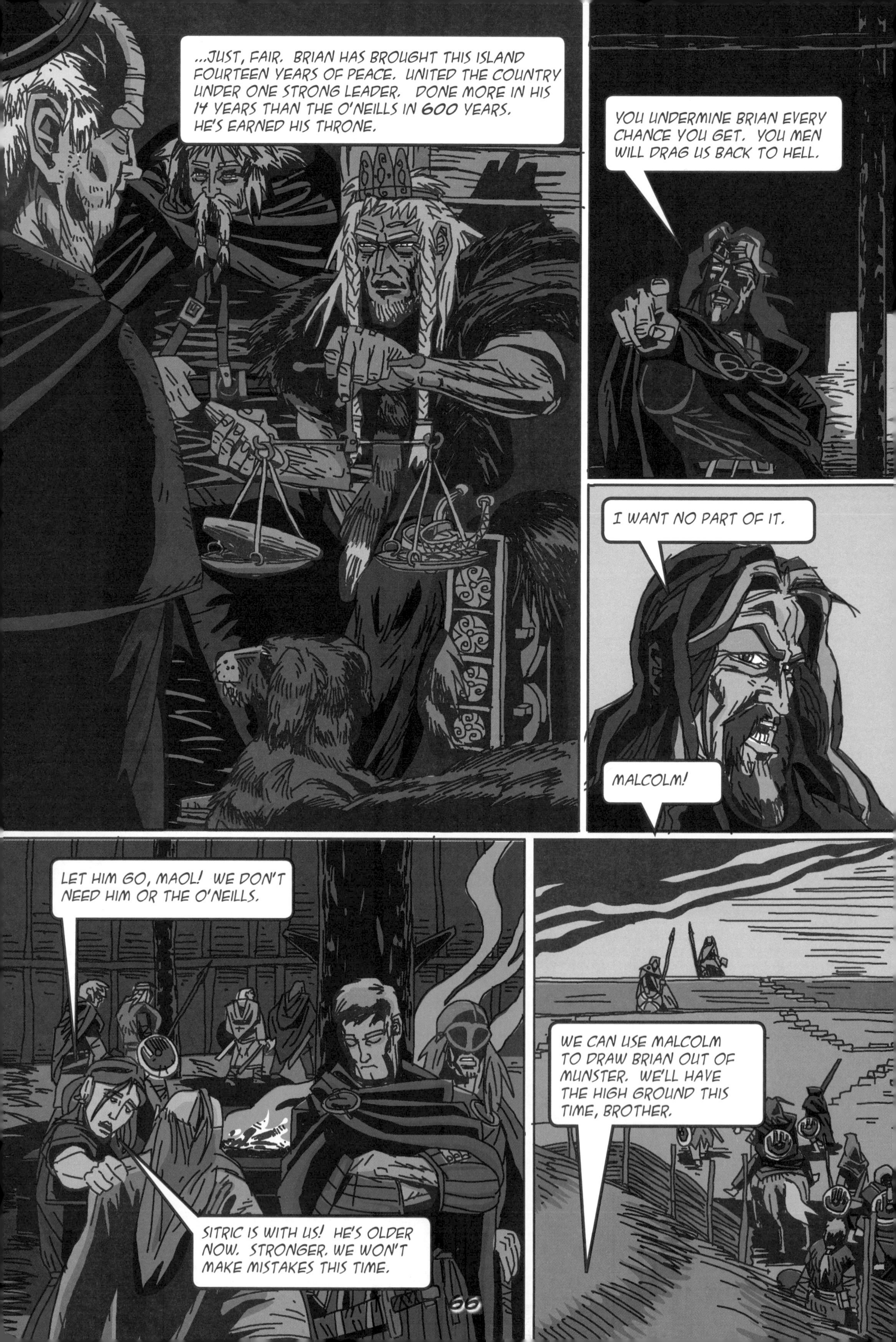
...JUST, FAIR. BRIAN HAS BROUGHT THIS ISLAND FOURTEEN YEARS OF PEACE. UNITED THE COUNTRY UNDER ONE STRONG LEADER. DONE MORE IN HIS 14 YEARS THAN THE O'NEILLS IN 600 YEARS. HE'S EARNED HIS THRONE.
YOU UNDERMINE BRIAN EVERY CHANCE YOU GET. YOU MEN WILL DRAG US BACK TO HELL.
I WANT NO PART OF IT.
MALCOLM!
LET HIM GO, MAOL! WE DON'T NEED HIM OR THE O'NEILLS.
SITRIC IS WITH US! HE'S OLDER NOW. STRONGER. WE WON'T MAKE MISTAKES THIS TIME.
WE CAN USE MALCOLM TO DRAW BRIAN OUT OF MUNSTER. WE'LL HAVE THE HIGH GROUND THIS TIME, BROTHER.

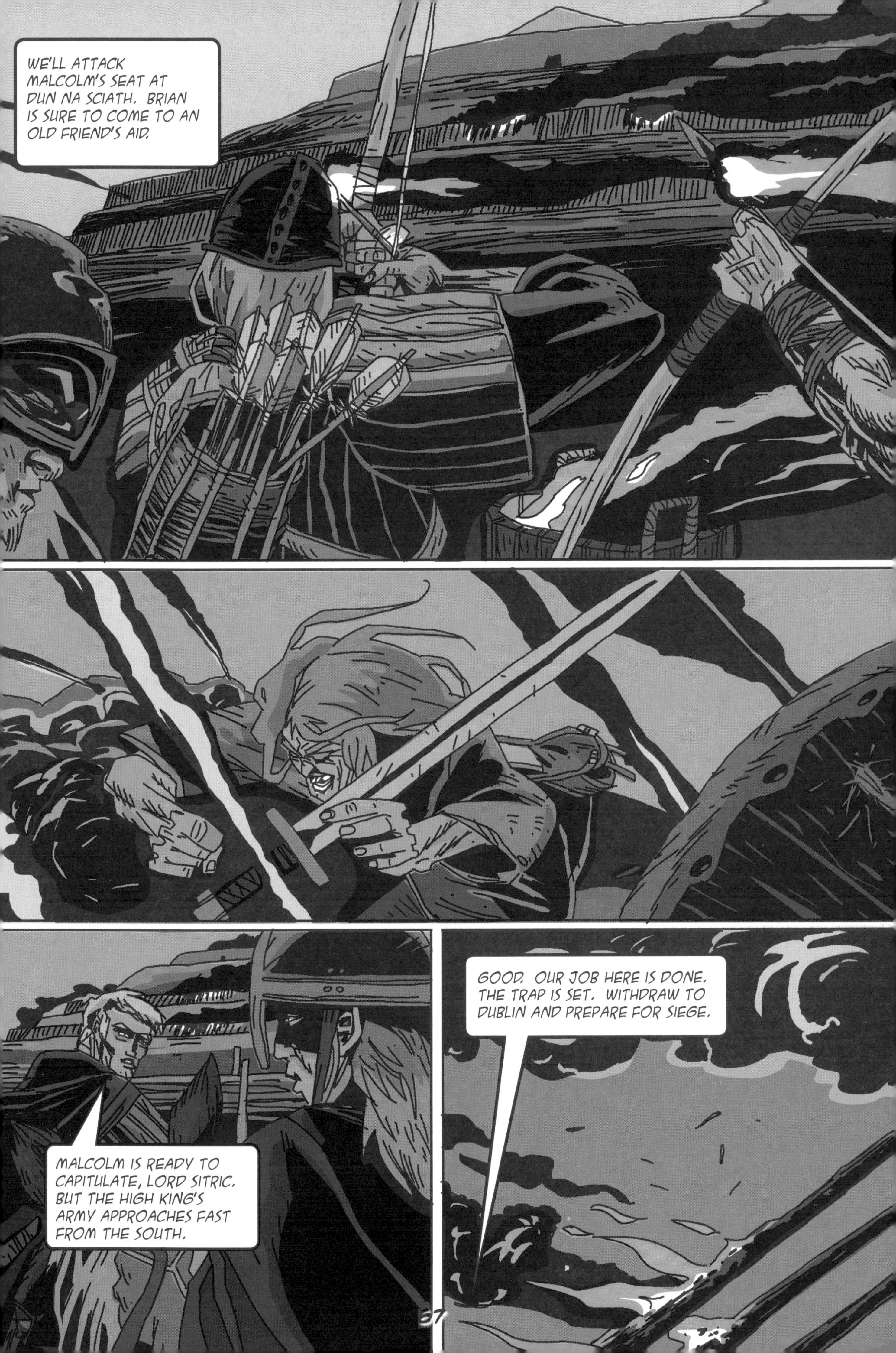
WE'LL ATTACK MALCOLM'S SEAT AT DUN NA SCIATH. BRIAN IS SURE TO COME TO AN OLD FRIEND'S AID.
MALCOLM IS READY TO CAPITULATE, LORD SITRIC. BUT THE HIGH KING'S ARMY APPROACHES FAST FROM THE SOUTH.
GOOD. OUR JOB HERE IS DONE. THE TRAP IS SET. WITHDRAW TO DUBLIN AND PREPARE FOR SIEGE.

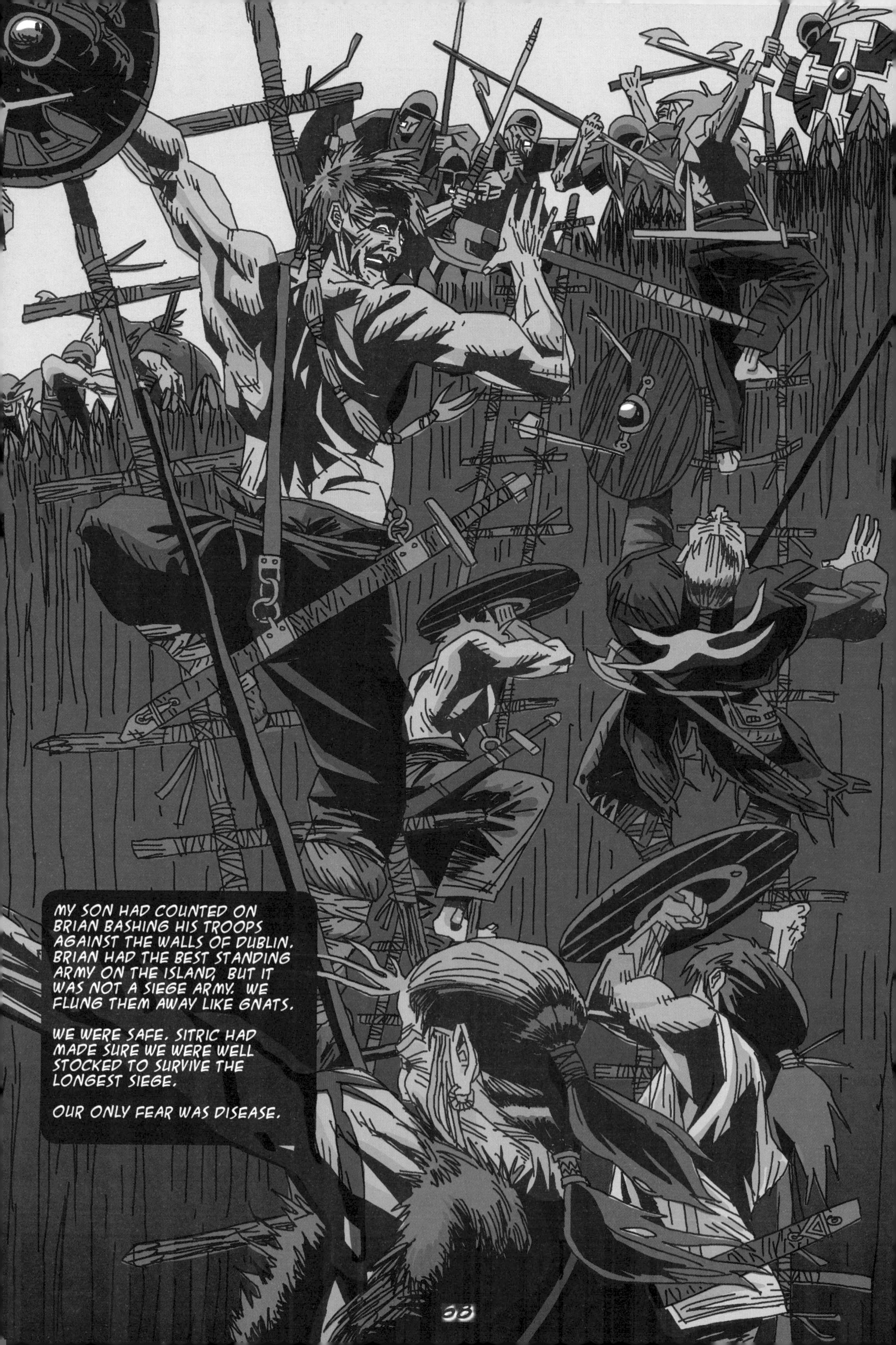
MY SON HAD COUNTED ON BRIAN BASHING HIS TROOPS AGAINST THE WALLS OF DUBLIN. BRIAN HAD THE BEST STANDING ARMY ON THE ISLAND, BUT IT WAS NOT A SIEGE ARMY. WE FLUNG THEM AWAY LIKE GNATS.
WE WERE SAFE. SITRIC HAD MADE SURE WE WERE WELL STOCKED TO SURVIVE THE LONGEST SIEGE.
OUR ONLY FEAR WAS DISEASE.

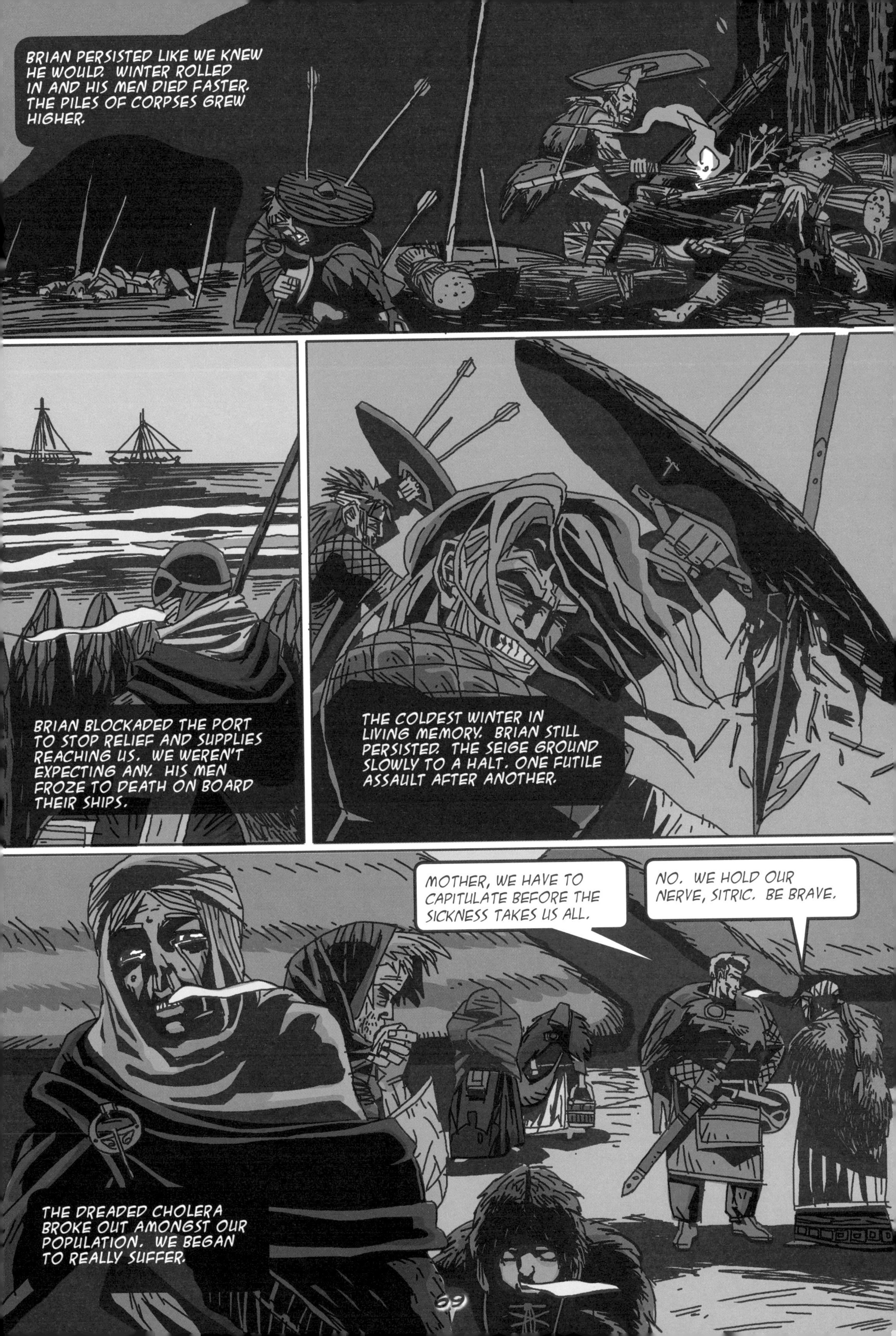
BRIAN PERSISTED LIKE WE KNEW HE WOULD. WINTER ROLLED IN AND HIS MEN DIED FASTER. THE PILES OF CORPSES GREW HIGHER.
BRIAN BLOCKADED THE PORT TO STOP RELIEF AND SUPPLIES REACHING US. WE WEREN'T EXPECTING ANY. HIS MEN FROZE TO DEATH ON BOARD THEIR SHIPS.
THE COLDEST WINTER IN LIVING MEMORY. BRIAN STILL PERSISTED. THE SEIGE GROUND SLOWLY TO A HALT. ONE FUTILE ASSAULT AFTER ANOTHER.
THE DREADED CHOLERA BROKE OUT AMONGST OUR POPULATION. WE BEGAN TO REALLY SUFFER.
MOTHER, WE HAVE TO CAPITULATE BEFORE THE SICKNESS TAKES US ALL.
NO. WE HOLD OUR NERVE, SITRIC. BE BRAVE.

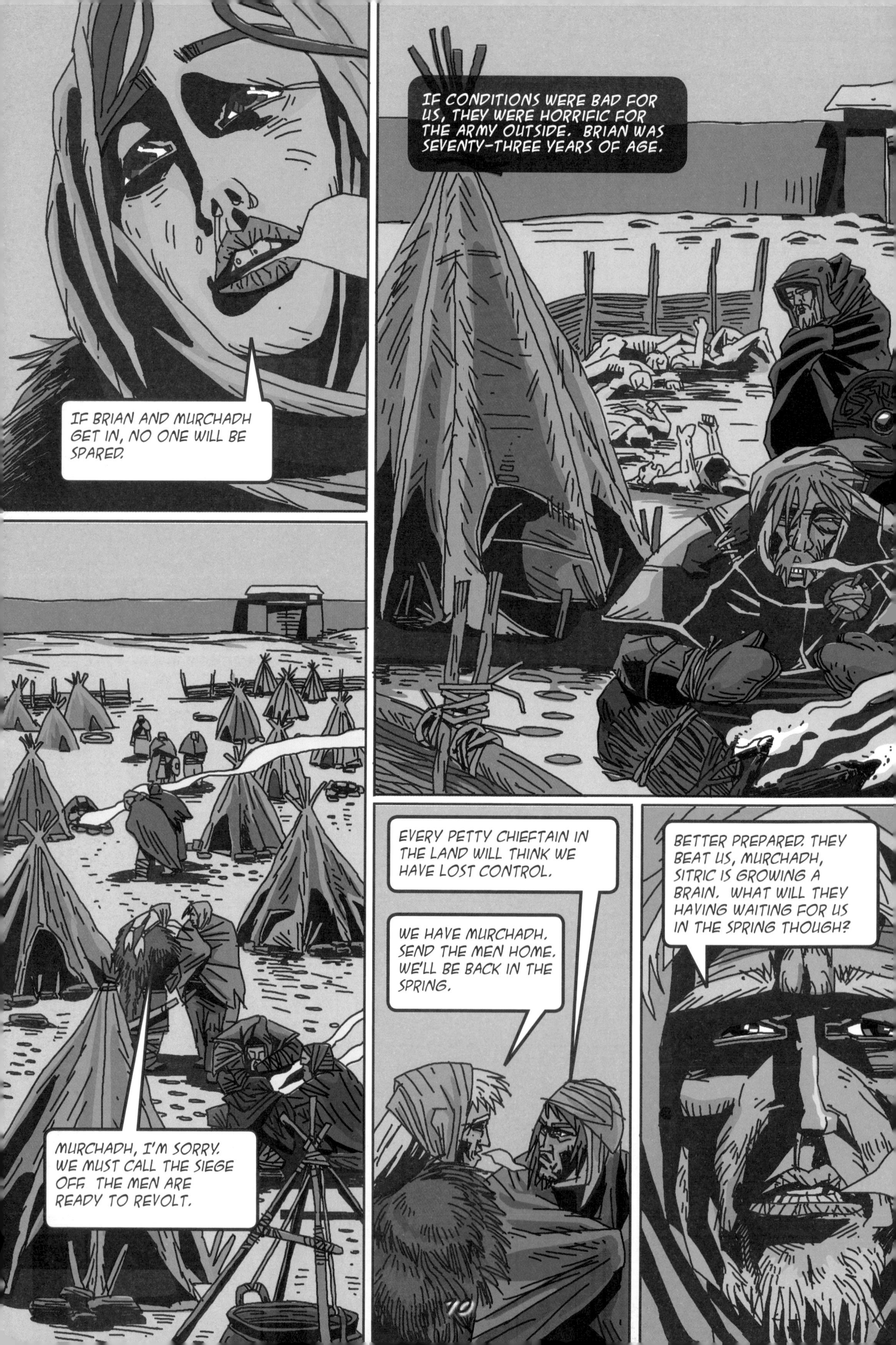
IF BRIAN AND MURCHADH GET IN, NO ONE WILL BE SPARED.
IF CONDITIONS WERE BAD FOR US, THEY WERE HORRIFIC FOR THE ARMY OUTSIDE. BRIAN WAS SEVENTY-THREE YEARS OF AGE.
MURCHADH, I'M SORRY. WE MUST CALL THE SIEGE OFF. THE MEN ARE READY TO REVOLT.
EVERY PETTY CHIEFTAIN IN THE LAND WILL THINK WE HAVE LOST CONTROL.
WE HAVE MURCHADH. SEND THE MEN HOME. WE'LL BE BACK IN THE SPRING.
BETTER PREPARED. THEY BEAT US, MURCHADH, SITRIC IS GROWING A BRAIN. WHAT WILL THEY HAVING WAITING FOR US IN THE SPRING THOUGH?

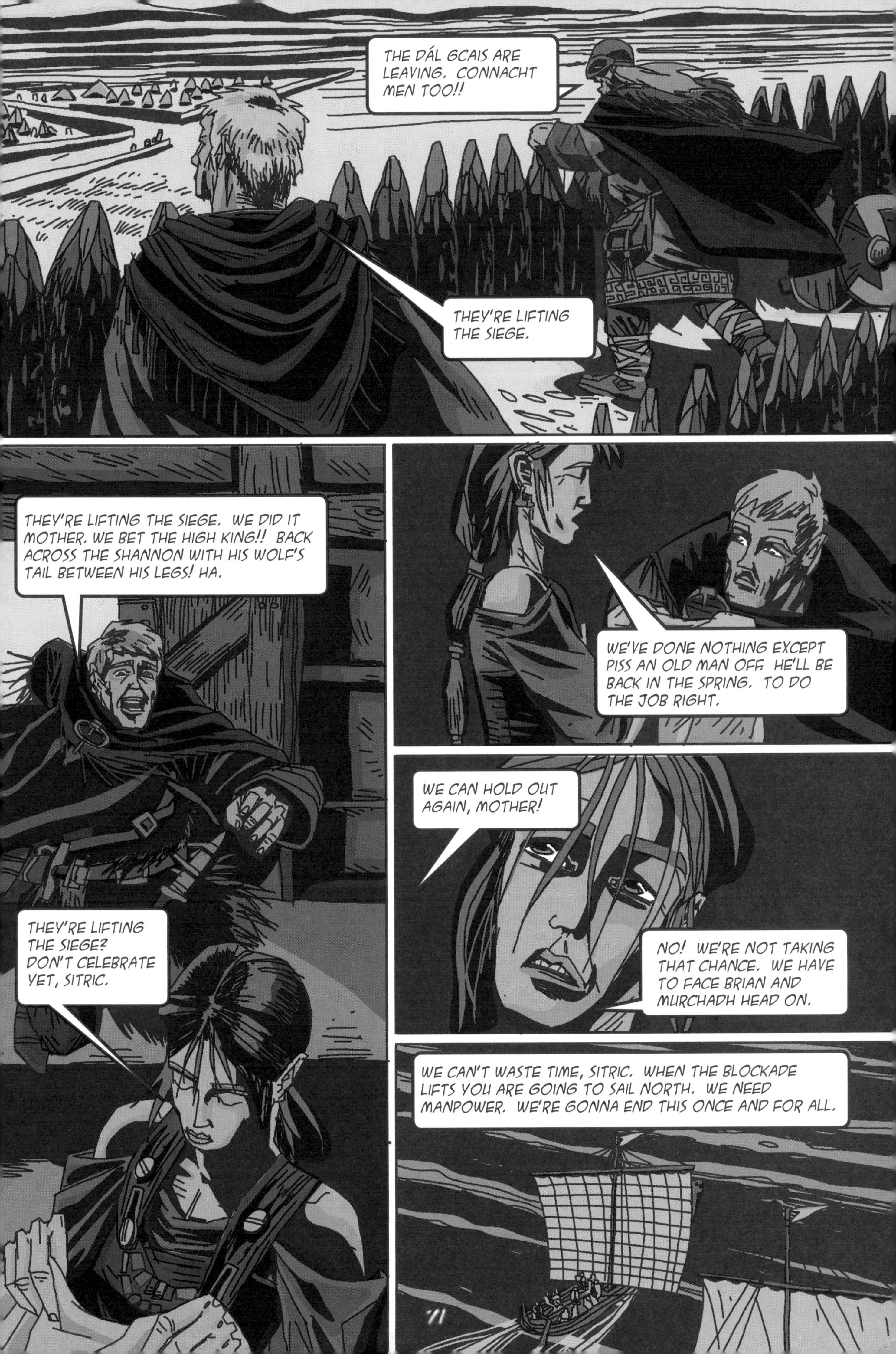
THE DÁL GCAIS ARE LEAVING. CONNACHT MEN TOO!!
THEY'RE LIFTING THE SIEGE.
THEY'RE LIFTING THE SIEGE. WE DID IT MOTHER. WE BET THE HIGH KING!! BACK ACROSS THE SHANNON WITH HIS WOLF'S TAIL BETWEEN HIS LEGS! HA.
THEY'RE LIFTING THE SIEGE? DON'T CELEBRATE YET, SITRIC.
WE'VE DONE NOTHING EXCEPT PISS AN OLD MAN OFF. HE'LL BE BACK IN THE SPRING. TO DO THE JOB RIGHT.
WE CAN HOLD OUT AGAIN, MOTHER!
NO! WE'RE NOT TAKING THAT CHANCE. WE HAVE TO FACE BRIAN AND MURCHADH HEAD ON.
WE CAN'T WASTE TIME, SITRIC. WHEN THE BLOCKADE LIFTS YOU ARE GOING TO SAIL NORTH. WE NEED MANPOWER. WE'RE GONNA END THIS ONCE AND FOR ALL.

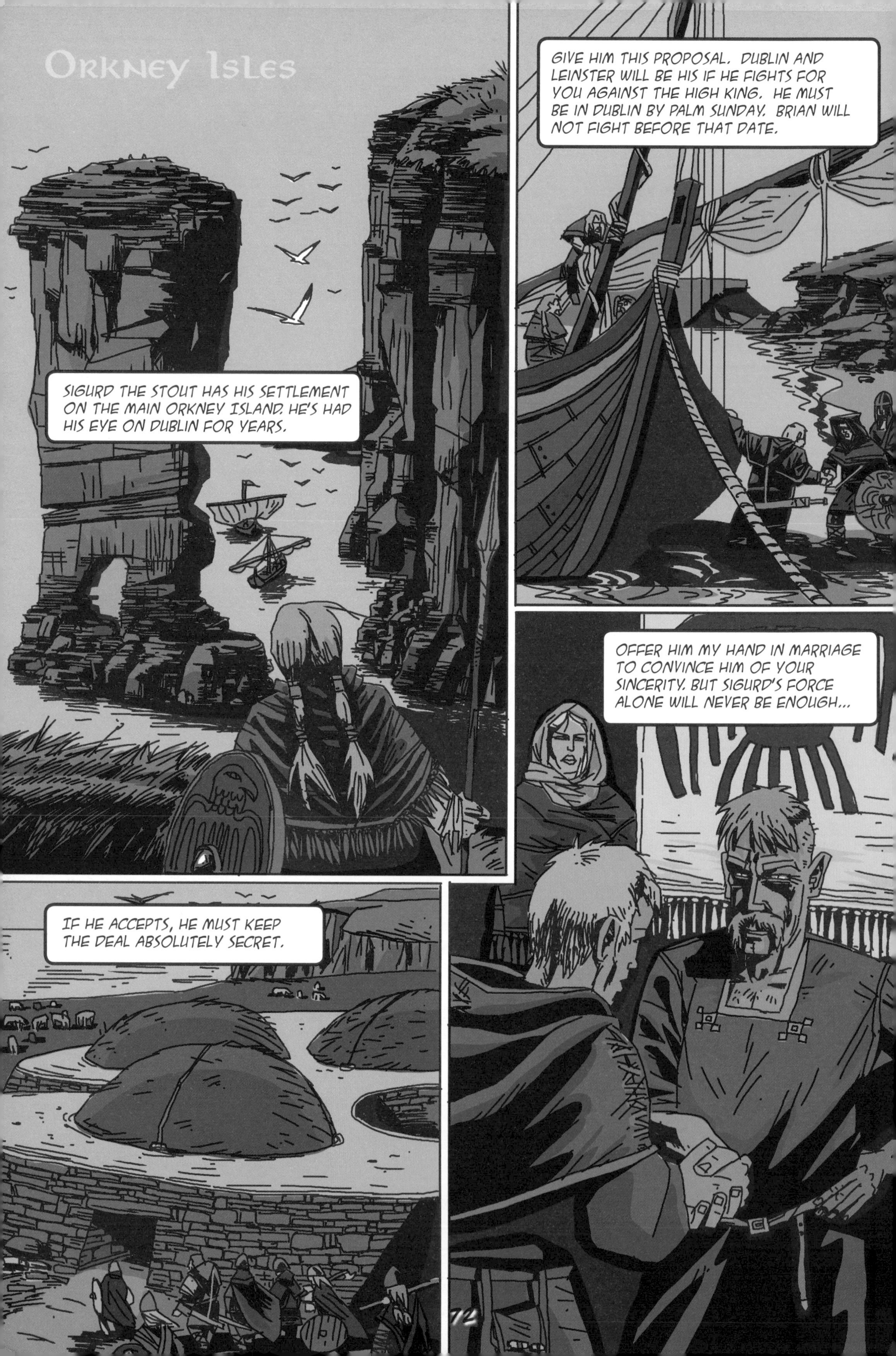
Orkney Isles
SIGURD THE STOUT HAS HIS SETTLEMENT ON THE MAIN ORKNEY ISLAND. HE'S HAD HIS EYE ON DUBLIN FOR YEARS.
GIVE HIM THIS PROPOSAL. DUBLIN AND LEINSTER WILL BE HIS IF HE FIGHTS FOR YOU AGAINST THE HIGH KING. HE MUST BE IN DUBLIN BY PALM SUNDAY. BRIAN WILL NOT FIGHT BEFORE THAT DATE.
IF HE ACCEPTS, HE MUST KEEP THE DEAL ABSOLUTELY SECRET.
OFFER HIM MY HAND IN MARRIAGE TO CONVINCE HIM OF YOUR SINCERITY. BUT SIGURD'S FORCE ALONE WILL NEVER BE ENOUGH...

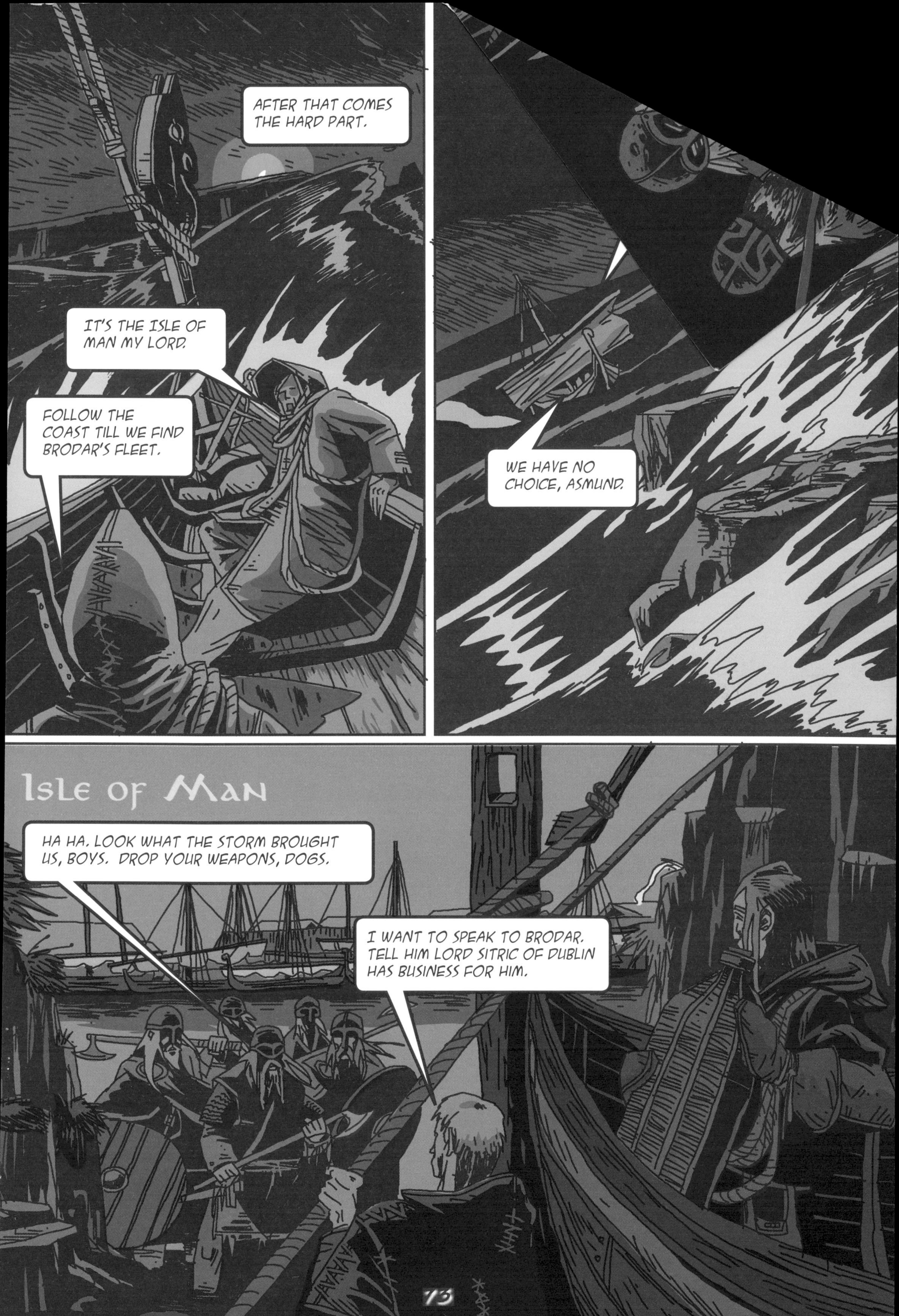
AFTER THAT COMES THE HARD PART.
IT'S THE ISLE OF MAN MY LORD.
FOLLOW THE COAST TILL WE FIND BRODAR'S FLEET.
WE HAVE NO CHOICE, ASMUND.
Isle of Man
HA HA. LOOK WHAT THE STORM BROUGHT US, BOYS. DROP YOUR WEAPONS, DOGS.
I WANT TO SPEAK TO BRODAR. TELL HIM LORD SITRIC OF DUBLIN HAS BUSINESS FOR HIM.

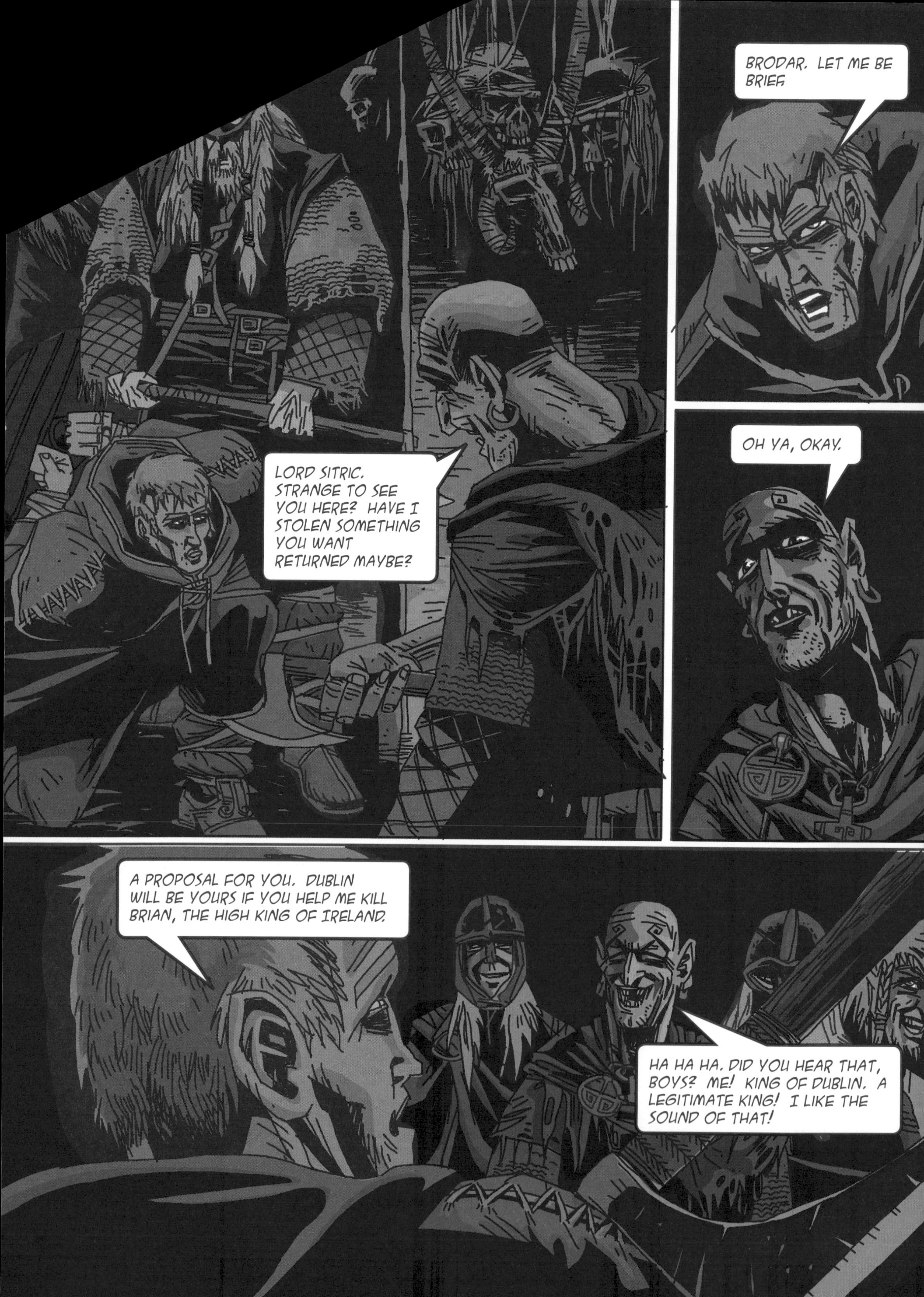
LORD SITRIC. STRANGE TO SEE YOU HERE? HAVE I STOLEN SOMETHING YOU WANT RETURNED MAYBE?
HAHAHAHAHA
BRODAR. LET ME BE BRIEF.
OH YA, OKAY.
A PROPOSAL FOR YOU. DUBLIN WILL BE YOURS IF YOU HELP ME KILL BRIAN, THE HIGH KING OF IRELAND.
HA HA HA. DID YOU HEAR THAT, BOYS? ME! KING OF DUBLIN. A LEGITIMATE KING! I LIKE THE SOUND OF THAT!

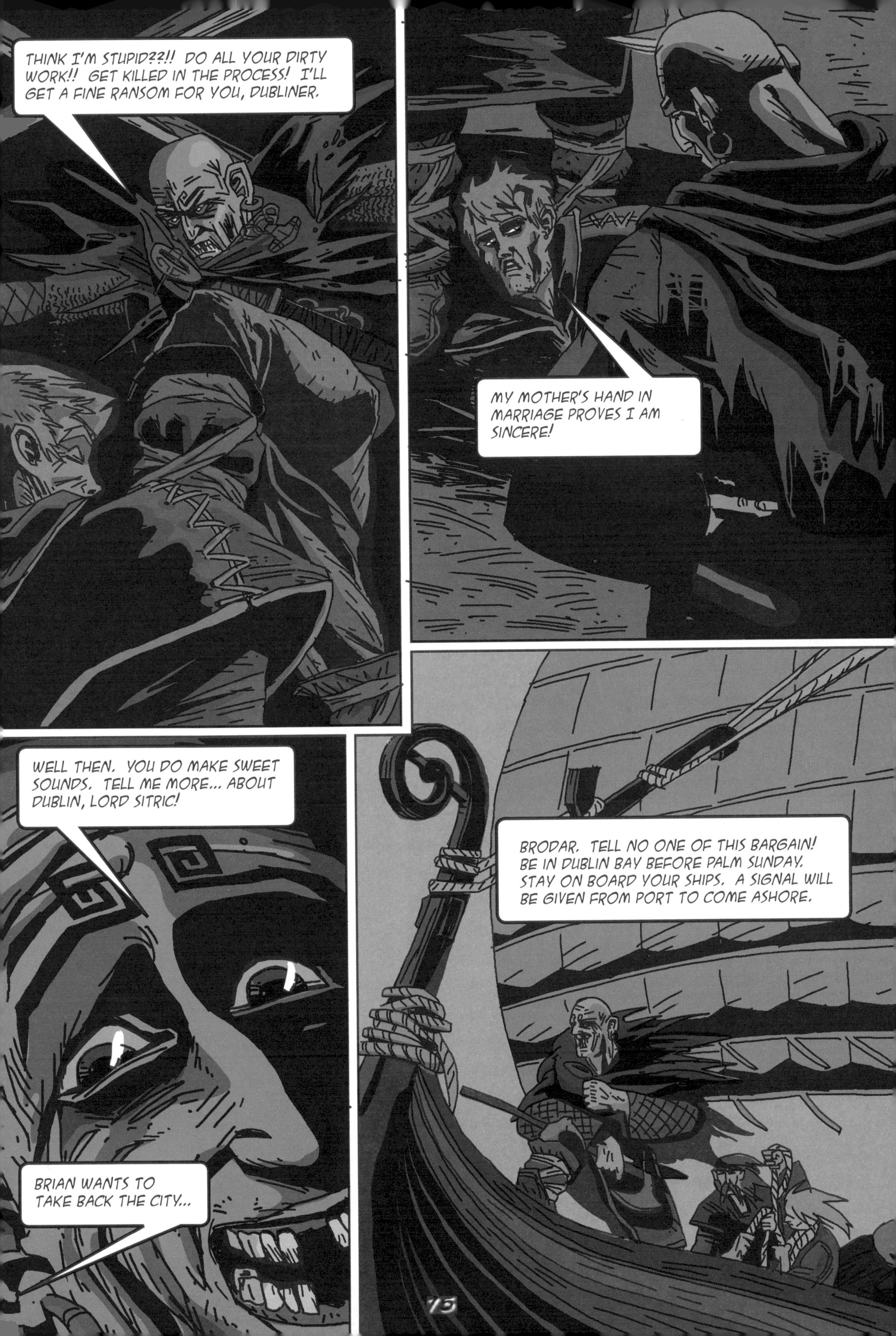
THINK I'M STUPID??!! DO ALL YOUR DIRTY WORK!! GET KILLED IN THE PROCESS! I'LL GET A FINE RANSOM FOR YOU, DUBLINER.
MY MOTHER'S HAND IN MARRIAGE PROVES I AM SINCERE!
WELL THEN. YOU DO MAKE SWEET SOUNDS. TELL ME MORE... ABOUT DUBLIN, LORD SITRIC!
BRIAN WANTS TO TAKE BACK THE CITY...
BRODAR. TELL NO ONE OF THIS BARGAIN! BE IN DUBLIN BAY BEFORE PALM SUNDAY. STAY ON BOARD YOUR SHIPS. A SIGNAL WILL BE GIVEN FROM PORT TO COME ASHORE.

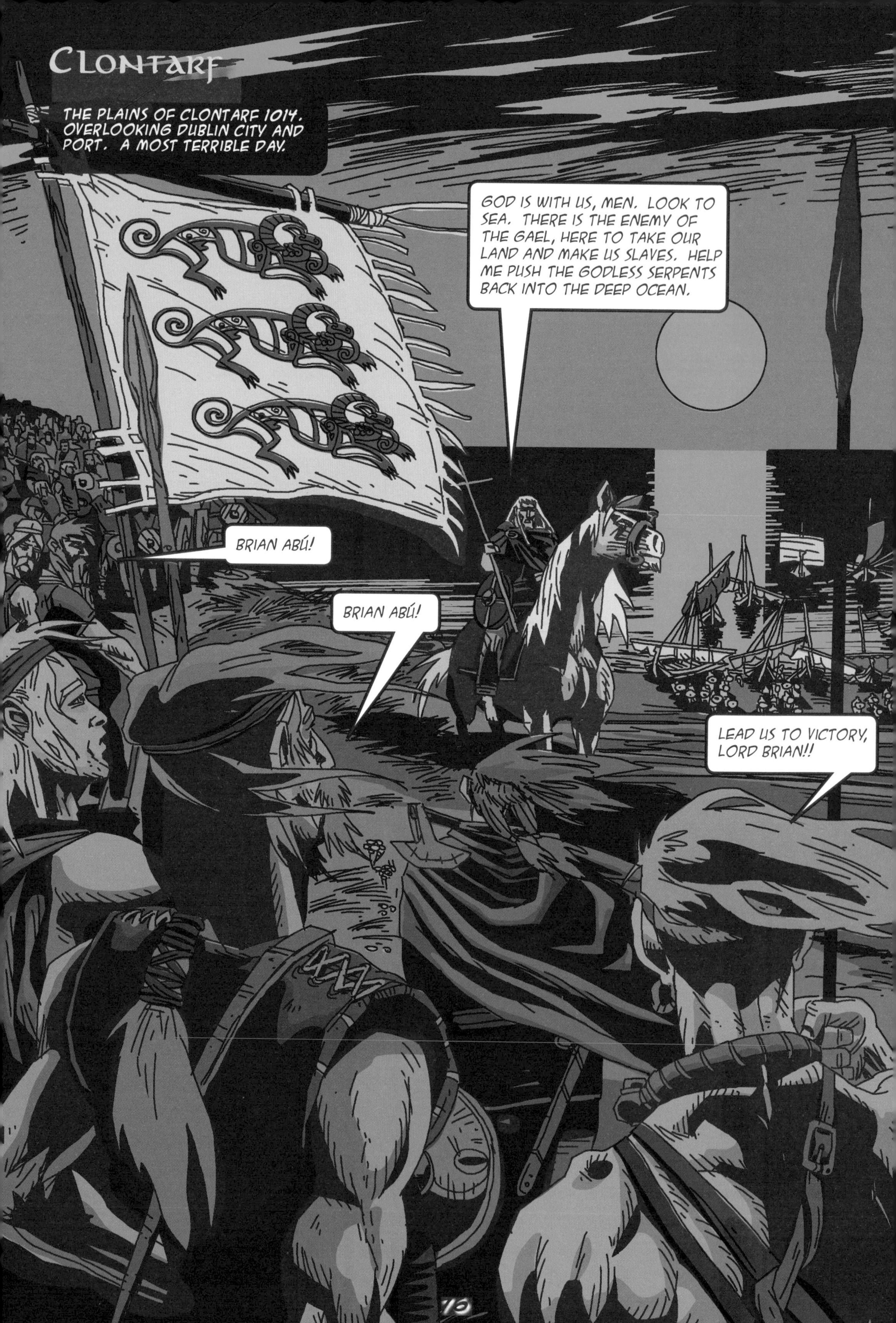
CLONTARF
THE PLAINS OF CLONTARF 1014. OVERLOOKING DUBLIN CITY AND PORT. A MOST TERRIBLE DAY.
GOD IS WITH US, MEN. LOOK TO SEA. THERE IS THE ENEMY OF THE GAEL, HERE TO TAKE OUR LAND AND MAKE US SLAVES. HELP ME PUSH THE GODLESS SERPENTS BACK INTO THE DEEP OCEAN.
BRIAN ABÚ!
BRIAN ABÚ!
LEAD US TO VICTORY, LORD BRIAN!!

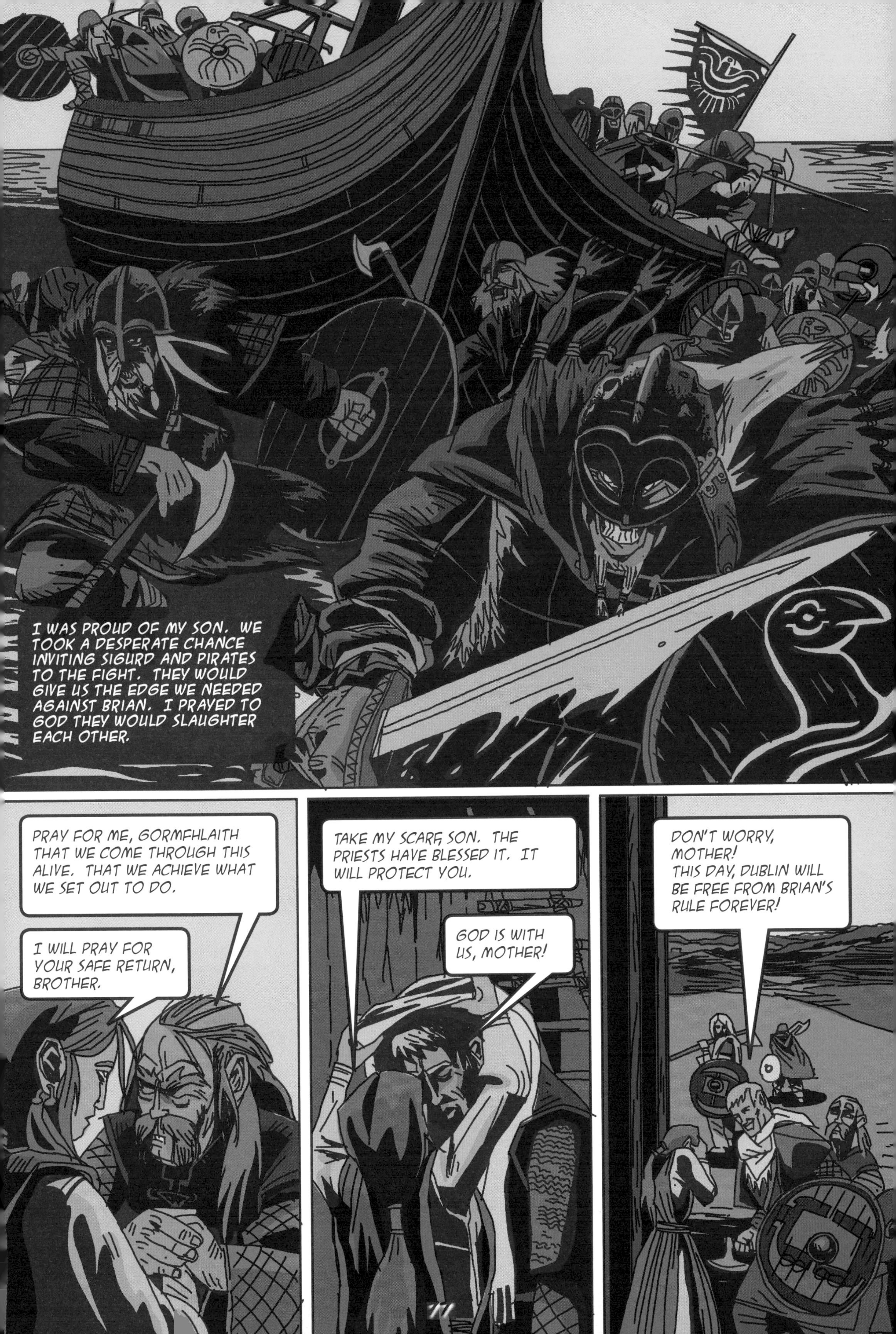

I WAS PROUD OF MY SON. WE TOOK A DESPERATE CHANCE INVITING SIGURD AND PIRATES TO THE FIGHT. THEY WOULD GIVE US THE EDGE WE NEEDED AGAINST BRIAN. I PRAYED TO GOD THEY WOULD SLAUGHTER EACH OTHER.
PRAY FOR ME, GORMFHLAITH THAT WE COME THROUGH THIS ALIVE. THAT WE ACHIEVE WHAT WE SET OUT TO DO.
I WILL PRAY FOR YOUR SAFE RETURN, BROTHER.
TAKE MY SCARF, SON. THE PRIESTS HAVE BLESSED IT. IT WILL PROTECT YOU.
GOD IS WITH US, MOTHER!
DON'T WORRY, MOTHER!
THIS DAY, DUBLIN WILL BE FREE FROM BRIAN'S RULE FOREVER!

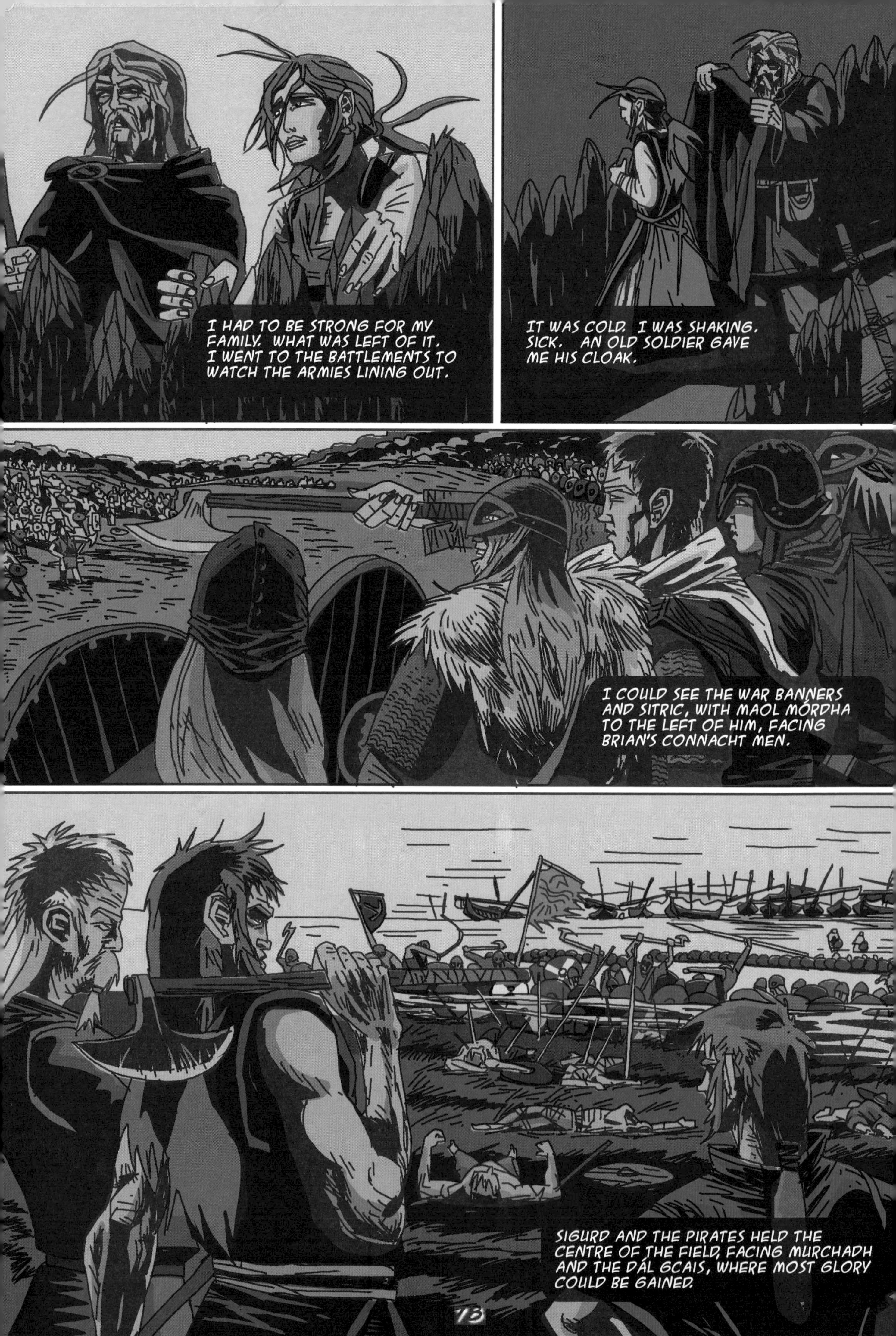
I HAD TO BE STRONG FOR MY FAMILY. WHAT WAS LEFT OF IT. I WENT TO THE BATTLEMENTS TO WATCH THE ARMIES LINING OUT.
IT WAS COLD. I WAS SHAKING. SICK. AN OLD SOLDIER GAVE ME HIS CLOAK.
I COULD SEE THE WAR BANNERS AND SITRIC, WITH MAOL MÓRDHA TO THE LEFT OF HIM, FACING BRIAN'S CONNACHT MEN.
SIGURD AND THE PIRATES HELD THE CENTRE OF THE FIELD, FACING MURCHADH AND THE DÁL GCAIS, WHERE MOST GLORY COULD BE GAINED.

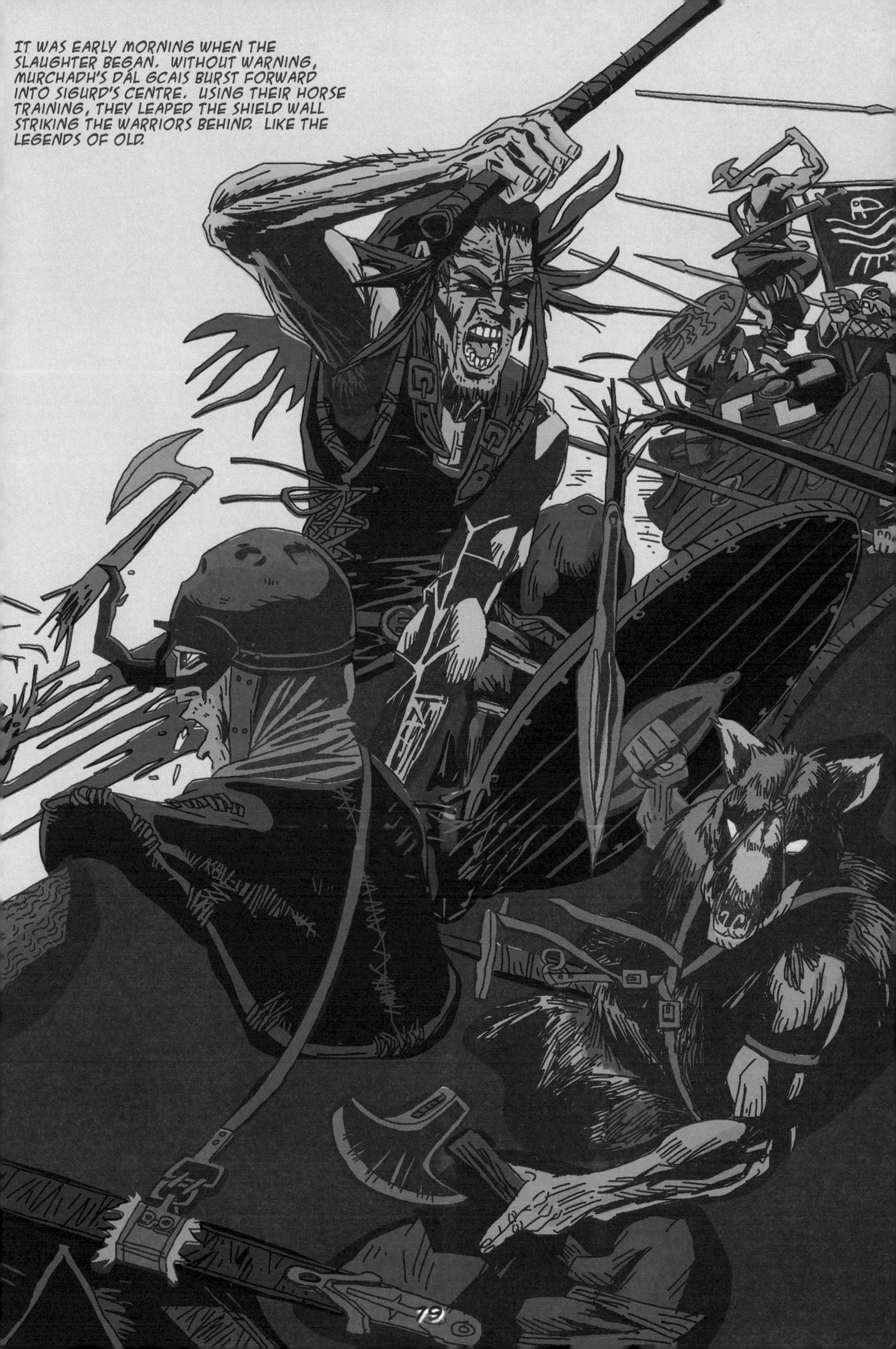
IT WAS EARLY MORNING WHEN THE SLAUGHTER BEGAN. WITHOUT WARNING, MURCHADH'S DÁL GCAIS BURST FORWARD INTO SIGURD'S CENTRE. USING THEIR HORSE TRAINING, THEY LEAPED THE SHIELD WALL STRIKING THE WARRIORS BEHIND. LIKE THE LEGENDS OF OLD.

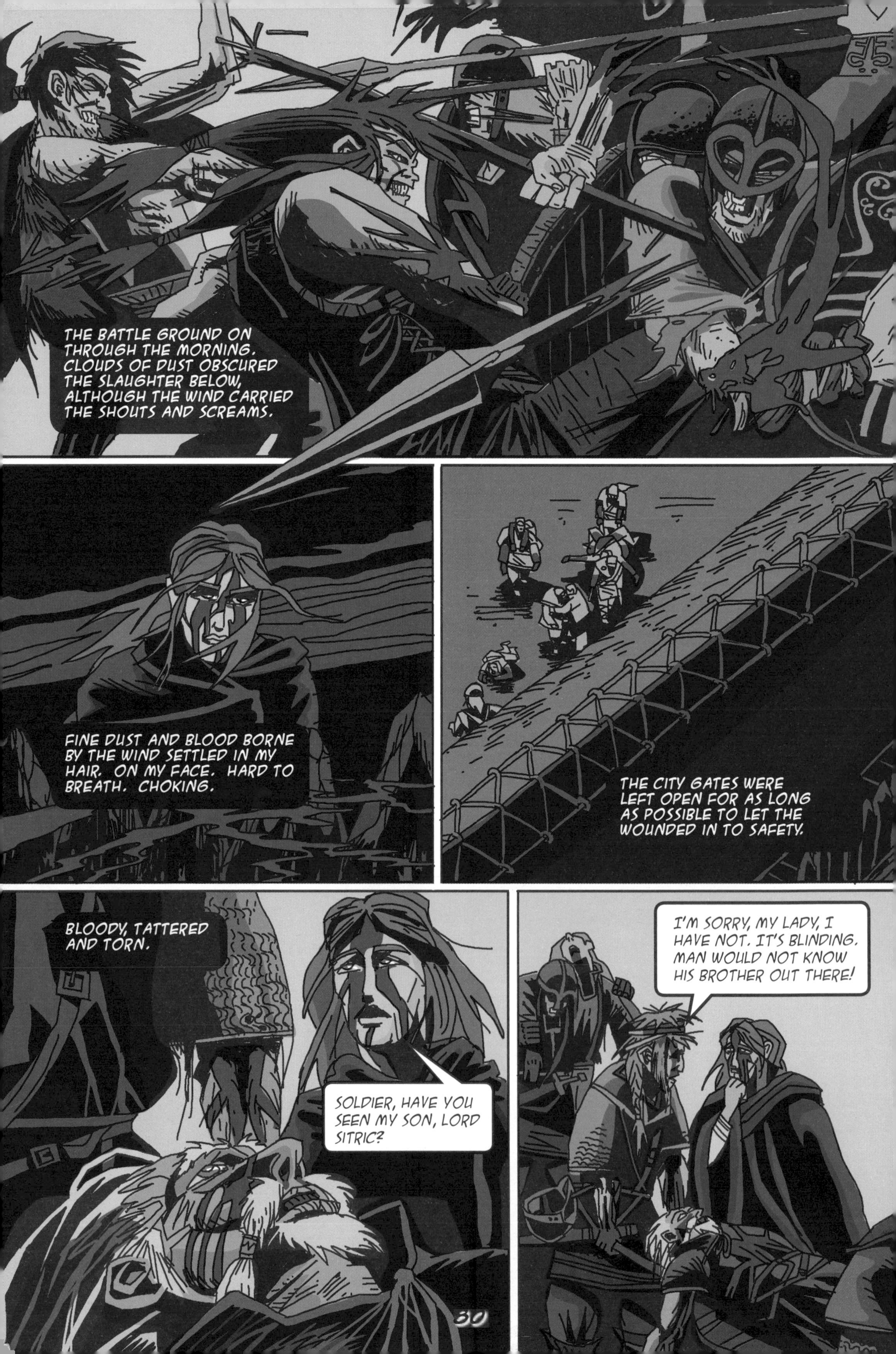
THE BATTLE GROUND ON THROUGH THE MORNING. CLOUDS OF DUST OBSCURED THE SLAUGHTER BELOW, ALTHOUGH THE WIND CARRIED THE SHOUTS AND SCREAMS.
FINE DUST AND BLOOD BORNE BY THE WIND SETTLED IN MY HAIR. ON MY FACE. HARD TO BREATH. CHOKING.
THE CITY GATES WERE LEFT OPEN FOR AS LONG AS POSSIBLE TO LET THE WOUNDED IN TO SAFETY.
BLOODY, TATTERED AND TORN.
SOLDIER, HAVE YOU SEEN MY SON, LORD SITRIC?
I'M SORRY, MY LADY, I HAVE NOT. IT'S BLINDING. MAN WOULD NOT KNOW HIS BROTHER OUT THERE!

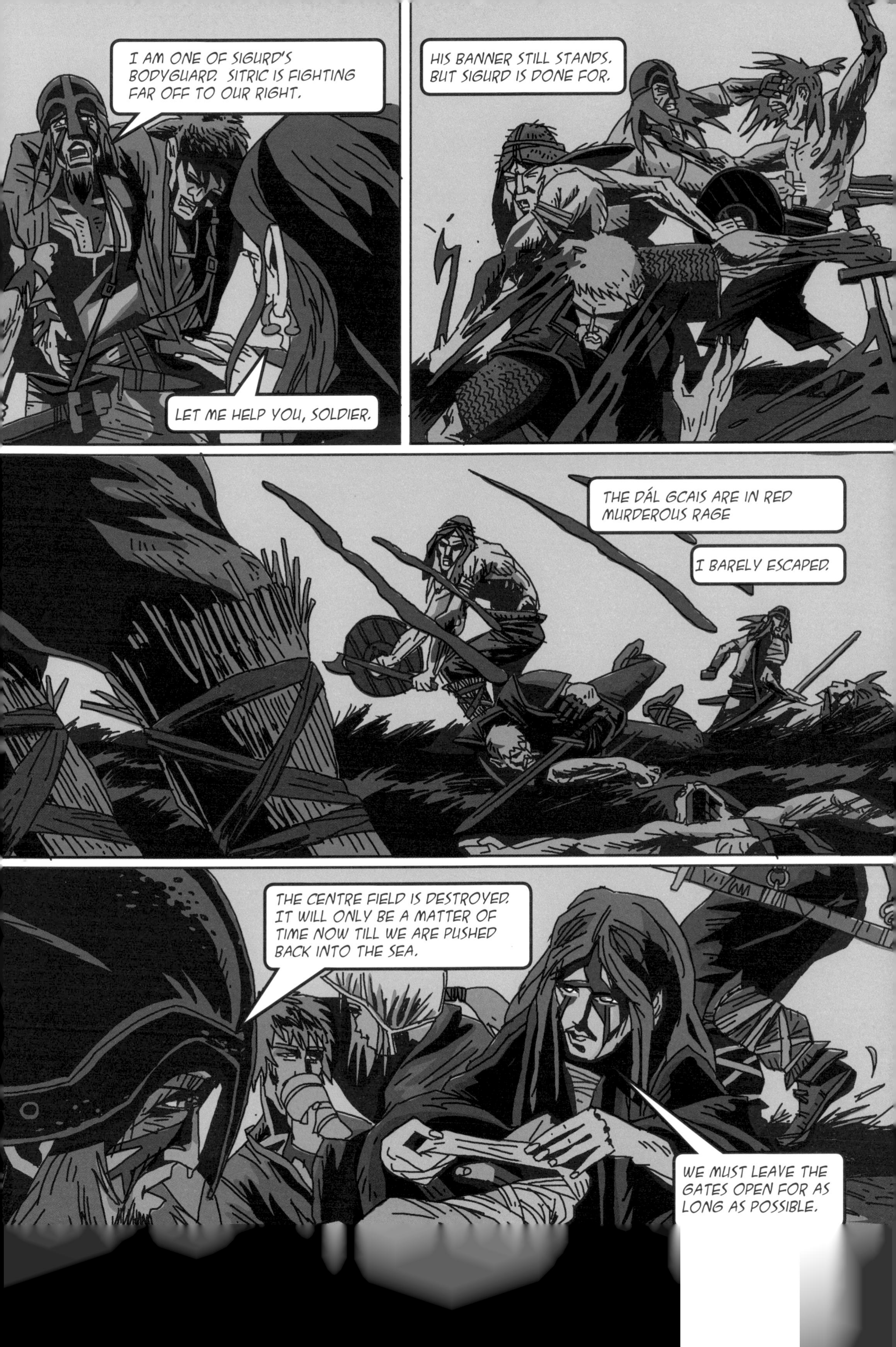

I AM ONE OF SIGURD'S BODYGUARD. SITRIC IS FIGHTING FAR OFF TO OUR RIGHT.
LET ME HELP YOU, SOLDIER.
HIS BANNER STILL STANDS. BUT SIGURD IS DONE FOR.
THE DÁL GCAIS ARE IN RED MURDEROUS RAGE
I BARELY ESCAPED.
THE CENTRE FIELD IS DESTROYED. IT WILL ONLY BE A MATTER OF TIME NOW TILL WE ARE PUSHED BACK INTO THE SEA.
WE MUST LEAVE THE GATES OPEN FOR AS LONG AS POSSIBLE.

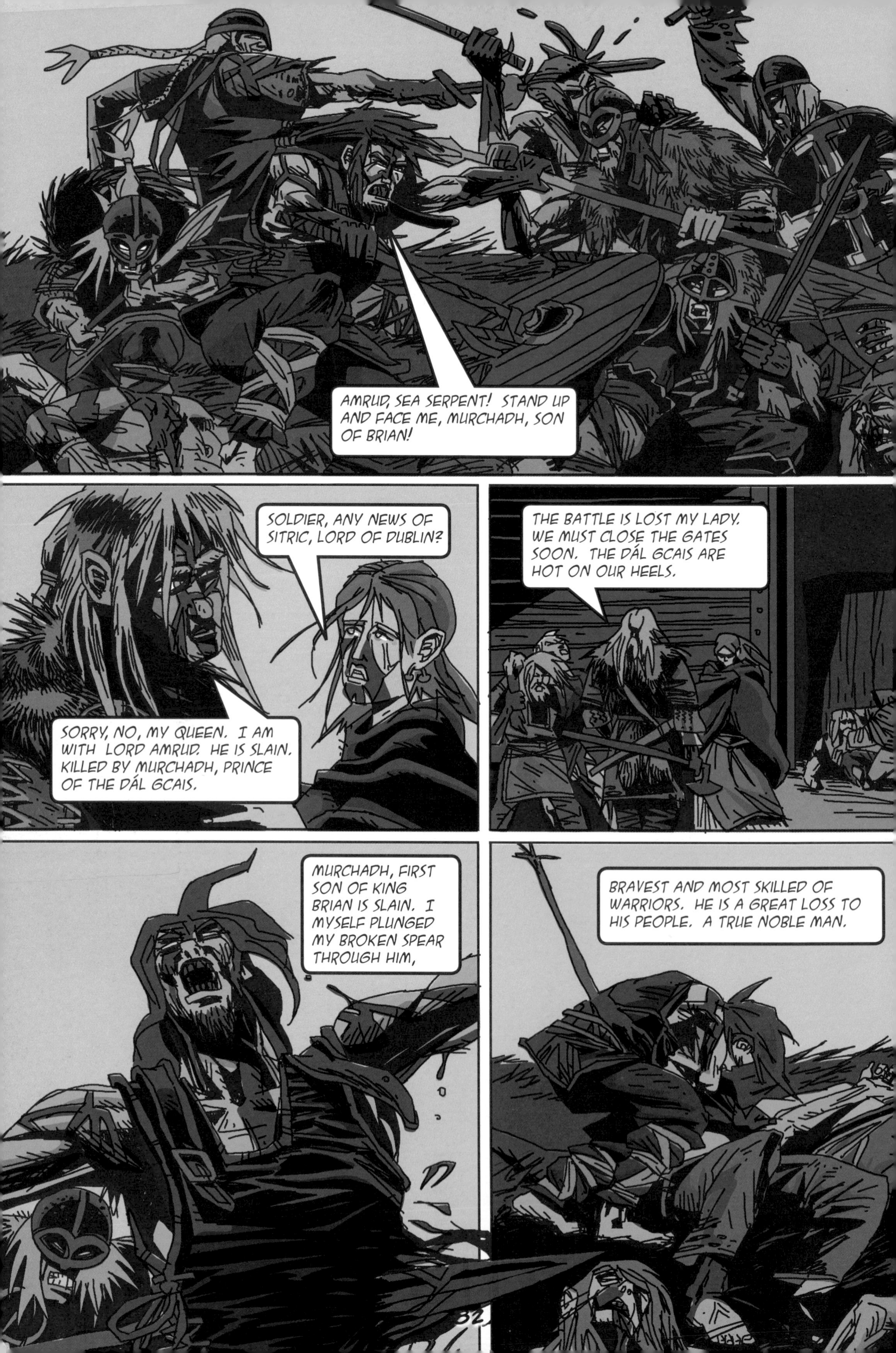
AMRUD, SEA SERPENT! STAND UP AND FACE ME, MURCHADH, SON OF BRIAN!
SOLDIER, ANY NEWS OF SITRIC, LORD OF DUBLIN?
SORRY, NO, MY QUEEN. I AM WITH LORD AMRUD. HE IS SLAIN. KILLED BY MURCHADH, PRINCE OF THE DÁL GCAIS.
THE BATTLE IS LOST MY LADY. WE MUST CLOSE THE GATES SOON. THE DÁL GCAIS ARE HOT ON OUR HEELS.
MURCHADH, FIRST SON OF KING BRIAN IS SLAIN. I MYSELF PLUNGED MY BROKEN SPEAR THROUGH HIM,
BRAVEST AND MOST SKILLED OF WARRIORS. HE IS A GREAT LOSS TO HIS PEOPLE. A TRUE NOBLE MAN.

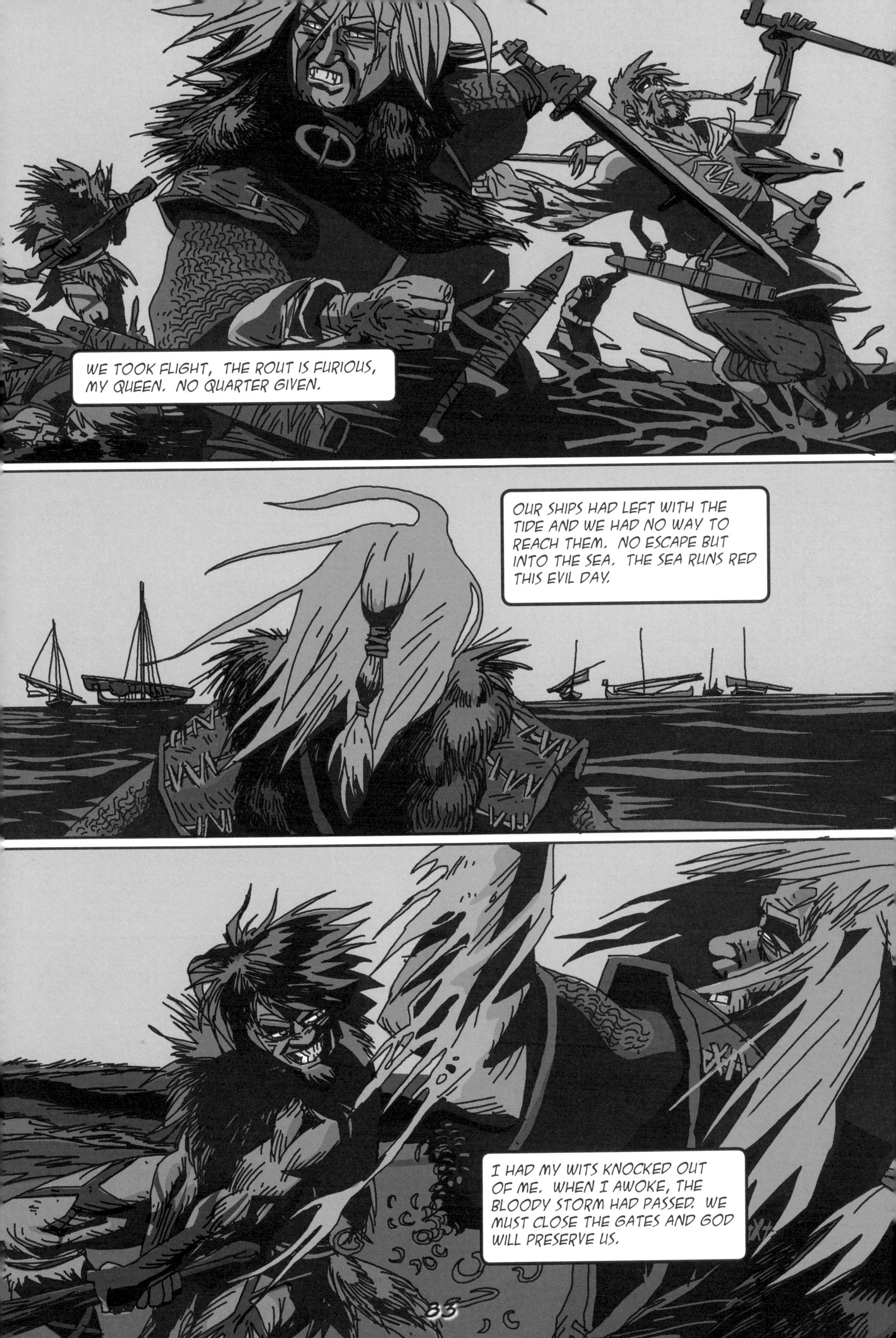
WE TOOK FLIGHT, THE ROUT IS FURIOUS, MY QUEEN. NO QUARTER GIVEN.
OUR SHIPS HAD LEFT WITH THE TIDE AND WE HAD NO WAY TO REACH THEM. NO ESCAPE BUT INTO THE SEA. THE SEA RUNS RED THIS EVIL DAY.
I HAD MY WITS KNOCKED OUT OF ME. WHEN I AWOKE, THE BLOODY STORM HAD PASSED. WE MUST CLOSE THE GATES AND GOD WILL PRESERVE US.

AS THE GATES ARE CLOSED MY HEART SHATTERS. HAD I LOST ANOTHER SON? YET HE DID NOT FEEL DEAD TO ME...

OPEN THE GATES QUICKLY. WOUNDED APPROACH!

IT IS LORD SITRIC!

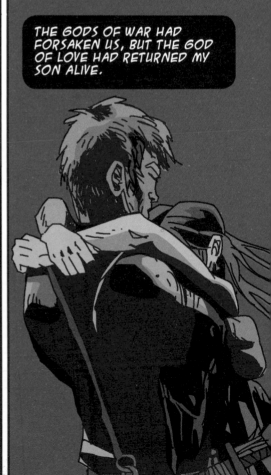

THE GODS OF WAR HAD FORSAKEN US, BUT THE GOD OF LOVE HAD RETURNED MY SON ALIVE.

84

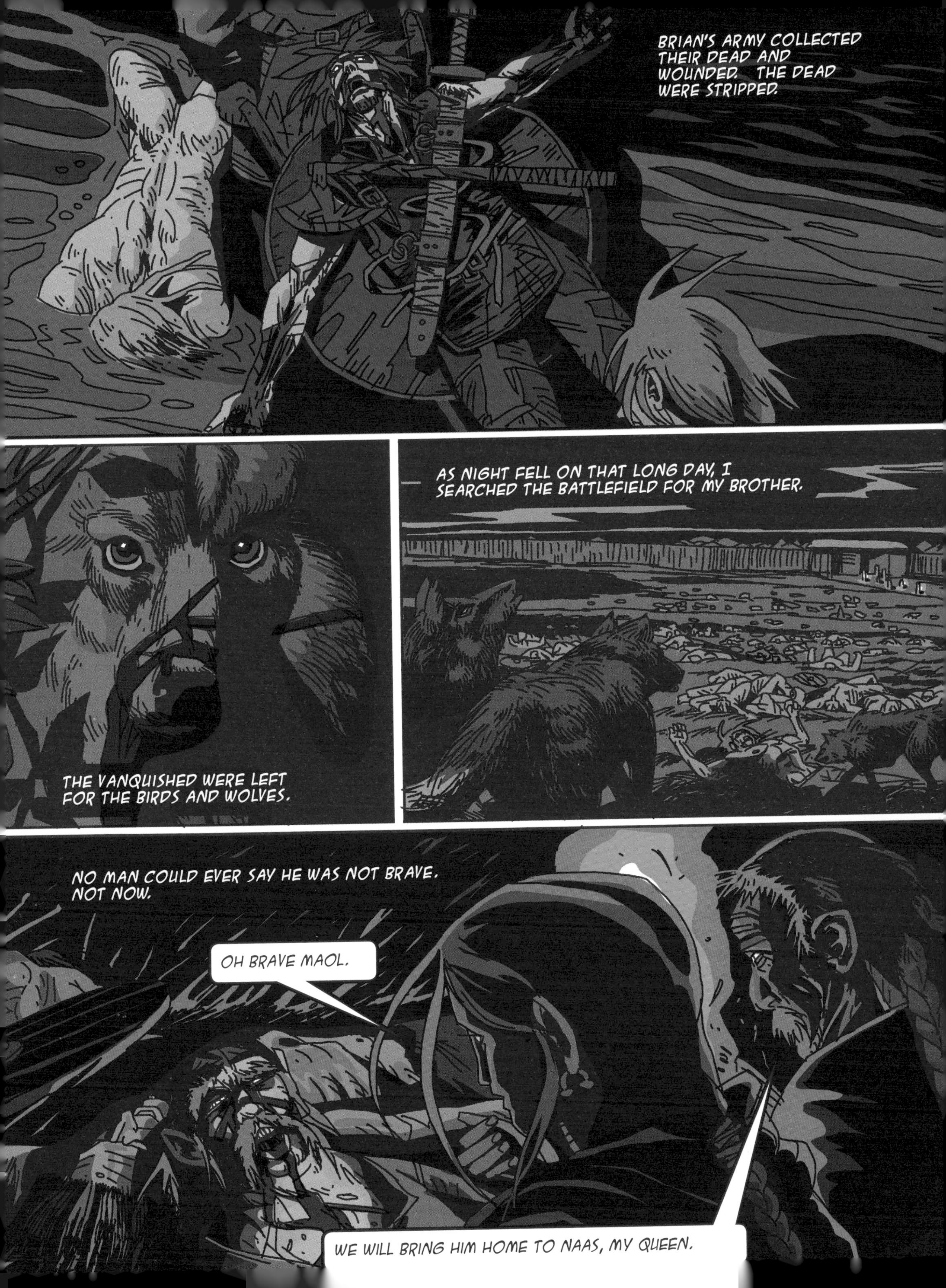
BRIAN'S ARMY COLLECTED THEIR DEAD AND WOUNDED. THE DEAD WERE STRIPPED.
THE VANQUISHED WERE LEFT FOR THE BIRDS AND WOLVES.
AS NIGHT FELL ON THAT LONG DAY, I SEARCHED THE BATTLEFIELD FOR MY BROTHER.
NO MAN COULD EVER SAY HE WAS NOT BRAVE. NOT NOW.
OH BRAVE MAOL.
WE WILL BRING HIM HOME TO NAAS, MY QUEEN.

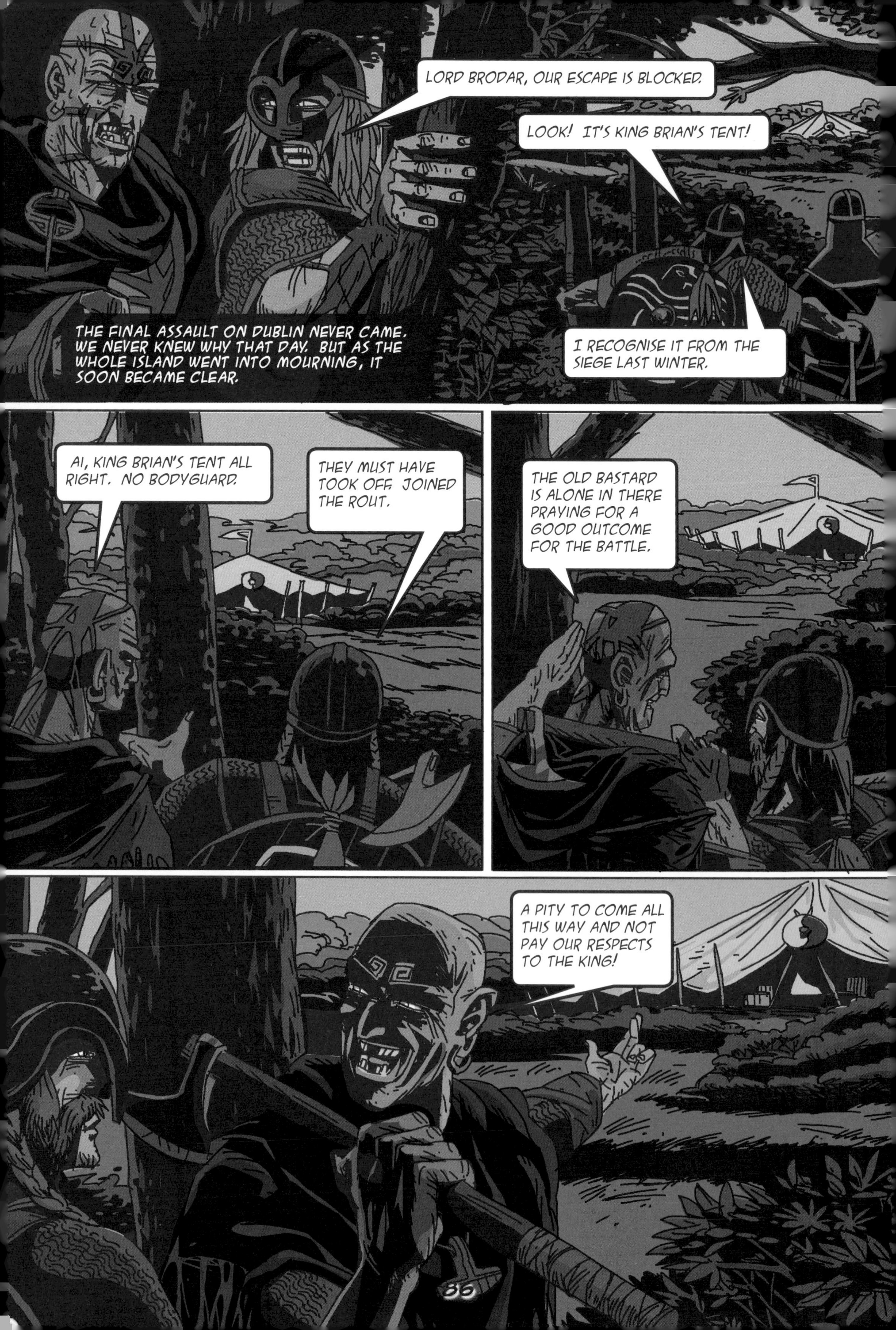
LORD BRODAR, OUR ESCAPE IS BLOCKED.
LOOK! IT'S KING BRIAN'S TENT!
THE FINAL ASSAULT ON DUBLIN NEVER CAME. WE NEVER KNEW WHY THAT DAY. BUT AS THE WHOLE ISLAND WENT INTO MOURNING, IT SOON BECAME CLEAR.
I RECOGNISE IT FROM THE SIEGE LAST WINTER.
AI, KING BRIAN'S TENT ALL RIGHT. NO BODYGUARD.
THEY MUST HAVE TOOK OFF. JOINED THE ROUT.
THE OLD BASTARD IS ALONE IN THERE PRAYING FOR A GOOD OUTCOME FOR THE BATTLE.
A PITY TO COME ALL THIS WAY AND NOT PAY OUR RESPECTS TO THE KING!

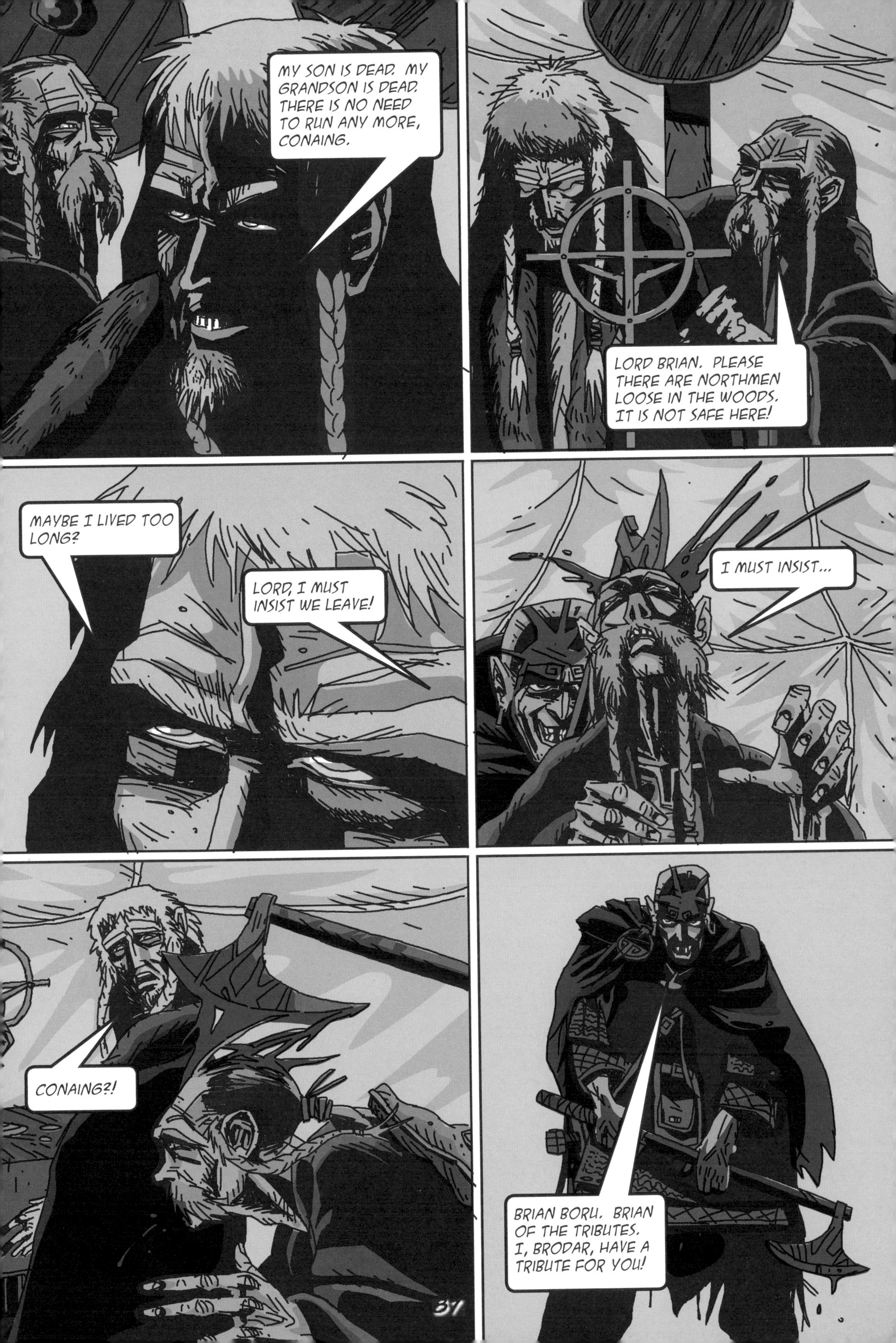
MY SON IS DEAD. MY GRANDSON IS DEAD. THERE IS NO NEED TO RUN ANY MORE, CONAING.
LORD BRIAN. PLEASE THERE ARE NORTHMEN LOOSE IN THE WOODS. IT IS NOT SAFE HERE!
MAYBE I LIVED TOO LONG?
LORD, I MUST INSIST WE LEAVE!
I MUST INSIST...
CONAING?!
BRIAN BORU. BRIAN OF THE TRIBUTES. I, BRODAR, HAVE A TRIBUTE FOR YOU!

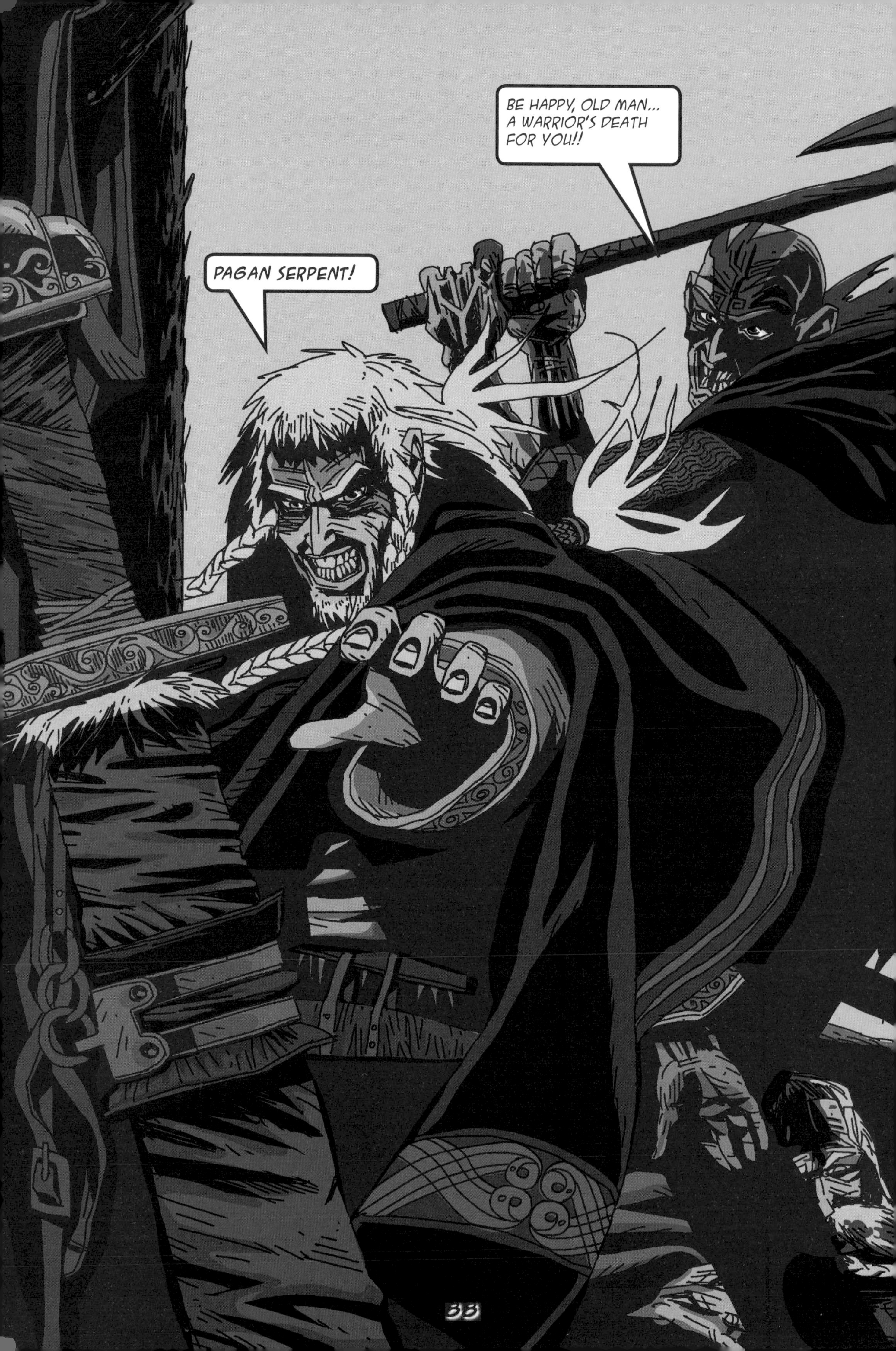
PAGAN SERPENT!
BE HAPPY, OLD MAN... A WARRIOR'S DEATH FOR YOU!!

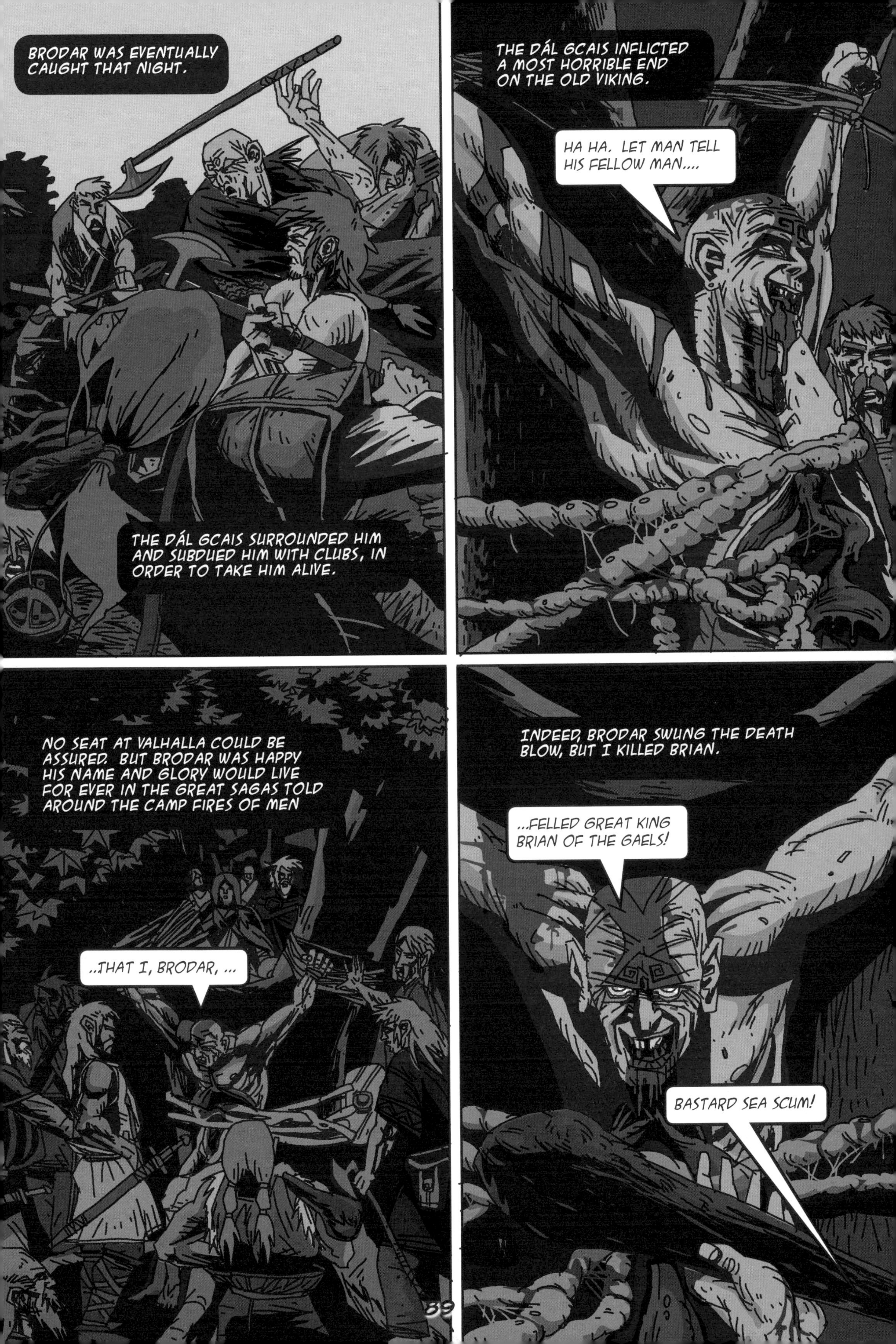
BRODAR WAS EVENTUALLY CAUGHT THAT NIGHT.
THE DÁL GCAIS SURROUNDED HIM AND SUBDUED HIM WITH CLUBS, IN ORDER TO TAKE HIM ALIVE.
THE DÁL GCAIS INFLICTED A MOST HORRIBLE END ON THE OLD VIKING.
HA HA. LET MAN TELL HIS FELLOW MAN....
NO SEAT AT VALHALLA COULD BE ASSURED. BUT BRODAR WAS HAPPY HIS NAME AND GLORY WOULD LIVE FOR EVER IN THE GREAT SAGAS TOLD AROUND THE CAMP FIRES OF MEN
..THAT I, BRODAR, ...
INDEED, BRODAR SWUNG THE DEATH BLOW, BUT I KILLED BRIAN.
...FELLED GREAT KING BRIAN OF THE GAELS!
BASTARD SEA SCUM!

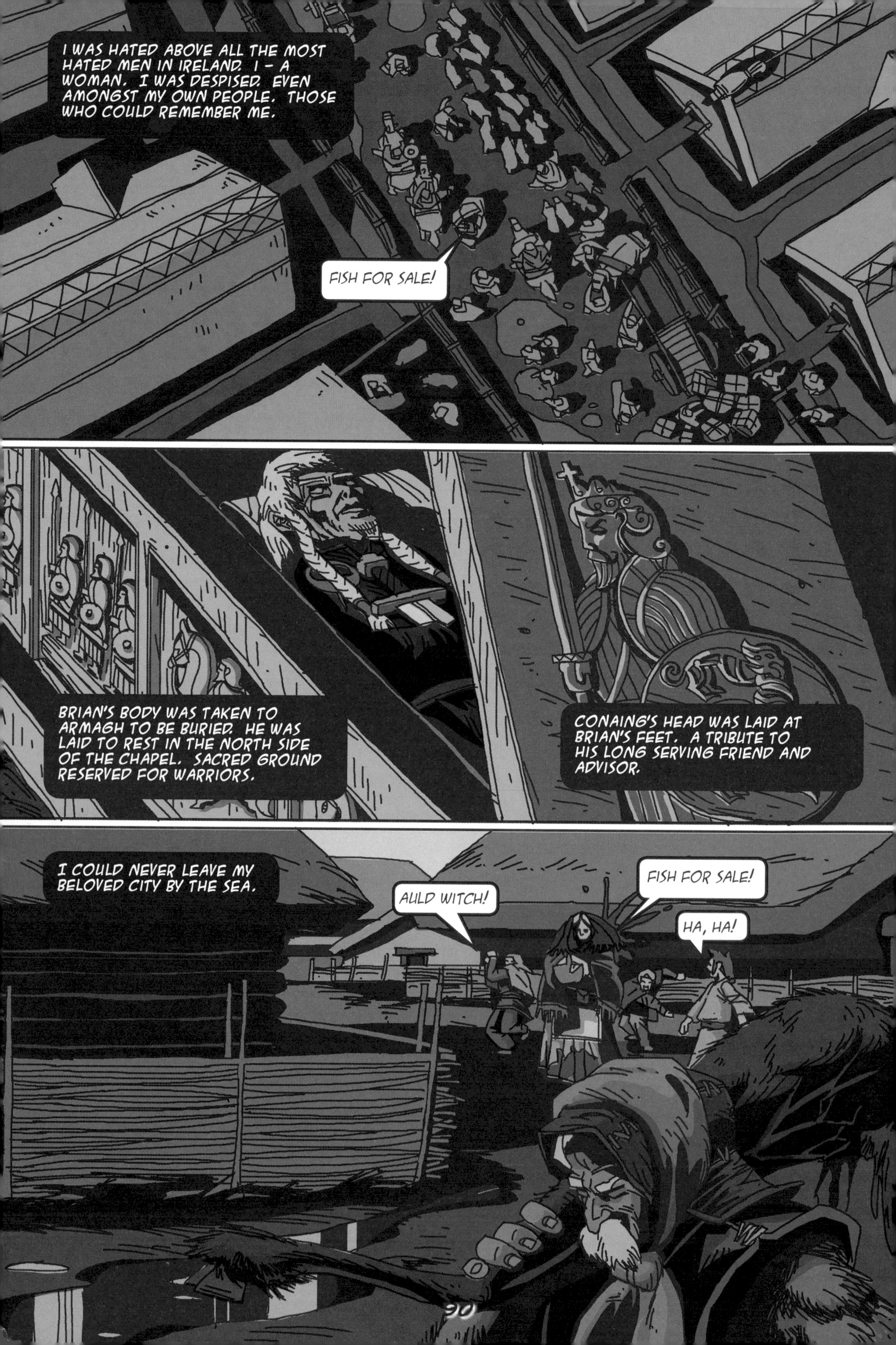
I WAS HATED ABOVE ALL THE MOST HATED MEN IN IRELAND. I - A WOMAN. I WAS DESPISED. EVEN AMONGST MY OWN PEOPLE. THOSE WHO COULD REMEMBER ME.
FISH FOR SALE!
BRIAN'S BODY WAS TAKEN TO ARMAGH TO BE BURIED. HE WAS LAID TO REST IN THE NORTH SIDE OF THE CHAPEL. SACRED GROUND RESERVED FOR WARRIORS.
CONAING'S HEAD WAS LAID AT BRIAN'S FEET. A TRIBUTE TO HIS LONG SERVING FRIEND AND ADVISOR.
I COULD NEVER LEAVE MY BELOVED CITY BY THE SEA.
AULD WITCH!
FISH FOR SALE!
HA, HA!

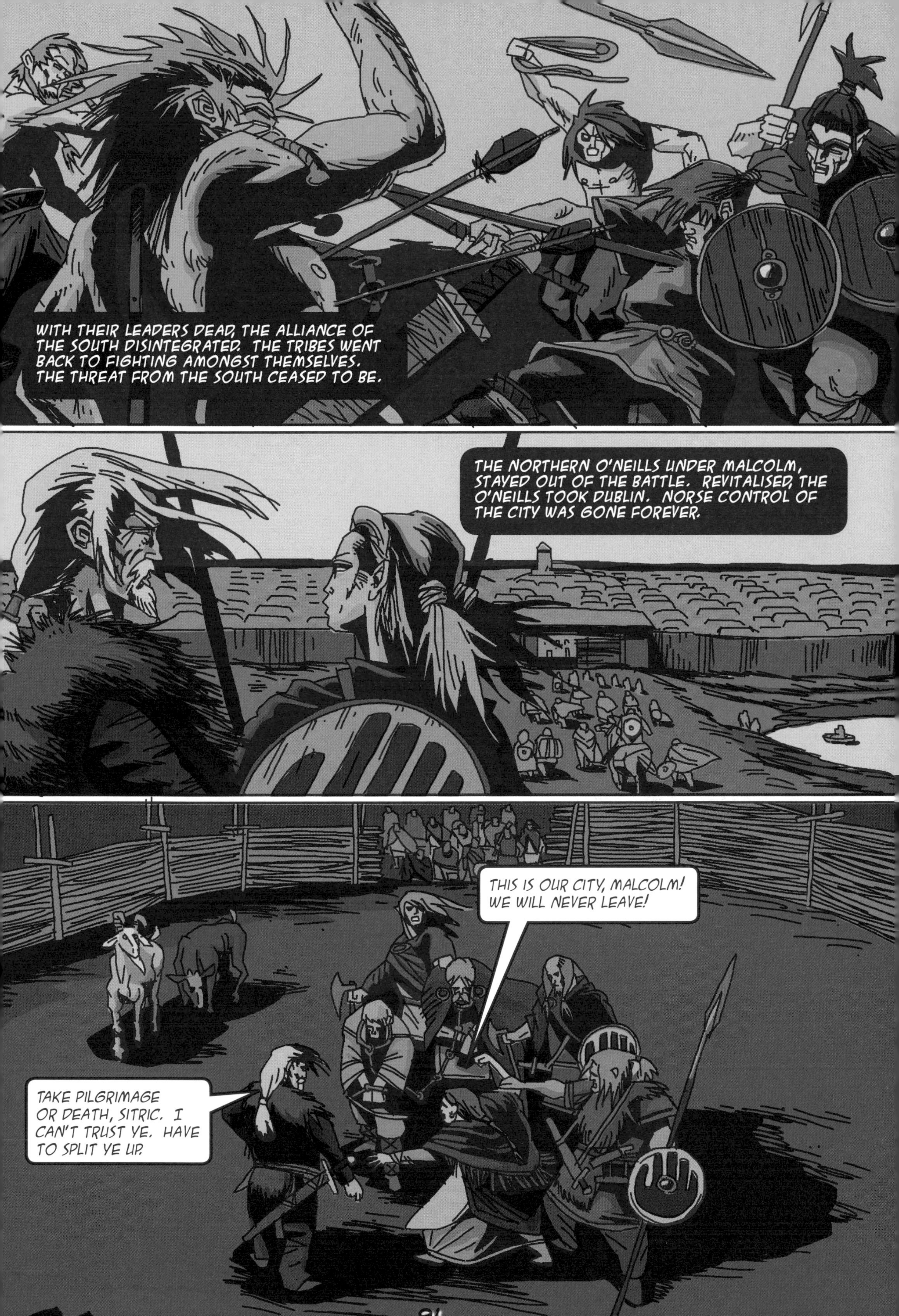
WITH THEIR LEADERS DEAD, THE ALLIANCE OF THE SOUTH DISINTEGRATED. THE TRIBES WENT BACK TO FIGHTING AMONGST THEMSELVES. THE THREAT FROM THE SOUTH CEASED TO BE.
THE NORTHERN O'NEILLS UNDER MALCOLM, STAYED OUT OF THE BATTLE. REVITALISED, THE O'NEILLS TOOK DUBLIN. NORSE CONTROL OF THE CITY WAS GONE FOREVER.
THIS IS OUR CITY, MALCOLM! WE WILL NEVER LEAVE!
TAKE PILGRIMAGE OR DEATH, SITRIC. I CAN'T TRUST YE. HAVE TO SPLIT YE UP.

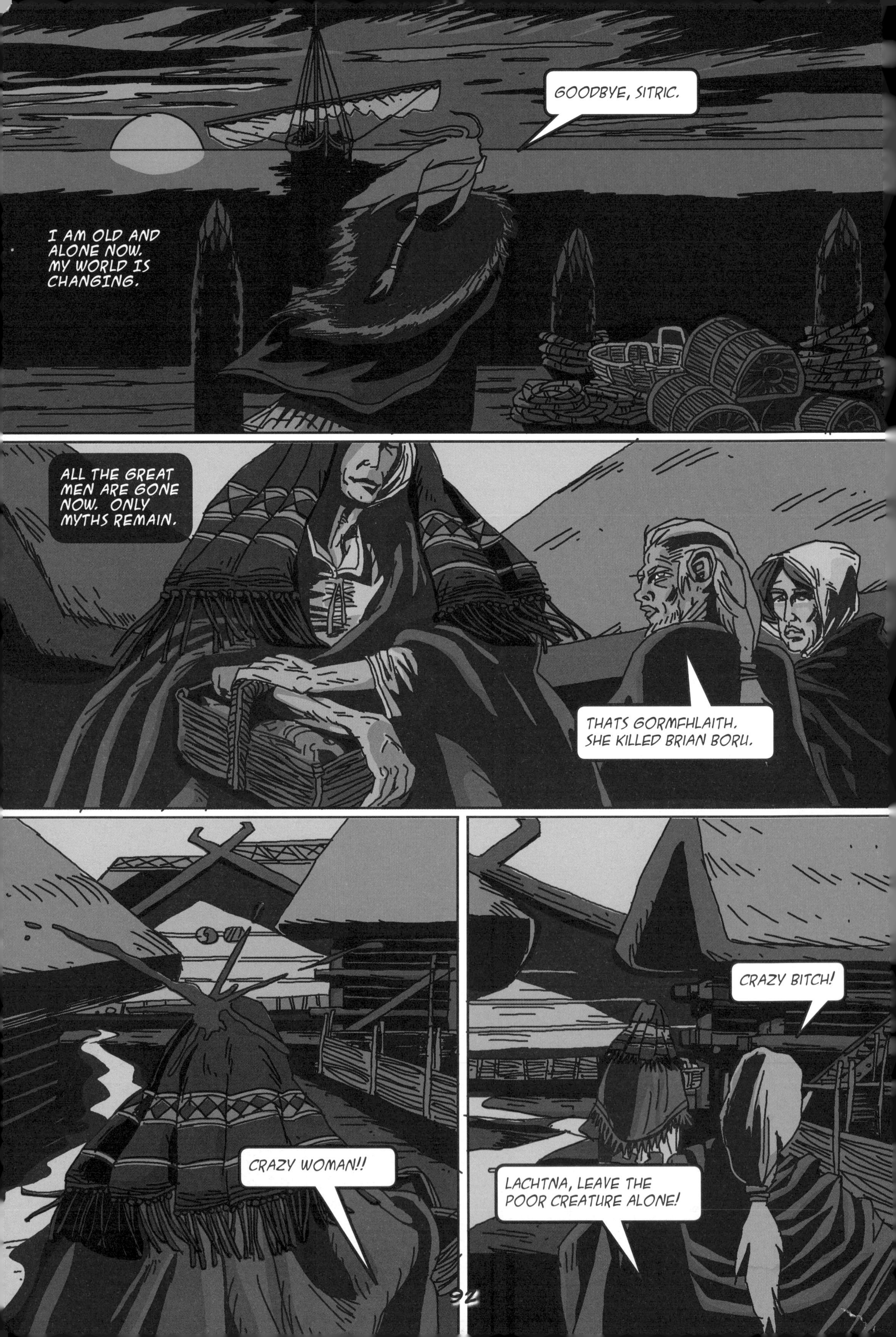
GOODBYE, SITRIC.
I AM OLD AND ALONE NOW. MY WORLD IS CHANGING.
ALL THE GREAT MEN ARE GONE NOW. ONLY MYTHS REMAIN.
THATS GORMFHLAITH. SHE KILLED BRIAN BORU.
CRAZY WOMAN!!
CRAZY BITCH!
LACHTNA, LEAVE THE POOR CREATURE ALONE!

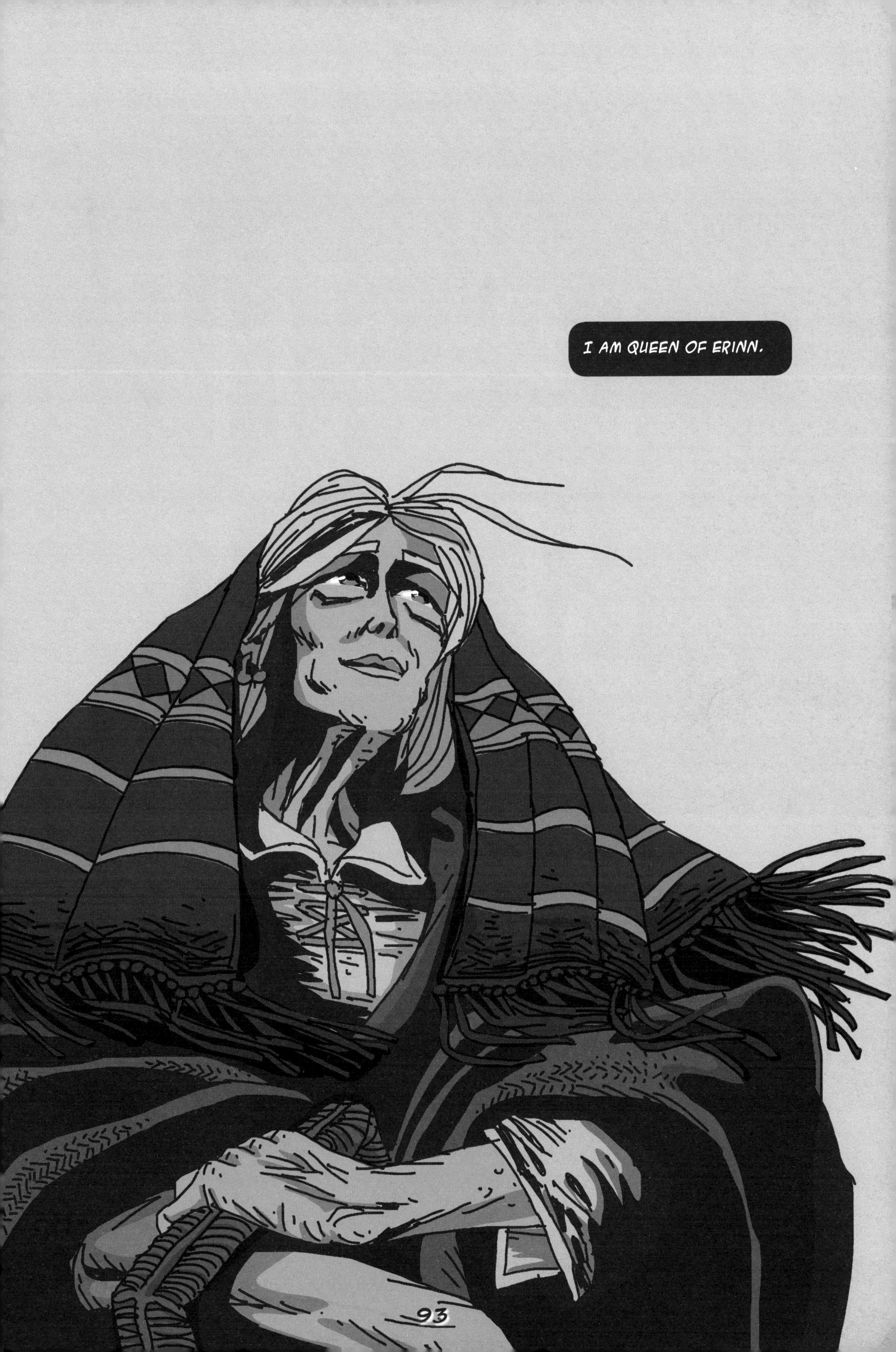
I AM QUEEN OF ERINN.

BRIAN BORU

Brian Boru, one of twelve sons of the king of the Dál gCais (Dalcassians), was an eleventh-century Irish High King, sometimes known as the 'Emperor of the Irish'. From his birthplace in Killaloe in the far west of Ireland (modern Co. Clare), he ended the domination of the O'Neill High Kingship of Ireland. A great military leader, he was crowned High King in Cashel, Co. Tipperary in 1002. Over the next decade, Brian Boru fought to retain his title and impose his rule on the whole island of Ireland, in the face of constant challenges from Ulster, Leinster and the Norse city of Dublin. His was a life of conflict, pitched battles, military strategy, intrigues, alliances and betrayals. His wife, Gormfhlaith, was the sister of Maol Mórdha of Leinster and the mother of Sitric of Dublin; she was hated by Brian's fiery son and heir, Murchadh, so the strife was complicated by family ties and power struggles. In 1014 Brian – the last great High King of Ireland – fought his last as his army faced the combined might of Leinster, Dublin and their hired mercenaries at Clontarf – he died on the battlefield along with his son, Murchadh, and grandson, Turlough. Brian's life was a meteoric rise to power and a lifelong battle to keep it, while his wife Gormfhlaith battled – just as violently, but through intrigues and alliances rather than on the field – to preserve the lives and status of herself and her sons by whatever means necessary.

First published 2011
by The O'Brien Press Ltd.,
12 Terenure Road East,
Dublin 6,
Ireland.
Tel: +353 1 4923333;
Fax: +353 1 4922777
E-mail: books@obrien.ie
Website: www.obrien.ie

ISBN: 978-1-84717-284-6

A catalogue record for this title is available from The British Library.

1 2 3 4 5 6 7 8 9 10
11 12 13 14 15 16

Printed and bound by W&G Baird

FSC
www.fsc.org
MIX
Paper from
responsible sources
FSC® C016201